Digitalization of Society and Socio-political Issues 1

Series Editor
Jean-Charles Pomerol

Digitalization of Society and Socio-political Issues 1

Digital, Communication and Culture

Edited by

Éric George

iSTE

WILEY

First published 2019 in Great Britain and the United States by ISTE Ltd and John Wiley & Sons, Inc.

ISTE Ltd
27-37 St George's Road
London SW19 4EU
UK

www.iste.co.uk

John Wiley & Sons, Inc.
111 River Street
Hoboken, NJ 07030
USA

www.wiley.com

Library of Congress Control Number: 2019948316

British Library Cataloguing-in-Publication Data
A CIP record for this book is available from the British Library
ISBN 978-1-78630-475-9

MIX
Paper from responsible sources
FSC www.fsc.org FSC® C013604

Contents

Acknowledgments

First of all, it is important to thank the Social Sciences and Humanities Research Council of Canada (SSHRC) and the *Fonds de recherche du Québec – Société et Culture* (FRQSC) for their financial support, without which the collaborations developed in Quebec, Canada and internationally between several of the authors of this book and the conference that hosted the vast majority of them could not have taken place.

I would also like to express my sincere thanks to the people who contributed to the production of this book: Oumar Kane, Associate Professor at the Université du Québec à Montréal (UQAM), member of the Executive Committee of the *Centre de recherche interuniversitaire sur la communication, l'information et la société* (CRICIS); Michel Sénécal, Full Professor at the Université TÉLUQ, member of the Executive Committee of CRICIS; Lena Hübner, doctoral candidate in communication studies at UQAM in charge of CRICIS' scientific activities, who evaluated texts; Karelle Arsenault, doctoral candidate in communication studies at UQAM, who performed the systematic review of all texts and made the preparatory layout; and Siavash Rokni, doctoral student in communication studies at UQAM, who proofread this book.

Acknowledgments written by Éric GEORGE.

Introduction

About the Digitalization of Society

Not everything that can be counted counts…
and not everything that counts can be counted.

William Bruce Cameron

What does digital mean? The question was asked on May 2, 3 and 4, 2018, at an international conference organized in Montreal by the *Centre de recherche interuniversitaire sur la communication, l'information et la société* (CRICIS). Under the title "*Numérisation généralisée de la société: acteurs, discours, pratiques et enjeux*" (Widespread Digitalization of Society: Actors, Discourses, Practices and Challenges), it brought together some 100 researchers who have devoted their thoughts to the theme of the digitalization of our societies, the discourse and social practices surrounding it, the actors who mobilize it, and the challenges that it brings to communicational, informational and cultural issues. This two-volume publication is a follow-up to this event. However, these are not conference proceedings for three reasons. First, this publication brings together the texts of about a third of the people who were present during these three days. Second, a significant number of proposals were rejected, and, for the other selected texts, significant editorial work was carried out. Third, some of the texts in this publication are from people whose contributions to the conference had been accepted but who were unable to attend. This opus is the result of this work.

The term *digital* is now present everywhere and applies to almost all the activities of our advanced capitalist societies (Bravo 2009; Cohen-Tanugi 1999;

Introduction written by Éric GEORGE.

Doukidis *et al.* 2004; Rushkoff 2012; Stiegler 2015). It is a question of digital technology about the economy (Illing and Peitz 2006; *Les Cahiers du Numérique* 2010), security and surveillance (Mathias 2008; Lévy 2010; Kessous 2012), identity (*Les Cahiers du Numérique* 2011), social relations (*Les Cahiers du Numérique* 2017) and many other fields (digital divide, solidarity, friendship, innovation, etc.). Almost all information circulates in the form of binary computer coding. Media, screens of all kinds (computers, televisions, tablets, video game consoles, multifunctional telephones and a whole range of so-called "connected" everyday objects) and networks (wired, satellite, microwave, etc.) are omnipresent in both the private and public spheres of our daily lives, two spheres whose boundaries tend to partly blur into each other. Big data (Big Data) circulates almost instantaneously and is processed by increasingly powerful computers and algorithms that bring to the fore the idea of artificial intelligence (AI), which has been regularly challenged since the 1950s, when cybernetic thinking had contributed to its development. Today, when we speak of "digital culture" (Gere, 2002; Greffe & Sonnac, 2008; Doueihi, 2011), we do so in reference to the usage of technologies that employ digitalization and algorithms necessitating a minimum of interactivity. Some even speak of the "digital age" or "digital revolution" (Collin and Verdier 2012; *Esprit* 2006). In short, digital technology is present in both a vast set of discourses and in countless practices. But what exactly does this term refer to? Who are the actors who talk about it and put it into practice? And what economic, cultural, political, social and technical issues does it raise, particularly from the point of view of communication studies? These are the questions to which the contributions in these two collective works attempt to provide answers.

However, we wanted to focus not only on digital technology as such, but also on the idea of the digitalization of our societies, and beyond. In doing so, we have made the scientific choice to approach digitalization as a long and constant process in which all domains of societal activities – from industries to entertainment, from art to academia, from health to environment – are concerned and are reconfigured by it. To this end, the two volumes of this book put emphasis on analyses of communicational, informational, and cultural phenomena and processes. This said, our goal is also socio-political in nature, since it is not only concerned with analyzing and understanding, but also contributing, though modestly, to changing the world, by proposing different critical reflections that accentuate the many ways the digital participates in relationships of power and domination, and contributes to eventual emancipatory practices. All these elements explain the title of the two books: *Digitalization of Society and Socio-political Issues*.

I.1. What does digital technology involve?

Speaking about the digital involves putting it in numbers, to represent the world, society and individuals. For a researcher in social and human sciences, this idea echoes numerous debates over the last few centuries regarding treating epistemology in relation to philosophy, natural sciences, human and social sciences. At the heart of these debates is the opposition between the merit of quantitative versus qualitative methods for better understanding the "real" (Pires, 1997). Do the digital data provide a more objective, representative view of reality than the participating observations and other life stories? Is it not the perspective that we use to understand different data that determines our position towards the knowledge that is produced – be it positivist, neopositivist, constructivist, critical or other? As we can see, the debate is not recent, but it has been updated in recent years with the production of a considerable amount of data, called *Big Data*. Would these mega data processed by algorithms provide us with a privileged mode of access to the world, or is it one mode of representation of the world among others?

That said, not unrelated to the above, the word *digital* also leads us to another field of research, that of information and communication technologies (ICTs), sometimes preceded by a "d" for "digital": digital information and communication technologies (DICTs). Perhaps it would be more relevant here to talk about socio-technical information and communication systems. The use of the word *device* refers to the idea of addressing different interdependent tools, the whole forming of an infrastructure, a system, and thus a device, which facilitates informational and communicational practices, at least some of them, because any device is both enabling and constraining. The material dimension of the device, starting with the choices made in terms of socio-technical design, provides a framework for the related communication processes (Proulx 1999). Nevertheless, no terminology standardization has been observed over the past five decades, as the terms used vary significantly over time. Thus, there have been alternating references to IT, then to ICT and now to DICT, as well as to "media technologies" and "new media" (George and Kane 2015). More recently, various syntagmas combining several of the words *media*, *networks*, *socionumeric*, *digital social* or *social* have emerged, such as "digital platforms".

Writing is therefore not standardized on this subject. However, behind this variety of expressions lie notable choices that are often not very explicit. Thus, emphasizing the "media" underlines the fact that these devices constitute organized groups from the cultural, economic, aesthetic, political, social and technical points of view. They are characterized by their interface, their mode of financing, the provision of access to a production of formatted cultural content and the way in which they create links between the supply of goods and services, on the one hand, and demand, on the other. Most of the time, private companies are behind these media, and not small companies, since the most important of the digital social media, Facebook, is part of the prestigious "GAFAM" (Google, Apple, Facebook, Amazon and Microsoft). This acronym is sometimes slightly modified, to GAFAN, for example, when we want to highlight the role of Netflix. On the other hand, speaking about networks rather highlights the reticulated technical dimensions of networked devices. This reminds us of the historical development of network technologies, such as the Internet, while taking us further back in history to the development of other networked technologies, such as the telegraph or even the railroads, from an Innisian perspective (Innis 1950, 1951), its fundamentally decentralized nature and the fact that these networks largely rely on the participation of their users in order to produce the famous User Generated Content (UGC).

That said, the only terminological issue is not the use of the words *media* and *network*. Thus, in some cases, we are talking about "social networks" or "social media". But doesn't such a use reveal a certain blindness, a new obliviousness of history when it comes to ICTs? Indeed, the very expression "social networks" refers to analyses that do not necessarily concern digital technology and that predate its development. As for the expression "social media", it is also questionable because all media are part of social processes, unless, as mentioned above, reference is made to a "digital platform", which means that neither the term *media* nor the term *network* can be used. Such websites that aim to link supply and demand can cover transport and accommodation activities, as well as cultural products and many other sectors of the economy. These new technological devices have become so widespread that we now speak of "platformisation" of the media, culture and even society (see Colin and Verdier, 2012; Guibert *et al.*, 2016; tic&société, 2019) in order to highlight the fact that they are at the heart of a very large societal transformation that jointly influences the forms of capitalism, democracy and sociability. We will also discuss these possible mutations in the chapters of these two volumes, and you will see that the analyses developed there are characterized above all by great finesse.

The term *digital* therefore has various meanings and, *de facto*, refers to objects and analyses that sometimes seem distant from each other. This is not surprising in a context where the scientific approach is increasingly oriented towards hyper-specialization, following the social division of labor that is characteristic of capitalist economies. However, if, to a certain extent, the development of disciplines and specializations brings new knowledge, it is possible to wonder, like Bernard Lahire (2012), whether this Balkanization does not lead to a loss "of the meaning of social totalities" (p. 322). However, while the terms "DICT", "digital platforms", "Big Data", "GAFAM" and others refer to analyses that are often separate from each other, they all reflect – and also participate in – more global changes that are underway, which can be presented in terms of the "digitalization of society".

We will therefore return to this in two stages, given that, by its scope, this publication is proposed in two volumes. This Volume 1, which has the subtitle *Digital, Communication and Culture*, consists of three parts that focus in turn on (1) the relationships between digital technology and current societal transformations, through the formation of Big Data, their treatment by algorithms and the relationship with surveillance and social control; (2) the relationship between digital technology and the changes in the culture and communication industries, particularly as a result of the role played by digital platforms and social and digital media (GAFAM) in the production and, in particular, the distribution/circulation of cultural works; (3) the relationship between digital technology and cultural and communication practices, with an emphasis on the so-called "digital native" generation, but not only this generation, as older people are also affected, as we will see.

I.2. Digital technology, Big Data and societal transformations

By mobilizing a socio-historical approach characteristic of all his work, **Armand Mattelart** (Chapter 1) recalls that our societies have always been governed by numbers as soon as mathematics became a model of reasoning and action. It was at the time of the scientific revolution, during the 17th and 18th Centuries, that the thought of the quantifiable and measurable became the prototype of any true discourse in the West. However, it was only in the 19th Century that the "calculable individual" was born, with the development of statistics and probabilities. Then cybernetics arrived, with the idea of governing human beings by machines that are supposedly more rational. At the same time, the visibility of the panoptic architecture designed by Jeremy Bentham and conceptualized by Michel Foucault gave way to the new invisibility of current surveillance. Voluntarily or not, we are revealing a great deal of information that is now considered massive data aggregates, or Big Data, the term (*Big Data → Big Brother*) to remind us that this is also about surveillance. Nevertheless, today, just as in the past, numbers can be mobilized for the purpose of surveillance and control but just as much they can contribute to progress – for example in the health sector when there is a risk of a pandemic. Therefore a factor of alienation, and also a possible tool for the emancipation of the other, hence the relevance of mobilizing the dialectical method (Ollman 2003). The risk, Mattelart believes, is that ultimately, only numbers would matter in decision-making in this new data-driven form of governmentality.

Megadata also contribute, says **Fabien Richert** (Chapter 2), to the colonization of the populated world. From now on, taking a growing place in our societies, they testify to the extent taken by the process of systematically decoding the social flows that have so far managed to escape capitalism. We are in a process of cold rationalization here, very far from all forms of singularity. In a way, Big Data collected on all facets of our daily lives tends to participate more than ever in the omnimarketing of the world (Latouche 1997). Finally, Richert asks, does digital labor itself reduce the individual to a set of partial and abstract functions? Here, we are in a new phase of consolidating Taylorism, where the scientific organization of work, Big Data and its algorithmic treatment is spreading in the ensemble of our activities.

Yanita Andonova (Chapter 3) examines how DICTs affect managerial practices, including human resources practices in contemporary organizations. She notes that, in the discourse, a vast set of mechanisms is mobilized in order to refer to the implementation of "flexible", "collaborative" and "transparent" organizational forms. However, these discourses are also accompanied by the implementation of practices that are based in particular on algorithmic applications, so much so that we are now talking about algorithmic management.

In combination with the practice of micro-targeting, algorithms are also mobilized in the constitution of political discourse and, beyond that, in the very development of political communication, as stated by **Samuel Cossette** (Chapter 4). This sector is increasingly characterized by automation, industrialization and hyper-personalization in the way citizens are targeted through algorithmic processes. In this respect, in the absence of a revolution, there are still significant transformations that must be taken into account.

A growing proportion of cultural practices, whether in literature, the performing arts, music, cinema, video games or museums, are themselves the subject of digital exploitation as part of Big Data, as pointed out by **Robert Panico** and **Geneviève Vidal** (Chapter 5). To support their thesis, they rely on empirical work carried out in the museum sector, which disseminates content and resources in a context of social acceptance, understood, on the one hand, in terms of an injunction to permanent and invasive digital innovation and, on the other hand, in terms of the use of surveillance and digital control devices.

Surveillance can help to challenge the notion of *privacy*, or at least to review what can be understood by this term. **Julien Rossi** (Chapter 6) develops the hypothesis that the very conception of this notion has changed between the Ancients and the Moderns. While traditionally there has been a clear and unambiguous separation between public and private, from now on, attachment to privacy would be more a matter of controlling information about oneself and its circulation in different contexts, as Helen Nissenbaum (2010) attests. The evolution of the meaning of this notion relates to the place in our daily lives progressively taken by computers since the 1960s. In this respect, the process of digitalizing society would be in certain continuity with that of social computerization.

Behind these cultural and communicational practices, **Rémy Rouge** (Chapter 7) reminds us, are large companies such as Facebook and Google, which provide media that favor the expression of subjectivity in digital practice precisely at a time when identity issues are ever more important in our societies. However, he adds that the services that are in place allow their managers to always produce more data with high market value and, therefore, likely participate in their valorisation on the financial markets. However, the issue of disclosing a great deal of data to the main economic and political actors, starting with GAFAM and national security agencies, does not seem to be a major issue for citizens (Kwok-Choon and George 2017).

I.3. Digital technology and changes in the cultural and communication industries

Who precisely are the social actors who are setting up this digitalization of the world? The acronym GAFAM refers to the corporate names of some of the most powerful companies on the planet and, in addition, to the strong symbols of the forms currently taken by capitalism: Google, Apple, Facebook, Amazon and Microsoft. These transnationals, all Western, and, more precisely, American, born on the west coast of the country, share a common point, namely the fact that their colossal profits are largely based on the large amount of data they collect and process tirelessly (Smyrnaios 2017) as well as on the massive use of advertising. However, as they accumulate data and develop an economy based on them, their very way of operating appears very opaque, hence the importance of working on them, just as it is now interesting to focus our attention on companies from China, such as BATX (Baidu, Alibaba, Tencent and Xiaomi), which are probably the only alternatives to GAFAM (Mosco 2017).

Maxime Ouellet (Chapter 8) contributes to the study of the new giants of the communications industry in his analysis of Facebook's strategy. We are now in a capitalist regime based on the domination of a few corporations in the formation of an oligopoly far removed from a competitive market regime. The textbook case of Facebook is a good example, according to Ouellet, of the fact that accumulation within advanced capitalism, an expression he prefers to that of digital capitalism, is based on the ability to accumulate from a "symbolic monopoly rent". The process of capital accumulation does not consist so much here in the accumulation of material wealth as in the extra-economic mechanisms of a "symbolic quantification of power". While profit formation remains important, for a company, it is first and foremost a matter of maximizing its ability to accumulate power.

But what are these companies doing? They mainly design digital intermediation platforms, says **Jacob Matthews** (Chapter 9), who focuses on their proliferation not only in the culture, information and communication sectors, which are of particular interest to us, but also far beyond, starting with health, personal services (care) and tourism. These platforms are both, and inseparably, institutions of ideological production and instruments of work organization and management. Matthews tells us that we can envisage that managers, freelancers and project leaders are all users of these platforms, certainly in different social positions, but all in the service of financial capital, which is taking up an ever-increasing share of the value produced and, in these specific cases, in the name of a supposed "collaborative economy".

Philippe Bouquillion (Chapter 10) focuses more specifically on audiovisual platforms that contribute to the development of the so-called bypass television. He sees it as a new stage in cultural globalization and renewed confrontations between cultural and communication industries. He had already highlighted this opposition in his book *Les industries de la culture et de la communication. Les stratégies du capitalisme* a little more than 10 years ago (2008), but this confrontation appears more intense than ever before, as the major groups in the communication industries increasingly try to control the downstream of cultural sectors, which implies, for example, a permanent increase in production. Nevertheless, content is obviously still necessary for these companies, and we see, for example, that Netflix invests significantly in audiovisual production (Perticoz, 2019). The analysis by Bouquillion shows that we are witnessing a proliferation of cultural offerings, the arrival of new entrants, a weakening of historical actors, defensive strategies on the part of several national actors and the development of public policies that oscillate between transnational logic and a more traditional national dimension. It is clear here that the roles of platforms are not negligible in the ongoing transformation of media and culture.

Édith Laviec (Chapter 11) is within the same theoretical framework, with work in the scientific book publishing sector. She wonders how the meeting between old and new actors in this sector took place, and what are the possible consequences on the transformation of the sector. Finally, she notes that, in the region studied in France, Rhône-Alpes, the new players who have been best able to integrate into the sector work in collaboration with the "historical" publishers on the basis of a sharing of the values and knowledge of traditional trades and their challenges. Nevertheless, other players – here she refers to Amazon, Google and, to a lesser extent, Apple – have benefited from their dominant international status to enter this sector. Here we find the idea that cultural industries have always been characterized by the coexistence at different industrial channels between large companies in a dominant situation and smaller ones in a competitive situation (Huet *et al.* 1978).

When it comes to changes related to technological innovations, the pornography industry is always one of the first, if not the first, to seize them. We have seen it in regard to videotapes, the Internet or even printing. Today, as **Arnaud Anciaux** (Chapter 12) points out, digitalization plays a significant role in promoting the formation of an oligopoly of publishing and distribution on a global scale, while also allowing the development of commercial exchanges that are built on the margins of this oligopoly. The development of sexcam platforms is evidence, at least in part, of the renewal of social relations between consumers, on the one hand, and performers, on the other hand, as well as the creation of new forms of remuneration. However, this is, again, an organizational mode that is quite largely industrialized. The projected discourse, namely that of relatively low intermediation, therefore appears to be out of step with a much more complex operating mode.

On the basis of these transformations, we can ask ourselves how political actors deal with digital technology. In many countries, it seems difficult to adopt a clear and firm attitude towards actors such as Facebook, Google, Netflix and others, who play on borders in different ways and undermine the very notion of sovereignty, at a time when states see themselves first and foremost as supporters (Vedel 1999). **Maud Boisnard, Destiny Tchéhouali** and **Michèle Rioux** (Chapter 13) also believe that the transformations brought about by digital technology in the cultural industries raise fears of an imbalance between English-speaking productions intended for the world market and "local" productions, for example in Canada and Quebec, which often have difficulty achieving visibility on the Web, even on a national scale, and attracting the attention of an audience. Boisnard, Tchéhouali and Rioux invite public action to better articulate three worlds, those of trade, culture and digital technology, which evolve according to different logics.

As for **Anne Bellon** (Chapter 14), she has worked on the various ways in which digital technology has penetrated the French Ministry of Culture. This researcher attempted to analyze how it is seized within a public institution and, on this occasion, highlighted two competing appropriations of the term. The ministry includes, on the one hand, supporters of the instrumentalization of digital technologies in the service of traditional cultural objects as part of a policy aimed at pursuing cultural democratization, and, on the other hand, parties who would like to rethink cultural content in light of the new technical tools made available, for example by addressing cultural diversity in the context of GAFAM.

I.4. Digital technology and cultural and communicational practices

As we have seen, the term *digital* also refers to the growing importance of a few giant companies in all the activities of our daily lives, including in the cultural sector. But, precisely, does the resulting multiplication of communicative socio-technical devices, the ever-increasing place of promotional discourses accompanying their marketing and the appropriation both by individuals and groups not contribute to the emergence of a certain "digital culture", especially among the youngest population (Fluckiger 2010), sometimes described as "digital natives"? On this subject, **Alma Betbout** (Chapter 15) discusses new youth practices in Tunisia by addressing the uses of digital social networks. The results of her survey lead her to conclude that a culture is developing – would it be better to talk about a "subculture"? – which is based on transgression in relation to traditional writing; on the use of phonetic writing with spelling errors; on participation in a Latinization of the Tunisian dialect, associated with different languages; on the mixing of numbers and letters, thus showing a desire to escape the normative; and finally on the development of invention and deciphering. All these communicative practices would strengthen the sense of these young people belonging to a youth culture and a connected community through the sharing of common references.

Young people are also the population *par excellence* concerned by the education sector. It so happens that **Marie David** (Chapter 16) was interested in how the uses of ICTs transform the academic knowledge learned. It can be seen that the students who participated in the research in France practice this knowledge collectively, through digital platforms and social networks, and that their practices modify the knowledge that is learned and thus have indirect effects on the teaching activity. However, **Cathia Papi** (Chapter 17) notes that in Quebec, while the place of these digital technologies appears to be constantly expanding, the education sector is often seen as a base with some resistance against this generalization of digitalization. This is not the case, at least not yet, despite the strategies and resources deployed. Papi notes that, on the one hand, teachers have rarely been trained in how to use these devices and, on the other hand, young people do not automatically transpose their familiarity with these technologies into practice in their learning activities.

When we think of culture and digital technology, it is therefore often young people who are mentioned. However, the elderly are also affected. They are confronted with various social incentives to participate in the development of a "digital culture". By asking whether it is possible to speak of "digital acculturation", **Lucie Delias** (Chapter 18) has argued that they are invited to consider incentives that take the form of normative injunctions linked to a model of "successful aging" that promotes activity and connectivity. In addition, these injunctions are supplemented by a *de facto* obligation to participate in the digital world induced by the dematerialization of administrative services. She concludes that members of the working classes are particularly disadvantaged in this situation.

Myriam Durocher (Chapter 19) also questions the relationship between culture and digital technology based on the notion of a "biomedicalized food culture". This growing culture contributes to the multiplication of content aimed at informing individuals about what constitutes contemporary "healthy eating", assessed according to its biochemical components, which are linked to the body processes that determine the intake of these nutrients. It also participates in the development of self-control practices, based on food, through socio-technical measures that promote personalized and real-time monitoring of what is consumed. It includes the notions of *biopolitics* and *biopower* developed by Michel Foucault (2004).

So much for the content of this Volume 1, which we finish with some summary elements in a short conclusion that also opens up Volume 2 of this publication.

Enjoy!

I.5. References

Bouquillion, P. (2008). *Les industries de la culture et de la communication. Les stratégies du capitalisme*. Presses universitaires de Grenoble, Grenoble.

Bravo, A. (2009). *La société et l'économie à l'aune de la révolution numérique : enjeux et perspectives des prochaines décennies (2015–2025)*. La Documentation française, Paris.

Cohen-Tanugi, L. (1999). *Le nouvel ordre numérique*. Odile Jacob, Paris.

Colin, N. and Verdier, H. (2012). *L'âge de la multitude : Entreprendre et gouverner après la révolution numérique*. Armand Colin, Paris.

Denouël, J. and Granjon, F. (eds) (2011). *Communiquer à l'ère numérique. Regards croisés sur la sociologie des usages*. Presses des Mines, Paris.

Doueihi, M. (2011). *Pour un humanisme numérique*. Le Seuil, Paris.

Doukidis, G., Mylonopoulos, N., and Pouloudi, N. (2004). *Social and Economic Transformation in the Digital Era*. Idea Group Pub, Hershey.

Esprit (2006). Que nous réserve le numérique ? *Esprit*, 5.

Fluckiger, C. (2010). *La culture numérique adolescente*. Les Cahiers de l'Orme. Available at: https://hal.univ-lille3.fr/hal-01613667/document.

Foucault, M. (2004). *Naissance de la biopolitique. Cours au Collège de France 1978–1979*. Gallimard, Paris.

George, É. (2006). Perspectives critiques et études en communication. In *Perspectives critiques en communication*, volume 2, Aubin, F., George, E., and Rueff, J. (eds). Presses de l'Université du Québec, Quebec.

George, É. and Kane, O. (2015). Les technologies numériques au prisme des approches critiques. Éléments pour l'ébauche d'une rencontre. *Canadian Journal of Communication*, 40(4), 727–735.

Gere, C. (2002). *Digital Culture*. Reaktion Books, London.

Greffe, X. and Sonnac, N. (2008). *Culture web : création, contenus, économie numérique*. Dalloz, Paris.

Guibert, G., Rebillard, F., and Rochelandet, F. (2016). *Médias, culture et numérique – Approches socioéconomiques*. Armand Colin, Paris.

Huet, A., Ion, J., Lefèbvre, A., Miège, B., and Peron, R. (1978). *Capitalisme et industries culturelles*. Presses universitaires de Grenoble, Grenoble.

Humbert, P. (2010). Piloter l'entreprise à l'ère du numérique. *Les Cahiers du Numérique*. 6(4), 49–75. Available at: http://www.cairn.info/revue-les-cahiers-du-numerique-2010-4.htm.

Illing, G. and Peitz, M. (2006). *Industrial Organization and the Digital Economy*. MIT Press, Cambridge.

Innis, H. (1950). *Empire and Communications*. Clarendon Press, Oxford.

Innis, H. (1951). *The Bias of Communication*. University of Toronto Press, Toronto.

Kessous, E. (ed.) (2012). *L'attention au monde : Sociologie des données personnelles à l'ère numérique*. Armand Colin, Paris.

Kwok-Choon, M.-J. and George, É. (2017). Vers de nouvelles formes de surveillance institutionnelle "post 9/11" au Canada. Les rapports informatique et liberté dans le contexte de l'adoption de la loi C-51. *Terminal*, 121. Available at: https://journals.openedition.org/terminal/1687.

Lacroix, J.-G. (2009). Conclusion. Pour une nouvelle éthique de l'émancipation. In *L'émancipation d'hier à aujourd'hui*, Tremblay, G. (ed.). Presses de l'Université du Québec, Quebec, 297–303.

Lahire, B. (2012). *Monde pluriel. Penser l'unité des sciences humaines et sociales*. Le Seuil, Paris.

Latouche, S. (1997). La mondialisation et la fin du politique : Diagnostic et perspectives. *La Revue du MAUSS*, 9, 137–150.

Les Cahiers du Numérique (2011). Identité numérique. *Les Cahiers du Numérique*, 7(1). Available at: http://www.cairn.info/revue-les-cahiers-du-numerique-2011-1.htm.

Lévy, A. (2010). *Sur les traces de Big Brother : la vie privée à l'ère numérique*. L'Éditeur, Paris.

Mathias, P. (2008). *Des libertés numériques : Notre liberté est-elle menacée par l'Internet ?* Presses universitaires de France, Paris.

Mosco, V. (2017). *Becoming Digital: Toward a Post-Internet Society*. Emerald, London.

Nissenbaum, H.F. (2010). *Privacy in Context: Technology, Policy, and the Integrity of Social Life*. Stanford Law Books, Stanford.

Ollman, B. (2003). *Dance of the Dialectic: Steps in Marx's Method*. University of Illinois Press, Chicago.

Perticoz, L. (2019). Filière de l'audiovisuel et plateformes SVoD : une analyse croisée des stratégies de Disney et Netflix. *tic&société*, 13(1–2).

Pires, A. (1997). De quelques enjeux épistémologiques d'une méthodologie générale pour les sciences sociales. In *La recherche qualitative. Enjeux épistémologiques et méthodologiques*, Poupart, J. (ed.). Gaëtan Morin, Montreal, 3–44.

Rushkoff, D. (2012). *Les 10 commandements de l'ère numérique*. FYP Éditions, Limoges.

Smyrnaios, N. (2017). *Les GAFAM contre l'Internet : une économie politique du numérique*. Institut national de l'audiovisuel, Paris.

Stiegler, B. (2015). *La société automatique. 1. L'avenir du travail*. Fayard, Paris.

tic&société (2019). Les industries culturelles à la conquête des plateformes ? *tic&société*, 13(1–2).

Vedel, T. (1999). La gouvernance des réseaux mondiaux de communication. *Politique et Sociétés*, 18(2), 9–36. Available at: https://www.erudit.org/fr/revues/ps/1999-v18-n2-ps2494/040171ar.pdf.

Viallon, P. (ed.) (2017). Bénévolat, lien social et numérique. *Les Cahiers du Numérique*, 13(2). Available at: http://www.cairn.info/revue-les-cahiers-du-numerique-2017-2.htm.

PART 1

Digital Technology, Big Data and Societal Transformations

1

For an Archaeology of the Cult of the Number

"Each 'piece of news' brings together movements of different origins and rhythms. Today's time is a combination of yesterday, the day before yesterday and in times past." This remark made by the historian Fernand Braudel in the 1950s about the need to free oneself from the cult of the present in order to understand the course of the world has not lost its relevance (Braudel 1958, p. 19). Quite the contrary. The digitalization of society tends to intensify the infinite race in the service of the present. It is the long duration and the simultaneous existence of different temporalities that give meaning to the trilogy I published in the 1990s: *Mapping World Communication* (1994), *The Invention of Communication* (1996) and *Histoire de l'utopie planétaire* (1999 – History of Planetary Utopia). The influence of the short-time view, or "presentism", encourages us to grant a patent of novelty, and therefore of revolutionary change, to what in reality reflects structural evolutions and processes that have been going on for a very long time. This is what Nicholas Garnham (2000, p. 118), one of the pioneers of the political economy of communication and culture, also reminded us on the threshold of the millennium: "As Braudel has reminded us in relation to the flexibility of capital within a space of flows, the answers are more likely to be inscribed in the *durée* of capitalist development than on the Information Superhighway." What I propose here is to retrace the path of a social project that risks generating, if we do not address its gray areas, a way of managing populations that is far from being emancipatory for all humanity.

Chapter written by Armand MATTELART.

1.1. Governing by numbers: an old and a new figure

Governing by trace, numbers, data, files or algorithms. These expressions, which have appeared over the past two decades, the logic that is at work in the digitalization process of contemporary society (Mattelart 2010; Marzouki and Simon 2010; Rouvroy and Berns 2013; Supiot 2015; Bonditti 2017). These expressions refer to the new rationality of government based on the market economy and are focused on the quantifiable individual. They are the product of various critical approaches that have sometimes developed from philosophy, law, political science, from sociology, information science, political economy of communication and even sometimes from mathematics or statistics. However, this diversity does not mean that there is not yet much to be done to decompartmentalize disciplines and fields of study.

The idea of a society governed by numbers appears to be brand new. However, it goes back long before cybernetics unveiled its potential and the notion of *information* made its way into the language and culture of modernity (Mattelart 2003, 2017, 2018). It is therefore already weighed down by a long history. It is indeed due to the Scientific Revolution, during the 17th and 18th Centuries, that the thought of the quantifiable and measurable became the prototype of any true discourse in the West. Mathematical thinking outlines the horizon of the quest for "perfectibility" or "progress" of human societies towards a "better state". It appears to be the model of thought in general. For the astronomer and physicist Galileo (1564–1642), for example, the whole creation is a book written in the language of mathematics and it is necessary for understanding anything in this world. Hope inspires belief in the power of numbers. Thus, when the German philosopher and mathematician Gottfried Wilhelm Leibniz (1646–1716) built "new knowledge compasses" by reducing numbers to the simplest principles, such as 0 and 1, in order to save thought, he hoped to contribute to the rapprochement of peoples, to the unification not only of Europe but of the "entire human race".

The same utopian faith in perfectibility framed the project of "universal language", a language with "geometric certainty", which the revolutionary philosopher and mathematician M.J.A. de Condorcet (1743–1794) set out in his *Esquisse d'un tableau historique des progrès de l'esprit humain* (English title: Sketch for a Historical Picture of the Progress of the Human Mind) (1793). He believed to have found, in the work of the Swiss Jacob Bernoulli (1654–1705) on the abstract logic of the probability calculation, the philosopher's stone of a moral and political science as "precise and exact" as the "physical sciences". Using past experience, i.e. the observation of the frequencies of events, "social mathematics", or "mathematized social science", as it is called, would make it possible to predict the future, in order to show the most probable historical scenario. The "*Fragment sur l'Atlantide*" (Fragment on the New Atlantis) with which Condorcet's *Esquisse* ends is a surprising evocation of the future of humanity. In it, he outlines a "Universal Republic of Sciences", a symbol of the "brotherhood of nations" through knowledge, guaranteeing a "general illumination of minds" (Condorcet 1988).

However, the enthusiasm for the quantifiable and the measurable did not meet with unanimous approval among the revolutionary circles of 1789. They themselves were divided on the "geometrical utopia". "Mathematical rage" is denounced. He was accused of ignoring life itself (Julia 1981).

1.2. The invention of the calculable individual

The pragmatic management of industrial society will test the "romanticism of numbers", to use Max Weber's expression.

It was not until the mid-19th Century that probability calculation was associated with statistics, according to the historians of the politics of large numbers (Desrosières 1993). Many of them are the work of the Belgian Adolphe Quételet (1796–1874), a pioneer in demography, the science of the state of populations and their flows, and the architect of the institutionalization of censuses and national and international statistical systems. He was "the man of the universalization of the calculation of probabilities – which is the universal exchanger" (Ewald 1986, p. 147). The risk technology developed in previous centuries by private insurance institutions was being transformed into "political technology". "Probabilistic reason" paved the way for a new mode of social regulation based on predictability, which Ewald calls "insurance society". Moral statistics helped define the profile of the "average man", in relation to whom the normality and deviances of a society were defined. The premise was that mathematical rules govern the occurrence and distribution of social pathologies and that these rules provide the legislator with tools to regulate flows in the face of "disruptive forces", i.e. everything that has a moral influence on people and determines them to act in one direction rather than another. Hence the research on innate tendencies towards crime, suicide and other indices of social instabilities. This led to the development of crime tables that provided information on the greater or lesser likelihood of committing a crime according to season, climate, gender, age, region and social group. Delinquency thus became the laboratory of carding and biotypology. Anthropometry or the science of measuring the human body and the "different faculties of individuals" was able to provide nomenclatures, indices and profiles that guided police officers, judges and forensic doctors in their hygienist mission of monitoring and standardizing "dangerous classes". The biotype "born criminal" or "delinquent man", forged by forensic scientist Cesare Lombroso, served as a reference to profile the multitudes in motion. Irrational, impulsive, emotional, hypnotized by the leaders, crowds can only be prone to crime. Delinquency was beginning to "function as a political observatory". What the positivist anthropology of delinquency then aimed to achieve through their criminalization were the newly conquered democratic freedoms of association and expression that have marked their emergence on the public scene, these "egalitarian chimeras", according to psychopathologist doctor Gustave Le Bon, author of the classic book on "crowd psychology". It was in this context that the first biometric identification techniques were developed at the end of the 19th Century, beginning with fingerprints (Mattelart 1994, 2010).

Extending biometric identification techniques to the entire population was the dream of the inventors of forensic science as well as of the assembly of legal scholars and doctors who, until the eve of World War I, gathered at international congresses on criminal anthropology in the major European capitals. For more than a century, however, Western democracies refused universal registration for fear of violating the privacy and fundamental rights of citizens. And many will have gone so far as to reject the very idea of an identity card for their nationals, except for certain categories, such as workers, nomads, itinerants and gypsies, who were imposed various types of passes, small notebooks, booklets or anthropometric traffic logs. On the other hand, the peripheral areas of the world will have offered life-size fields of experimentation to colonial empires. In the 1890s, British eugenist Francis Galton was able to study digital drawings, the first steps in the discovery of fingerprints, because a senior official of the Victorian Empire administration in Bengal provided him with a sample of the indigenous thumbprints he had collected for nearly four decades to authenticate public records.

With the exception of periods of war and crisis, it can be said that surveillance will only become a mass phenomenon when the imperative of security requires a policy that embraces the entire population.

1.3. Control as a mass phenomenon

The industrial era is over. We are on the same level in the age of cybernetic imagination. Surveillance and control have become a mass phenomenon, the individual has become quantifiable, devices have become sophisticated and universalized, and the usage of digital information technologies has become hybrid: military or civil, commercial or public. The very nature of social control has changed. How does it differ from the specificity of previous forms?

For more than three centuries, from the 16th to the 19th Century, it was disciplinary and panoptic systems in the West that made individuals both "docile and useful". This is what Michel Foucault shows in his book *Discipline and Punish: The Birth of the Prison* (1977). The confinement in closed places (not only the prison, but also hospitals, schools, colleges, barracks, workshops) and the subjugation of bodies have ensured social normalization and the positive production of behaviors. The originality of the change that digitalization brings to the way populations are controlled lies in the following: unlike traditional surveillance that is based on the visibility of panoptic architecture, the efficiency of control technologies lies in their invisibility. While, in the discipline, the observed person placed under the gaze of the controller participates in their own normalization through self-constraint and self-control, they are now, in the name of prevention, relieved of this work in the light of the information that has been collected from them, whether they give it up voluntarily or without their knowledge. In addition, this collection is mobile and automatic, and data processing is deterritorialized. This is what *Le profilage des populations. Du livret ouvrier au cybercontrôle* (translation: Population Profiling: From the Employment Record Book to Cybercontrol) elaborates (Mattelart and Vitalis 2014).

Control can be associated with profiling or *profilage*, understood as the result of statistical correlations and personal data banks, in order to "evaluate certain personal aspects relating to a natural person, in particular to analyze or predict elements concerning the work performance, economic situation, health, personal preferences, interests, reliability, behavior, location or movements of this "natural person", as defined by the new European Directive on the protection of personal data, which came into force in May 2018. This administrative definition of profiling meets the academic definition of *surveillance* proposed by *Surveillance Studies*, a new field of interdisciplinary studies that emerged, especially in the English-speaking academic world, shortly after the attacks on the Twin Towers: "To study surveillance is to provide an understanding of the procedures by which personal data are collected, stored, transmitted, controlled and used as means of influencing and managing the population" (Lyon 2002, p. 1). "Influencing and managing the population" is precisely what Foucault meant by "biopolitics" in his analyses of the "security society". It is the whole of society, the multiplicity, the "public", i.e. the "population taken on board by their opinions, their ways of doing things, their behaviors, their habits, their fears, their prejudices, their demands, what has been taken over by education, by campaigns, by convictions" (Foucault 2004, p. 77).

As intrusive technologies advance, the way populations are approached by profiles and the file has taken on an ever-wider extension. The expansion of GAFA (Google, Apple, Facebook, Amazon) is an example of how fast this process can be, affecting all aspects of our lives. In a way, these gigantic advertising agencies and their approach to consumers are the culmination of a long process that began in the 1930s and 1940s with the rise of advertising tools. Gradually, consumption has created an inexhaustible field of experimentation for the development of techniques for tracking and recording consumer behavior. Throughout this process, which should be called the "taylorization of consumption", companies and marketing devices have constantly broken down the movements and gestures of individuals, seeking their interests, preferences, needs and desires (Mattelart 1989).

Like today, in a world governed by highly integrated ultra-liberal capitalism, the boundaries are porous between geopolitics and economics, and security strategies guided by reason of the State can hardly do without the capital in personal data that these *data brokers* have collected and continue to feed. Nothing attests to this reality better than the revelations made in June 2013 by Edward Snowden, the young computer scientist working for the National Security Agency (NSA), on the clandestine Prism (*Planning tool for Resources, Integration, Synchronization and Management*) program: this agency and the FBI had access to foreign Internet users' data stored by the transnationals on the Net. Moreover, it is not only in terms of security strategy that the latter give up personal data without the consent of third parties. The Cambridge Analytica case, named after the consumer research firm, shows that these data can also be coveted by other companies, for example for election advertising purposes.

From the prevalence of new forms of control, invisible, mobile, automatic and deterritorialized, it cannot be concluded that the logic of panopticism has disappeared from the management modes of multitudes. The "security society", as Michel Foucault understood it, does not erase the disciplinary society. It integrates it, completes it, without deleting it. The two are articulated. The society of disciplinary closure remains a sediment of the traffic society. The proliferation of walls and border barriers, whether high-tech installations or barbed wire, indicates that coercive mechanisms in disciplinary societies remain the common horizon for the mass of migrants, refugees and others excluded from the global techno-economic system.

1.4. The techno-security paradigm

Modern wars, whether global or not, have played a decisive role in defining basic concepts such as national security, internal enemy, state of siege, emergency, counter-insurgency and pacification, as well as their corollaries: psychological action, psychological warfare, winning hearts and minds, all of which are privileged sources of innovation in social control doctrines and techniques. All these concepts have endorsed (and continue to support) State terrorism as the supreme rule in very different latitudes. This is what I have tried to report on, in particular in *Multinational Corporations and the Control of Culture* (1979), *Mapping World Communication* (1994) and *The Globalization of Surveillance* (2010).

In the proceedings of the *2001 Bogues: Globalisme et pluralisme* symposium, held at the University of Quebec in Montreal in 2002, since it was postponed following the attacks of September 11, 2001, Professor Gaëtan Tremblay and I rightly recalled that "one of the major risks is that the global integration process, in the context of the fight against terrorism, is driven by the globalization of the security state. All the more reason to be vigilant about all restrictions on the exercise of freedom of expression and democratic rights" (Mattelart and Tremblay 2003, p. 16).

The fight against terrorism has undoubtedly legitimized the multiplication of techno-social control systems. In this respect, it has acted as a powerful trend accelerator. The violations of the rule of law by the democratic regimes in their fight against the "new threats" have shown the links between concepts, institutional logics and technological developments that had hitherto appeared in isolation. The measures taken by the United States in the aftermath of the attacks of September 11, 2001 have a paradigm value: creation of an *ad hoc* ministry; new anti-terrorist legislation (Patriot Act); implementation of the TIA (Total Information Awareness) mass surveillance project, later renamed Terrorism Information Awareness; and the transfer of military control and surveillance technologies to police applications. More generally, "national security", which might have been thought of as obsolete with the end of the Cold War, made a strong comeback during the response to the attacks. The tightening of institutions around this principle reactivated the Cold War era patterns of a military–industrial complex and cooperation between university research, industry, military and civilian intelligence organizations (Giroux 2007). Lines of study have resumed the preoccupations of the counter-insurgency wars of the 1960s and 1970s, which were abandoned as soon as the Vietnamese conflict was over. New bridges have been built between the national territory and the global space, external security and internal security, the police universe and the military universe, the secret services and information in open environments. The slogan of "interoperability" between organizations reflects this fundamental logic that helps to drive the globalization of safety standards. Agencies whose official mission was previously confined to the national territory have set up relays abroad, and agencies that could only operate outside have extended their area of intervention to the national territory.

As security systems, procedures and protocols are standardized at the global level. This has affected the control of the entire mode of communication and movement of people, goods and ideas. The fight against terrorism has endorsed advances in intrusion techniques throughout society. Surveillance practices that were previously illegal have become common practice. Under the pretext of protecting citizens, they have often made them feel "insecure". Under the pressure of urgency, governments struggling with the attacks sought to incorporate emergency measures into the common law. The abundance of reforms of penal codes, codes of criminal procedure and laws on intelligence and security in everyday life attest to the variable geometry of the new nomenclature of penalties and the categories of individuals and groups likely to "disturb public order". The old positivist concept of "dangerousness" has returned to the legal–police system, bringing with it the one just as marked by "dangerous classes". It presupposes that an individual can be considered guilty (and therefore jailable) not for the acts they have committed, but for those they *could* commit. It abuses such as this that make Giorgio Agamben (2014) say that "the securitarian obsession makes democracy mutate". While the impact of the mass surveillance paradigm is global in nature, its resonance at the level of each nation, region or continent depends on their position on the geopolitical map of the globe. Moreover, as in any process of internationalization, there is an interaction between global logic and the singular realities in which it is territorialized. This geolocation, or local anchoring of the "safety culture", is a decisive factor.

1.5. The fascination for Big Data

Profiling can also be associated with Big Data. With the great leap forward in artificial intelligence (AI) and autonomous systems, software such as algorithms have intruded wherever massive digital data, or Big Data, are being processed in order to infer rules that allow foresight and prediction in the most diverse dimensions of human activity, and this, in an environment of digital data from multiple sources (administrations, companies, scientific communities, Internet users) that are varied, both in terms of their production and use (Mabi, Plantin and Monnoyer-Smith 2017). For large transnational companies, data accumulation is a guarantee of a new form of capital, a basic factor of production and a competitive advantage. For medicine, it offers the possibility of anticipating pandemics or making medical diagnoses more reliable, for hospital services, to control patient flows and, for the education system, student flows. For the so-called "predictive security" programs, it offers a tool for identifying "high-risk populations". For criminal policy, it is the promise to relieve the courts of their workload by preventing acts of recidivism. For the police, it is about measuring the risk of crime in time and space.

The fact is that Big Data have triggered fantasies of omnipotence, despite uncertainties about their exploitation. "Massive data processing can lead to massive errors, and ultimately to catastrophically bad decisions", according to a mathematician at the University of Berkeley[1]. "Weapons of mathematical destruction", a mathematician rightly adds, which increase inequalities, threaten democracy and leave the real human world outside the universe of algorithms (O'Neill 2016). Resistant statisticians continue to warn against abuses of the new governance by numbers and data. The desire to detect *risky* behavior at all costs leads to the "distortion of official statistics", they argue. Because "the developments of computerized intelligence are not only used for control, they also concern the implementation of social policies and the reduction of inequalities". And to ask the question: "Can we find a compromise between knowledge and filing?" (Marzouki and Simon 2010, description). Nevertheless, the controversies over the possibility of governing algorithms and the confrontation between autonomous machines and human intelligence raise both hope and fear.

Another issue is that of continental and global policies on the protection and circulation of personal data, a long-term process, as indicated by the genesis of the disputes that have been going on between the European Union and the United States government since the 1980s over the transatlantic transfer of such data, the latter wanting at all costs to impose its doctrine of the free flow of data. The 2016 European Directive on the protection of personal data, which came into force in May 2018, aims to rebalance Internet users' relationships with major Internet operators. It also aims to unify the rules throughout Europe, as well as to extend the application of these rules to companies located outside its borders that process data from EU citizens. But the showdown is also played out at other levels, that of global governance. This is the case of the World Trade Organization (WTO), which, during the negotiations on electronic commerce, is also moving towards the deregulation of all types of standards, as we saw at the eleventh ministerial conference, the Organization's supreme decision-making body, held in Buenos Aires in December 2017. In addition, regional free trade treaties, such as the Trans-Pacific Partnership (TPP) or the Transatlantic Trade and Investment Partnership (TTIP), or less identified treaties, such as the Trade in Services Agreement (TISA), are proving to be places where governments' legislative capacity is under attack and where the liberalization of data flows is decided, directly or indirectly.

1 M. Jordan, quoted in Reverchon, A. (2015, October 31). "Le défi de tous les superlatifs". *Le Monde*, section "Cultures et Idées".

1.6. The shadows of the number cult

Where do we stand today? The risk is that, in the end, only numbers count. The prophetic vision of a better world, which originally inspired the Western dream of a harmony based on calculation, has faded. The algorithmic "reason" shows the dystopic or anti-utopic face of the "information society" project. The reality is that, by being quantifiable, the individual appears more and more transparent in the eyes of power systems, which, in turn, continue to unfold in opacity. As the fundamental rights lawyer Alain Supiot, a professor at the Collège de France, attests: "Governance by numbers and data aims at the effective achievement of measurable objectives rather than obeying fair laws, leaving individuals, or States, with no other way out than to make allegiance to someone stronger than themselves in contempt of social law"[2].

Scientists have, in their own way, clearly understood this set of challenges and issues when today they examine AI and autonomous systems in the light of ethics and question the dynamics of research in digital science and technology. The argument of the 2017 edition of the *Entretiens du Nouveau Monde Industriel* (New Industrial World Talks), whose theme was "Artificial intelligence and stupidity", is a living example of this act of resistance and in the face of systems of exclusion and isolation:

> "Technologies derived from mathematics applied to networked computing tend to impose themselves on the scientific world based on the efficiency criteria prescribed by the markets… The result is an extreme and highly paradoxical threat to the possibilities of exercising, cultivating and developing scientific knowledge if it is true that it cannot submit to the processes of proletarianization that are induced by the 'black boxes' that the instruments and devices come from for scientists now as much as for the common people" (ENMI 2017, paragraphs 1–2).

We can see it. There are many reasons to share knowledge. This pooling can only exist if the struggles and reflections to stop the commodification of the new intangible resource are aimed at challenging the relationships of knowledge and consequently at bringing about a new social contract between science and society, between science and researchers, that is capable of freeing the imagination and collective intelligence and that opens up new rights and new forms of citizenship. This is a necessary condition for the development of new democratic uses of the potential of the network of networks.

---

2 On the University of Nantes' WebTV, 2015. Available at: https://webtv.univ-nantes.fr/fiche/6463/alain-supiot-la-gouvernance-par-les-nombres.

1.7. References

Agamben, G. (2014). Comment l'obsession sécuritaire fait muter la démocratie. *Le Monde diplomatique*, 133, 56–61.

Bonditti, P. (2017). Violence and the modern international: An archaelogy of terrorism. In *Foucault and the Modern International*, Bonditti, P., Bigo, D., and Gros, F. (eds). Palgrave Macmillan, London, 155–173.

Braudel, F. (1958). Histoire et sciences sociales : la longue durée. *Annales Économies, Sociétés, Civilisations*, 13(8), 725–753.

CNIL (2018). *Règlement (UE) 2016/679 du Parlement européen et du Conseil du 27 avril 2016*. Available at: https://www.cnil.fr/fr/reglement-europeen-protection-donnees/.

de Condorcet, N. (1988). *Esquisse d'un tableau historique des progrès de l'esprit humain.* Flammarion, Paris.

Desrosières, A. (1993). *La politique des grands nombres*. La Découverte, Paris.

ENMI (2017). *Onzièmes entretiens du Nouveau Monde industriel : "Argumentaire"*. Available at: https://enmi-conf.org/wp/enmi17/argumentaire/.

Ewald, F. (1986). *L'État-providence*. Grasset, Paris.

Foucault, M. (1975). *Discipline and Punish: The Birth of the Prison*. London, Allen Lane.

Foucault, M. (2004). *Security, Territory, Population*. New York, Palgrave Macmillan.

Garnham, N. (1998). Information society theory as ideology: A critique in Society and Leisure, 21(1), 97–120. Presses de l'Université du Québec.

Giroux, H.A. (2007). *The University in Chains: Confronting the Military-Industrial-Academic Complex*. Paradigm Publishers, Boulder.

Julia, D. (1981). *Les trois couleurs du tableau noir, La Révolution*. Belin, Paris.

Lyon, D. (2002). Editorial: Surveillance studies understanding visibility, mobility, and the phenetic fix. *Surveillance and Society*, 1(1), 1–7.

Mabi, C., Plantin, J.-C., and Monnoyer-Smith, L. (eds) (2017). *Ouvrir, partager, réutiliser, Regards critiques sur les données numériques*. Maison des sciences de l'Homme, Paris.

Marzouki, M. and Simon, P. (eds) (2010). Sous contrôle. Gouverner par les fichiers. *Mouvements*, 62, 7–10.

Mattelart, A. (1979). *Multinational Corporations & the Control of Culture*. Harvester Press, New Jersey.

Mattelart, A. (1994). *Mapping World Communication*. The University of Minnesota Press, Minneapolis.

Mattelart, A. (1996). *The Invention of Communication*. The University of Minnesota Press, Minneapolis.

Mattelart, A. (1999). *Histoire de l'utopie planétaire*. La Découverte, Paris.

Mattelart, A. (2003). *The Information Society*. Sage Publications.

Mattelart, A. (2005). *Advertising International*. Routledge, London.

Mattelart, A. (2010). *The Globalisation of Surveillance*. Polity Press, Cambridge.

Mattelart A. (2017). The word and the things: An archaelogy of an amnesic notion. In *Foucault and the Modern International*. Bonditti, P., Bigo, D., and Gros, F. (eds). Palgrave Macmillan, London.

Mattelart, A. (2018). *Histoire de la société de l'information*, 5th edition. La Découverte, Paris.

Mattelart, A. and Tremblay, G. (eds) (2003). *2001 Bogues, tome 4, Globalisme et pluralisme : communication, démocratie et globalisation*. Les Presses de l'Université Laval, Quebec.

Mattelart, A. and Vitalis, A. (2014). *Le profilage des populations. Du livret ouvrier au cybercontrôle*. La Découverte, Paris.

O'Neil, C. (2016). *Weapons of Math Destruction. How Big Data Increases Inequality and Threatens Democracy*. Crown Publishing, New York.

Rouvroy, A. and Berns, T. (2013). Gouvernementalité algorithmique et perspectives d'émancipation. *Réseaux*, 177, 163–196.

Supiot, A. (2015). *La gouvernance par les nombres*. Fayard, Paris.

2

Big Data as a Device for Generalized Decoding of the Social Field[1]

Big Data[2] has often been described as a huge disruption in the social field. While profound changes are taking place here and there (generalized surveillance of goods and people, endless extension of sensors and connected objects, etc.), we could say that the much-anticipated "Big Data Revolution" has never really taken place. On the one hand, because its production never stops in all levels of the social field and sometimes on a molecular scale (e.g. data mining techniques that apply to the sequencing of the human genome). On the other hand, because this permanent revolution, often with indistinguishable effects, is part of a dynamic that is nothing new: the search for new spheres of market value. In this way, Big Data expresses the tendency to integrate more and more things from the lifeworld[3] in the process of valorization and commodification.

Big Data is reviving with ever greater urgency the theory of the colonization of the world experienced by the subsystems of economics and the State, whose regulatory means, money and power, penetrate even the most intimate aspects of

Chapter written by Fabien RICHERT.

1 This text takes up the argument and part of the subject of the chapter "*Le Big Data à l'ère du sémiocapitalisme : décodage et axiomatisation généralisés du champ social*" (Richert 2018), published in the book *Big Data et Société* (2018), edited by André Mondoux and Marc Ménard.

2 We usually talk about a large amount of data produced continuously on a global scale; thinking in the plural, we talk about mega data (Big Data). In this chapter, it is mainly a question of taking Big Data as a set of techniques, devices and discourses that support the process of duplicating the world experienced in data.

3 "Lifeworld" is understood in the sense of Jürgen Habermas (1987): a concrete subjective reality whose resources are structured by the culture, society and personality of individuals.

subjectivity. This colonization was thematized by Deleuze and Guattari by the notions of *coding*, *decoding* and *axiomatization*; aspects to which I propose to return to shed a singular light on Big Data.

2.1. Coding, decoding and axiomatization

Deleuzoguattarian anthropology is marked by a singular reading of Marx, marked by a series of reinterpretations, diversions and conceptual reworking against a background of a break with a certain Marxist tradition. Deleuze and Guattari share the Marxist project of establishing a universal history from the point of view of capitalism by targeting the process of coding–decoding that runs through the different forms of society, i.e. a universal history considered in the light of its end: capitalism as the supreme and terminal decoding authority.

Deleuze and Guattari then analyzed the different modes of investment of desire specific to a machine of social production. To ensure and determine social reproduction, each type of society must intervene directly in the desirable production in order to limit its mad and indeterminate productivity in the form of subordination to its own dominant authorities. In other words, if the desire for production springs up from all angles, it is up to societies, in varying historical forms, to close the vanishing lines in order to fix and stabilize the social order. And this stabilization constitutes a kind of "coding" operation that involves the construction and assimilation of symbolic, institutional or legal content that determines how to govern the production, circulation, distribution and consumption of a multiplicity of social flows[4]. Coding, therefore, plays a role in determining deviant and illegitimate flows, as well as in promoting flows that are authorized and legitimized by the social order.

Deleuze and Guattari undertook a comparative analysis of the ways in which different social formations adopt particular and specific instances to code their flows. The coding process itself is related to a kind of evolutionary curve (coding, overcoding, decoding and axiomatization) to the extremities from which so-called "primitive" societies would face capitalist societies. It is necessary in advance to dispel doubts and equivocations regarding the analysis delivered by Deleuze and Guattari, which is not evolutionary, but rather genealogical. Thus, in a way, the ramifications of the different social machines studied cross and overlap as much

4 For Deleuze and Guattari, the flows refer to a reality in perpetual movement and which refers in an undifferentiated way to desire, to *objects* or to forces and powers that circulate permanently in the social field. And while some flows precipitate into flight movements, others settle and stratify.

synchronously as diachronically in a way that any evolutionary temptation is rejected in advance by Deleuze and Guattari. Thus, capitalism is not associated with some form of mythology of progress that would see a conquest of civilization in the development of science, technology and, more generally, reason in opposition to the so-called "primitive" or "barbaric" societies, maintained at a less evolved stage. For Deleuze and Guattari, it is more simply a question of considering capitalist societies as a specific state of social and desirable. In fact, the latter shares a methodological proximity with that of Marx, insofar as capitalism offers a retrospective point of view for establishing a universal history of human societies.

The idea of coding, overcoding and axiomatization then corresponds to the typology of three major social machines. Primitive societies function from a territorial machine that encodes flows on land, which becomes an investment of collective desire and quasi-cause of the fertility of women and soils. State-owned societies overcode the flows of primitive societies to channel them into the despot's body and its bureaucratic apparatus of power. It was first necessary to decode the primitive codes to reinvest desire on despotic machines. Finally, capitalist societies proceed by axiomatization. They tend towards a threshold of generalized decoding of flows in order to facilitate the conjunction between labor and capital. The body of capital becomes the general authority that subjugates the bulk of productive forces according to its logic of valorization, which is why Deleuze and Guattari (1972) define capitalism as "the only social machine [...] that is constructed on the basis of decoded flows, substituting intrinsic codes with an axiomatic of abstract quantities in the form of money" (p. 167).

Therefore, coding involves the creation and assignment of symbolic, institutional or legal content that condition the ways of governing the production, circulation and consumption of a multiplicity of flows. In *Anti-Oedipus* (1972), Deleuze and Guattari repeatedly discuss one of the non-exhaustive descriptions of these codes which regulates the activity and circulation of the trade flows of pre-capitalist societies: prestige and alliance objects, the logic of gift and counter-gift, sumptuary expenses, tribute, slavery, major works, etc.

From the point of view of economic anthropology, coding corresponds first and foremost to a process of qualifying flows. The codes themselves refer to extra-economic instances. Deleuze and Guattari then set out some of these instances, drawing on the work of Étienne Balibar and Louis Althusser, which show, for example, that legal relations are "determined to be dominant" in economic relations from the feudal era, or that alliance and filiation relations[5], which are observed in so-called "primitive" societies, prevail in the way that exchange and consumption

5 Deleuze and Guattari rely in particular on Africanist anthropology, which had developed, in the 1960s, an ethno-historical approach to lineage and filiative societies.

are structured (p. 298). In other words, coding establishes a form of mediation that organizes the meeting of qualified flows. The qualification itself is based on beliefs, symbolic content or an "instituting imaginary" (Castoriadis 1975).

Deleuze and Guattari are more precisely interested in the impact of the capitalist mode of production on the different codings adopted by pre-capitalist societies in order to organize their production and give meaning to their practices. From this point of view, capitalism is organized as the only social formation that functions from a process of generalized decoding of flows of all kinds and natures. By extending the theories of Pierre Clastres (1974), Deleuze and Guattari showed that pre-capitalist societies have not ceased to conjure up a generalized decoding of all flows with all their might, so that "in a sense, capitalism has haunted all forms of society, but it haunts them as their terrifying nightmare, the fear and panic that they have of a flow that eludes them of their codes" (Deleuze and Guattari 1972, p. 268). Although different, the territorial machine and the despotic machine are haunted by the same nightmare, that of a diversion from a generalized decoding of flows that would result from an empowerment of economic flows. As Deleuze and Guattari (1972, p. 183) point out:

> "The primitive machine is not ignorant of exchange, commerce, and industry; it exorcises them, localizes them, cordons them off, encastes them, and maintains the merchant and the blacksmith in a subordinate position, so that the flows of exchange and production do not manage to break the codes in favor of their abstract or fictional quantities".

Sibertin-Blanc (2013) showed that the concept of decoding refers first and foremost to Marxist analysis of primitive accumulation. Primitive accumulation is characterized by a process of generalized dissolution of the symbolic, institutional and political factors that would structure social relationships. This decoding is essential insofar as extra-economic codes always block, at different levels, the empowerment of the abstraction value as a universal equivalent and an undifferentiating factor with respect to the quality of all decoded flows. Thus, when the flows encoded by these instances lose their old identity, when they escape their own code, they are caught in a decoding movement: a monetary flow will constitute a capital by decoding the relations of prestige and personal allegiance; a flow of slaves or producers will constitute the conditions of the proletariat by decoding the relations of servitude and professional orders; a flow of merchants or bankers will constitute the conditions of the bourgeoisie by decoding the castes and ranks (Deleuze and Guattari 1972).

But the demonstration is not yet quite obvious since, starting from the sole point of view of a flow that would escape these old identities coded by multiple extra-economic instances, decoding is not yet a process exclusive to capitalism. Despotic societies also decode the elements of primitive societies, but in the form of an overcoding of flows that are dominated and subordinated to a transcendent unity, embodied in empires by the half-human, half-divine figure of the despot.

This is because the decoding movement is twofold insofar as the decoding of flows is carried out simultaneously against the background of their axiomatization: "it axiomatizes with one hand what it decodes with the other" (Deleuze and Guattari 1972, p. 296). Rather than using the terms coding, recoding or overcoding, Deleuze and Guattari favor the idea of axiomatic. An axiom generally presupposes a set of absolute rules and statements that are considered generally indemonstrable and undecidable. In the context of capitalism, axioms "are evidently neither theoretical propositions, nor ideological formulas, but operative statements that constitute the semiological form of Capital, and that enter as component parts into assemblages of production, circulation and consumption" (p. 577).

The distinction between coding and axiomatic is then made in this way: coding establishes a form of mediation that organizes the meeting of qualified flows and implies, *a fortiori*, "a system of collective appraisal and evaluation" (Deleuze and Guattari 1972, p. 270) based on beliefs, symbolic content or even instituted and instituting imaginary creations (Castoriadis 1975). Rather, axiomatic indicates a collapse of codes, because it proceeds by dissolving and destroying the symbolic content of the conditions of existence of these social formations. The old codes are as if they were guarded, tied up and suffocated for an implacable logic. Departing from Marx's fundamental analyses of the categories that underpin capitalism, Deleuze and Guattari find one of the best illustrations of the specificities of capitalist axiomatization in value form: value abstraction as a master axiom and as the most deterritorialized flow capable of abstracting the sensitive quality of all things to enable exchange. Expressed in the form of money, the value form opposes the code in that it assigns an abstract quantity to all the flows it encounters, regardless of their own qualities. Deleuze and Guattari (1972) then described capitalism as the only social machine "that was built as such on decoded flows, replacing intrinsic codes with an axiomatic of abstract quantities in the form of money" (p. 167). Consequently, the accumulation of capital is carried out immediately and without the intermediary of a transcendent body, if by this we mean extra-economic forms of mediation that symbolically and institutionally code the organization of social relations. The economic authority becomes autonomous and ends up subordinating itself to all other forms of authority (political, familial, associative, etc.). We understand here that the generalized axiomatization of flows, therefore, comes back to the idea of a real subsumption of the social field by capital.

In addition, the logic of endless accumulation raises the problem of the very limit that capitalism constantly pushes back by opening up new markets to compensate for recurrent crises of overaccumulation and chronic problems of declining trends in profit rates:

> "If capitalism is the exterior limit of all societies, it is not because it does not have an exterior limit on its own, but only an interior limit, which is capital itself, and which does not encounter, but reproduces by always displacing it" (Deleuze and Guattari 1972, p. 277).

The decoding operation of all flows, operated by capitalism, is therefore limited internally in the conditions of production and circulation of merchandise. And this "immanent limit" is constantly confronted with problems of the depreciation of existing capital and crises of overproduction temporarily resolved by renewed forms of primitive accumulation intervening in the destruction (unemployment, factory closure, deregulation of the labor market, etc.) and creation (relocation of production centers, privatization of the public sectors, etc.) of new high added-value markets.

In short, if capitalism is the "universal truth", it is because it occupies the borderline position of all previous societies in terms of what they are able to code and overcode. And if the Deleuzoguattarian history undertaken from the point of view of the capitalist mode of production is called "universal", it is in the sense that, at the heart of this mode of production, an orientation and a dynamism have been maintained that have eventually become universal. From this point of view, we pose the current phenomenon of Big Data as one of the ongoing avatars of this tendency to decode and axiomatize all flows of the social field.

2.2. The role of Big Data

Big Data, sometimes requalified as new black gold, results incidentally from this shift in boundaries, so that the code–decode–axiomatization relationship does not only serve as an analogy to approach the process of reducing the world after 0 and 1. Moreover, Big Data illustrates in its own way the process of decoding a multiplicity of flows that still managed to escape capitalistic axiomatization. Big Data appears as a machine for unifying flows of all kinds for immediately becoming a source of profit. We can think of areas as strategic as consumption (prediction of purchasing behavior or the ability to repay a loan, etc.), health (determination of the trajectory of influenza epidemics, automated detection of physical anomalies, etc.), insurance (proposal of tailor-made insurance contracts following a hyper-responsibility of policyholders in managing their own risks) or politics (prefabrication of campaign arguments on the basis of detailed profiling).

Moreover, the translation of any event (communication, travel, banking transaction) into data for market valuation purposes induces a deep distance as for the existential richness inherent to this event, an abstraction of its qualitative dimension. Big Data completes the reign of equivalence; it makes "what is heterogeneous comparable by reducing it to abstract quantities" (Adorno and Horkheimer 1974, p. 29). From this point of view, databases can be considered as warehouses or banks that store data flows regardless of their content and awaiting market activation for the highest bidders. Think of applications such as Facebook, Uber and Airbnb, where a large part of the business model depends on a "smart" analysis of Big Data.

2.3. Semiocapitalism

An important part of Big Data relating to human activities is intimately linked to the subjectivity of individuals, as well as to their movements, relationships, desires, bodies, etc. Consequently, the slightest part of their existence can be translated into data, and then analyzed, correlated and commoditized.

It is in this spirit that I am currently working on the concept of *semiocapitalism*, of which Big Data is one of the current expressions of the accumulation regime. The concept of semiocapitalism informs the idea that the semiotic activity of individuals – language, thought patterns, as well as gestures and behaviors – has become directly productive, because it is largely subject to a logic of market value. There are two aspects to this valuation: the first aspect refers more specifically to the particular modalities of a certain type of intangible work that emerges in the era of digital social media, digital labor (to which we will return in the next section); the second aspect concerns more specifically the modes of subjectivity and desire that are concretized by the enthusiastic, even addictive participation and the use of interconnected devices, applications and web platforms. This second point should be qualified by specifying that these forms of subjectivity and desire are always constrained and disciplined by the imperatives of production and valorization. For example, the imagination and inventiveness of the creative class, which would be essential for the economic development and attractiveness of urban centers in the era of semiocapitalism (Florida 2002), are largely determined by modern market standards. Therefore, the creativity that manifests itself, for example, in the design of algorithms, graphics and interfaces for renowned platforms, such as Uber, Airbnb and Facebook, aims first and foremost to develop, maintain and perpetuate functionalities that are driven by market logic: transport and hosting services are offered, a network of knowledge is accumulated and optimized, self-promotional strategies are developed, etc.

Large semio-corporations such as Facebook and others exploit part of the mental activity, which is translated into computer technology and stored in databases. This exploitation increases the axiomatization potential of the psyche and the social field through the endless extension of calculating rationality: a cold and distant rationality from any form of singularity, that of algorithmic governmentality (Rouvroy and Berns 2013).

2.4. Digital labor

In the semiocapitalist regime, Big Data refers less to immaterial labor than to a dynamic of digital labor, which refers to a generalized decoding of our activities involving, at different levels, the use of interconnected devices. As Félix Guattari (2012) noted, while the duration of a worker's incarceration in a factory is easily measurable, its effects are much less so. To paraphrase Guattari, the semiocapitalist regime extorts not only working time, but a highly complex semiotic process, a semiotic surplus value (and no longer just mechanical), where the semiotic capital of the individual in a digital labor situation becomes an important commodity for the valorization process. By seizing "human beings from within" (Guattari 2012, p. 102), semiocapitalism decodes the semiotic flows themselves. Whether in the management of digital social networks, in the creation of a graphic charter or in the writing of a line of code for a computer program, semiocapitalism seeks to exploit the capital of competence and knowledge of a flexible and polyvalent infoworker.

From this point of view, Big Data virtually expresses this decoding by allowing the commodification of decoded flows, so that we should rather speak of "dividual" production to illustrate digital labor, which Antonio Casilli and Dominique Cardon (2015) define as the reduction of our digital activities "at some point in the production cycle" (p. 13). In the semiocapitalist regime, *digital labor* refers to a generalized decoding of our various activities involving, at several levels, the use of interconnected devices. The individual production of *digital labor* continues the fragmentation of human activity and the reduction of the individual in the form of a plurality of partial and abstract functions which have no other purpose than that of capital accumulation.

The integrative power of semiocapitalism is based on a fully automated operating mode that is not solely observed between the different material operations that connect sensors to databases and individuals to the Internet. This automation is observed at the level of the individual and collective psyche: an automation of semiotic processes. Franco Berardi (2016) and Bernard Stiegler (2012) examine this automation in its most deadly aspects through a detailed analysis of the conditions and causes of spectacular acts.

Berardi (2016), to whom we owe the term *semiocapitalism*, proposes a figure, that of the spasm "as a moment of brief and sudden energy" (p. 208). A spasm is the body's unconscious and automatic response to the endless exploitation of individual and collective semiosis in a context of technical and social acceleration. The spasmodic condition, when it becomes widespread, undeniably induces a pathological state of social misery where impulse and addiction – which engage routines, habits of thought and ways of being affected – in return become directly exploitable by semiocapitalism. However, this spasmodic condition is not only expressed through the spectacular passages to action analyzed by Berardi and Stiegler. To fully understand the parallel between machine–human automation, Gary Genosko (2016, p. 110) gives the example of an online banking platform: remote access to his banking information presupposes the implementation of a disparate series of so-called "a-signifying" semiotics, identified here in the computer code, which allow access to a server at the rate of stop and access points, locks and openings in network connections. Moreover, the invisibilization of these mechanical interactions has an effect on the individual, for whom account management and the carrying out of various transactions involve a unique emotional relationship with the banking paradigm. Activation is the key to the functioning of a-signifying semiotics, which "issue start and stop commands" (Guattari 1992, p. 75) and allow or prohibit connections that far exceed the simple human gestures considered in a banking transaction, a geolocalized movement or a simple message sent over digital social networks.

This last point leads us to the fundamental idea that we seek to link to the phenomenon of Big Data from the point of view of a theory of semiocapitalism of a Deleuzoguattarian nature: as a current manifestation of the semiocapitalist accumulation regime, Big Data illustrates in its own way the process of decoding a multiplicity of flows that still managed to escape capitalist axiomatization. Big Data appears as a machine for unifying flows of all kinds to become an immediate source of profit. In this way, Big Data can be thought of as the digital recording of a decoded and potentially axiomatic individual and collective semiosis.

2.5. Conclusion

I wish to draw a picture here that seems distressing and pessimistic. However, it is not a question of falling into the Adornian trap of total reification, since if it were totally reified, we could not say anything about it. However, it is still necessary to maintain theoretical and empirical work on the unprecedented conditions of domination exercised by Big Data in the social field. In other words, thinking of emancipation is dialectically based on a critique of forms of domination, some aspects of which were sketched out under the Deleuzoguattarian term, which in particular made it possible to analyze Big Data as a process that participates in the decoding and axiomatization of social flows, resulting in a profound limitation of their symbolic content.

Particularly, by translating the process of primitive accumulation from a semiotic description (coding, decoding, axiomatic), Deleuze and Guattari define capitalism as the negative of all social formations, given its tendency to dissolve extra-economic codings that block to varying degrees the displacement of its immanent limit. Sociocapitalism embodies this displacement of limits up to the individual and collective psyche, which we have summarized by the idea of a real subsumption of all types of semiotic activity. From this point of view, Big Data, understood as one of the current modes of expression of the semiocapitalist accumulation regime, opens up new conditions for valorization through data mining techniques to analyze feelings on socio-digital networks (*opinion mining*), or predicting decisions and purchasing behaviors on the basis of supposedly precise and neutral inputs of activities in the social field under the influence of monitoring and control mechanisms.

To consider Big Data from the angle of semiocapitalism is to first of all consider that abstraction and indifference towards everything imposed by digital reason first affect subjectivities and sensitivities. The virtually unlimited production of insignificant information is a consequence of a semiotic collapse that can be observed through a standardization of lifestyles and thinking, an oppressive "mass mediatization", or a strengthening of control and monitoring systems.

Moreover, the Deleuzoguattarian perspective tells us that the political terrain should precisely invest in the possibilities of a recoding of social flows that would not coincide purely and simply with capitalist axiomatization. In the social field, proposals abound on all sides, such as the concept of the *notion of the commons* developed by Dardot and Laval (2014) and the requirement of an inappropriate standard, the subversive use of the institution of salaried employment proposed by Bernard Friot (2012) to imagine the possibilities of a lifetime salary, or the project to restructure the concept of *social* by Franck Fischbach (2017), articulated with a reflection on the elements of socialist governmentality. All these proposals aim to formulate new forms of mediation, to imagine another way of encoding social organization.

2.6. References

Adorno, T. and Horkheimer, M. (1974). *La dialectique de la raison*. Gallimard, Paris.

Berardi, F. (2016). *Tueries : forcenés et suicidaire à l'ère du capitalisme absolu*. Lux, Montreal.

Cardon, D. and Casilli, A. (2015). *Qu'est-ce que le Digital Labor* ? INA, Bry-sur-Marne.

Castoriadis, C. (1975). *L'institution imaginaire de la société*. Le Seuil, Paris.

Clastres, P. (1974). *La Société contre l'État. Recherches d'anthropologie politique*. Éditions de Minuit, Paris.

Dardot, P. and Laval, C. (2014). *Commun : essai sur la révolution au XXIème siècle*. La Découverte, Paris.

Deleuze, G. and Guattari, F. (1972). *L'anti-Œdipe*. Éditions de Minuit, Paris.

Deleuze, G. and Guattari, F. (2004). *A Thousand Plateaus*. University of Minnesota Press, Minneaplis.

Fischbach, F. (2017). *Qu'est-ce qu'un gouvernement socialiste ?* Lux, Montreal.

Florida, R. (2002). *The Rise of the Creative Class*. Basic Books, New York.

Friot, B. (2012). *L'enjeu du salaire*. La Dispute, Paris.

Genosko, G. (2016). *Critical Semiotics: Theory, from Information to Affect*. Bloomsbury Academic, New York.

Guattari, F. (1992). *Chaosmose*. Galilée, Paris.

Guattari, F. (2012). *La révolution moléculaire*. Les Prairies ordinaires, Paris.

Habermas, J. (1987). *Théorie de l'agir communicationnel*. Fayard, Paris.

Rouvroy, A. and Berns, T. (2013). Gouvernementalité algorithmique et perspectives d'émancipation. Le disparate comme condition d'individuation par la relation ? *Réseaux*, 177, 163–196.

Sibertin-Blanc, G. (2013). *Politique et État chez Deleuze et Guattari*. Presses universitaires de France, Paris.

Stiegler, B. (2012). *États de choc : bêtise et savoir au XXIème siècle*. Mille et une nuits, Paris.

3

Algorithmic Management, Organizational Changes and the Digitalization of HR Practices: A Critical Perspective

Recruitment, remuneration, training, social dialog, the promotion of professional equality, quality of life at work, diversity, etc. are all areas that the vast Human Resources (HR) function is called upon to deal with on a daily basis within contemporary organizations, who are constantly confronted with market uncertainties, increased competitiveness and digital transformations. Experts agree that the HR function is changing rapidly (see ANDRH reports[1], managerial literature and the many publications of management researchers). Thus, traditionally oriented towards the administrative management of staff, it would have become a strategic function (Peretti 2018). The purpose of this chapter is to critically examine the transformations underway related to the massive use of digital tools (platforms, professional social networks, chatbots, predictive models) that affects HR – practices, whether in terms of recruitment, training or internal communication – and which have profound consequences on management within companies. The approach is part of the field of organizational communication and draws from research in sociology related to work in large companies as well as from Information and Communication Sciences (ICS). To what extent does digital technology contribute to the transformation of HR processes and business developments? How does it affect managerial practices in organizations? What are the social consequences on individuals and info-communication processes?

Chapter written by Yanita ANDONOVA.

1 The *Association nationale des DRH* (ANDRH), created in 1947, is a key player in the French professional landscape.

From a methodological point of view, the following analysis is based on our own field observations and *in situ* studies, carried out over the past 15 years in different types of organizations (large companies, associations, local authorities, project-based organizations, etc.), as well as on examples of case studies examined as part of a university master's degree. In this chapter, we will successively address the following points: 1) digital transformations and the evolution of professions; 2) the digitalization of the HR function[2]; 3) the analysis of these social transformations in a communication approach, taking into consideration issues of visibility, agility, disruption and creativity.

3.1 Digital transformations and business developments

The term *digital* has invaded managerial literature, delighted consultants and become a permanent feature of the discourse of different companies. In one of our observation areas in a major French telecommunications group[3], for company management, "digitalization" is presented as an opportunity, while being a constrained and inevitable choice, to face the contemporary challenges facing this telecommunications group: increased competition and reduced margins on traditional activities (telephony, data). More generally, this digitalization is inscribed in the digital transformation of companies. It implies the emergence of new agile, collaborative, transparent organizational forms, and refers to a set of supposedly innovative professional practices, while omitting the new forms of surveillance and social control that they impose. From SMEs to large multinational companies, they are all rethinking their organization in terms of digital technology. This has a profound impact on working practices, forms of apprenticeships within organizations and, more generally, the conditions under which certain professions are carried out.

Many sectors of activity are affected within the increasingly digitalized "information society" (Lacroix and Tremblay 1997; Mattelart 2001; Miège 2000). IBM's Watson program, the virtual assistant capable of answering user questions, analyzes a huge amount of data and is deployed in the banking sector (Crédit Agricole and Orange in France). The use of artificial intelligence (AI) has already revolutionized journalistic practices (robot-journalist at the *Washington Post*). Algorithms for automatic translation mark a turning point, and the digitalization of

2 Through this chapter, we use the expression "the digitalization of HR practices". While this may generate enthusiasm among professionals and business consultants, our analysis of the subject is in a resolutely critical perspective.

3 This includes a qualitative study on digital skills, carried out in 2015–2016. The objective was to understand the perception of the group's strategic management's discourse on digital transformation in order to identify the transversal skills required by digitization/digitalization and the ways in which these skills are acquired.

press relations, based on interactions with e-influencers, which have become, according to some authors, media in their own right through digital social networks, is disrupting professional practices. Robotics is also transforming healthcare professions, remote healthcare solutions and remote surgical operations with remote assistance. Connected objects are becoming more common. Telemedicine plays an important role in optimizing the quality of patient care. We even speak of "social robotics" when we talk about the care of robots.

As a result of the automation of tasks, computerization and robotization, new professions are emerging, while others, such as reception and assistance, are evolving in depth[4]. Many companies in France use the Pepper robot including Renault, with the deployment 120 robots in its showrooms, the *Cité des sciences de l'industrie*, and Carrefour, the first player in Europe to have tested the robot's functionality in stores. At Axa Banque, a robot, whose activities are to inform customers about new services and to simulate loans, is deployed in various branches. Aico Chihira is the first humanoid robot to work as a hostess in a Tokyo store. Julie Desk is the virtual secretary "made in France", specialized in appointment management, relaunching unreactive contacts and booking restaurants. She manages all activities by email, the purpose being to call her by copying her in a message containing the people you want to meet. She sets an appointment after each party has validated the request, proposes slots according to everyone's availability and takes care of the rest concerning the appointment booking: it is she who sends the invitations, enters the appointments in the participants' calendar, sends a reminder message, etc.[5].

Beyond these few examples of robotization, we are witnessing profound changes in the structure of jobs. A cashier's job, turned hostess, has undergone major changes. It has evolved a lot in recent years from grocery stores to hypermarkets, with the appearance of barcodes and optical scanners, fast cash registers, payment by scanner, carts connected to smartphones, etc. The computerization has made it possible to monitor the performance of each cashier on a daily basis and thus increase productivity: how many references per minute did she scan during the day? How many customer payments did she collect per hour? Is it efficient? The computerization of the cash registers has therefore strengthened the supervision and hierarchical controls of these employees, which are mainly evaluated on quantitative

4 According to an OECD study, the demand for highly skilled jobs has increased dramatically, leading to the robotization of repetitive tasks. The International Federation of Robotics indicates 10 main reasons for employers to robotize in the tertiary sector: improving the quality of agents' workstations; increasing efficiency; improving health and safety conditions at the workplace; reducing labor turnover and recruitment difficulties; and reducing training costs.

5 Julie Desk's creators opted for a hybrid system in which humans support AI, as a small team monitors the virtual assistant.

criteria and are then classified according to their individual performance. But the hunt against idle time does not stop there, since it became more pronounced in the 2000s, when automatic registers flourished in most supermarkets. The automation of the cash registers has redesigned the work of the cashiers (since they are now responsible for several cash registers at the same time) and has led to an intensification of work, as shown by the national surveys of the DARES, from 2014 on working conditions[6].

Another particularly significant example of the evolution of professions since the arrival of the Internet and digital tools in the professional world is that of the postman, whose profession is currently under threat. The historical model is being challenged by the development of digital exchanges (emails, SMS, phone calls, digital social networks and other means of communication). In France, La Poste group has been diversifying its original business in recent years by extending it to the banking (*La Banque postale*) and telephone (*La Poste mobile*) sectors, as well as to the digital sector (*Coffre digital*, which makes it possible to secure data). These activities reflect the gradual disappearance of the "conventional" postman profession in favor of new tasks. The company reorients the tasks of its postmen towards other activities, which require new skills (and consequently new training), in order to carry out several types of tasks: home delivery of medication; paper collection for the purpose of recycling; home visits; detection of anomalies on the road; conducting driver's license exams; reading parking meters; etc. Diversifying the missions makes it possible to limit the dismissals and reclassification of employees whose activity is significantly reduced. But can we still call their job a "postman"? We can also note the use of drones, tested by La Poste in 2016. These drones, which are responsible for delivering parcels to the homes of users in hard-to-reach areas, are responsible for one of the main tasks of the "traditional" postmen. Indeed, the modernization of mail and parcel distribution processes, which is faster and more efficient, makes it possible to meet the needs of customers who have become more demanding in terms of service quality and delivery times.

If we believe the results of the study published in 2017[7] by Dell Technologies and the Institute for the Future (IFTF), a Californian think tank based in Palo Alto, and widely reported by the general public press in France and elsewhere in the world, then the world of work will undergo profound changes within the next 10 years. Drawing on a panel of experts from the high-tech economy and the academic world, this study states, not without claim, that 85% of the jobs that will be created by 2030 do not yet exist. The main reason, according to the study, is the omnipresence of the digital

6 The results are available on the website of the Ministry of Labor (France): https://dares.travail-emploi.gouv.fr/IMG/pdf/2014-049.pdf.

7 The results of the study are available at: https://www.delltechnologies.com/content/dam/delltechnologies/assets/perspectives/2030/pdf/SR1940_IFTFforDellTechnologies_Human-Machine_070517_readerhigh-res.pdf.

and robotization in organizational processes, which could contribute to the partial destruction of some trades. Without debating the effects of automation, computerization, robotization and then digitalization on employment[8], it is certain that prospective studies are flourishing (especially concerning the future of intelligent automatons) and are undoubtedly contributing to the structuring of representations while feeding collective imaginaries. However, the central questions, those of developments in skills and quality, seem to be somewhat omitted.

Web developers and code geniuses remain the market's biggest favorites, but new web experts are gaining power. Thus, data scientists, web analysts and cybersecurity experts (who protect companies against cyberattacks) have a meteoric career. We see the emergence of *the chief digital officer*, *the social media manager*, *the digital evangelist*, *the e-influencer*, *the creative technologist*, *the brand content manager* (who helps brands to be present on digital social networks and positions themselves in relation to the competition), all designated professions thanks to a predominantly English vocabulary. The IT sector remains the main source of employment in the digital sector, but the range of jobs sought is wider. Scientific, creative and marketing profiles are in the spotlight and are categorized by companies as "talents". The *web designer*, both creator and computer scientist, creates the visual identity of a web interface; the *UX designer* makes the site accessible on a computer, tablet or smartphone; the *motion designer*, the *community manager*, the *traffic manager*, etc. are solicited by recruitment agencies for "creative" people. Following the interviews we conducted in 2018 with recruiters of "creative" people, they unanimously affirmed that the "digital has shaken up the creative professions". "Finding talent" has become a central activity for companies, as several recruitment managers working in specialized agencies have told us. Often, they use massive data analysis methods, allowing the recruitment of diversified and sometimes geographically distant profiles. We will come back to this issue in the third part of our argument.

3.2. Digitalization of the HR function: practices and tools

HR practices are also part of the transformations induced by the massive use of digital platforms and tools (Cousserand-Blin and Pinède, 2018). Companies are now recruiting through job boards, Facebook and Twitter. Human Resources digitalization is more common nowadays, considering all these new usages of digital technologies for the services of HR. Traditional sourcing techniques (sending paper CVs, handwritten cover letters) have been extended to online tools made available to

---

8 See *Conseil d'orientation pour l'emploi* (2017, January). *Automatisation, numérisation et emploi*. Volume 1: Impacts on the volume, structure and location of employment. Report. Available at: http://www.coe.gouv.fr/IMG/pdf/COE_170110_Synthesis_of_the_report_Automatisation_numerisation_et_emploi_Tome_1.pdf.

recruiters via the Internet. New software offers that are more advanced in terms of ergonomics, functionalities and configuration facilities have been very successful. Automating the administrative dimension of candidate search is the primary objective sought by companies, who have already been using algorithms to sort and choose CVs. What is the situation today? Is it really possible to be recruited by a robot? Algorithms are used to recruit, to retain employees who are inclined to leave the company, and to monitor and improve HR management (People Analytics at Google). Free search engines allow you to identify "rare profiles" on professional platforms (LinkedIn, Viadeo, Twitter, Facebook, etc.), find their contact details and approach them directly.

Behind the neutrality of the recruitment platforms façade lies fundamental ethical issues (on the use of personal data and the question of social control, for example). The neutrality of data and algorithms, being of course quite relative (O'Neil 2016), requires an urgent awareness of civil society, consumers, employees and managers. A critical approach in communication sciences makes it possible to focus questions on the themes of traceability, visibility and self-exposure on professional social networks, topics that we will discuss in the following. This refers to the reflections of Antoinette Rouvroy and Thomas Berns (2013) on algorithmic governance, which is a crisis of representation, i.e. "a crisis of truth regimes".

HRIS (HR Information Systems) are also part of a company's tools for "building a digital culture" and aim to simplify HR management by streamlining processes, streamlining communication and relieving managers of low value-adding activity. Thus, strategies for digitalization HR practices are inspired by start-up enterprises, so often praised for their "agility" and capacity for innovation, which have become models of creativity and flexibility for heavier and more hierarchical bureaucratic organizations.

In addition, many companies use chatbots, which are conversational agents, most often presented as avatars to answer customer questions. Some companies even use them to recruit new employees online. The economic impact is significant: since there is no longer a need to employ recruitment managers (due to the usage of algorithmic management), costs are greatly reduced and the company can claim that it has gained productivity and speed. Other companies use chatbots to automatically handle time-consuming tasks and thus improve the speed of HR processes, i.e. they shorten the time it takes to answer employees' questions about their payslips or the current rules. This is the case with YODA (Your Own Digital Assistant), a chatbot launched at the end of 2016 by the *Société Générale* which is accessible on the group's Intranet. It concerns 140,000 employees and is part of the overall digital transformation strategy announced in the group's annual report (2016). The name chosen is the result of the group's narrative strategy in terms of communication and is a nod to the *Star Wars* saga, whose character of the same name embodies the wisdom it instills in its apprentices (the "Padawans"). This communication story promotes a tool, available in several languages, all the time, whose goal is to improve the responsiveness of HR departments to multiple requests by improving response time and reducing the workload of overwhelmed and small numbers of HR administrative staff. However, we lose space for words, because the suffering or distress of some colleagues cannot be expressed in the chatbot. Can we talk about a deterioration in working conditions (Klein and Ratier 2012), with the dehumanization of relations between employees and the departments responsible for personnel management? The loss of speaking space deserves a thorough communication analysis (see AFCI's White Paper *Parole au travail & parole sur le travail*, 2017 (Word at work & word about work)).

These changes have significant consequences on managerial practices. With teleworking, open space, flex-office, third locations, etc., the proximity manager is expected to manage dispersed, flexible and agile teams in shortened time frames. Will the proximity manager soon have to deal with robots as well? The "disembodied management" (Dujarier 2015) that we have been witnessing for more than a decade, disconnected from the reality of work, based on quantified indicators, is reinforced by algorithmic management. We observe the implementation of managerial practices based on the use of algorithms: machine learning, voice recognition, facial biometrics of employees, implementation of RFID chips, etc. Moreover, job boards, professional social networks (LinkedIn, Viadeo, Xing), chatbots, conversational platforms, microblogging tools, geolocation tools, etc. are used in recruitment processes. What are the risks for individuals and work collectives? What are the consequences for social cohesion?

3.3. Which communication approach for studying these phenomena and their social consequences?

It is therefore necessary to put the above questions into a "communicational perspective". It can be deployed in different registers. Our approach falls within the field of organizational communication and focuses on both the communication devices, practices and processes that constitute the dynamics of social construction of organizations (d'Almeida and Andonova 2006). Organizational communication has become an established field between normative and critical models (Delcambre 2000; d'Almeida and Carayol 2014) at the intersection of scientific issues and professional practices. Reflecting on the digitalization of the HR function and the consequences of algorithmic management implies that we must take a close look at both communication and organization (Grosjean and Bonneville 2011), i.e. we must closely examine the relationship between organizational communication and communicating organization. To do this, we propose to question ourselves here on two central points: 1) the problem of visibility, chosen or experienced by individuals, and 2) that of creative disruption and the social inconsequences of the use of agility.

The issue of visibility, addressed in ICS work, helps to shed light on the analysis of new managerial practices linked to the digitalization of the HR function. The algorithmic management of recruitment is based on digital traces (Merzeau 2013), omnipresent on the social web. The algorithms used make it possible to perform numerous calculations, filter the results and provide refined data for decision-making (recruitment or not of a candidate). As we have shown above, these digital tools are intended to help human resources managers by providing them with an initial automated analysis. The latter is allegedly considered neutral, i.e. free of any risk of discrimination. Nevertheless, digital traces reveal the candidates' editorial qualities, their networks of contacts, their lifestyles (through photographs that go well beyond the traditional identity photo), as well as certain sensitive information that can give rise to prejudice and discrimination: political opinion, trade union involvement, sexual orientation, medical situation, religious sensitivity, etc. These themes remain taboo subjects within companies, as internal communication often considers them to be sensitive, relating more to the intimate than to the professional life of individuals. The new European framework – the GDPR[9] – takes this aspect forward, which has so far received little attention, by offering greater protection to individuals in the management of personal information about customers and employees of companies.

There are also internal issues related to the management of personal data and the social control of employees. For companies, HRIS, chatbots and internal digital social networks allow them to refocus the HR function on a more strategic, less administrative management. For employees, it is a matter of developing new strategies for visibility in the face of the tools now available to them, adopting new codes while maintaining flexibility. Issue 44 of the journal *Communication & Organisation*, "*Nouvelles formes de visibilité des individus en enterprise : technologie et temporalité*" (Communication & Organization, "New forms of visibility for individuals in companies: Technology and temporality"), addresses this theme in the internal and external frameworks of organizations[10] and demonstrates how employees juggle on a daily basis between what can be revealed and what must remain hidden, between spaces for visibility and forms of withdrawal (Andonova and Vacher 2013). The question of the alleged neutrality of algorithmic models is central to this.

9 The General Data Protection Regulation (GDPR) entered into force on May 25, 2018 in the European Union, and concerns the processing and circulation of personal data used by companies to sell services or goods.

10 See Valérie Laroche's article (2013), which analyzes in particular the professional visibility of employee ambassadors 2.0 with recruiters based on an analysis of the Backstage platform, initiated by BNP Paribas' brand and employer department.

The issues of “e-reputation” and “digital identity” have also become unavoidable. Fanny Georges (2009) proposed a study of digital identity through three sets of signs: declarative identity (data produced by the user), active identity (concrete activities of the user on digital social networks) and calculated identity (variables calculated by the algorithm and interpreted quantitatively by the user). Algorithms count the digital traces left by individuals, interpret them according to opaque criteria and categorize them (Cardon 2015). In addition, the question of visibility raises the question of invisibility. The invisibility of algorithmic systems leads to a dissolution of responsibilities as well as a reduction in the opportunities for conflict (Sadin 2016).

Another question, which deserves careful consideration, but which we can only outline here, concerns the problem of disruption and agility in relation to the creativity so sought by companies. The “talents” and “creative” that we mentioned earlier are considered as “nuggets”, which stimulate new ways of acting and working in organizations that are often very hierarchical. Flexible, autonomous, adaptable and fast learning, these employees have an agility of thought that is deployed through *design thinking* and project modes. Disruption, an overused term that has become commonplace and initially falls within the lexical field of marketing (disruption marketing), is supposed to “trigger creative jolts”. Disruption would not only not restrict creativity, but would also free it from the constraints of routine, allowing new perspectives and ideas to emerge. Agility postures and in the moment learning are expected to quickly adapt to contexts of permanent change. The considerable acceleration of technological innovations and disruptive innovation are disrupting individuals, and thus induce new managerial practices (algorithmic management based on the calculation of millions of data on individuals and correlations with the company’s economic model) to the detriment of social systems (Stiegler 2016). Creativity in companies is expressed through agility and disruption that shake up pre-established patterns.

This terminology is similar to the artistic field of talent rating. Expert employees qualified as “high creative potential” are sought, recruited and retained by HR specialists who are ready to do anything to keep them. The question of “talent management”, a fully fledged HR technique, deserves to be studied in the light of research on injunctions to creativity (Andonova 2015; Andonova and Kogan 2017). How to characterize “talent” in the company? What are the explicit criteria and who has the legitimacy to define them?

The social inconsistencies of the use of agility, disruption and creativity in companies deserve to be analyzed in a specific approach in communication sciences, focusing on the devices, practices and discourses related to the use of digital technology and, in particular, the implementation of predictive models, which affect managerial practices, the vast HR function and, more generally, info-communication processes in contemporary organizations. Digital technology does not change everything, but it accompanies the societal transformations already underway, which leads to a joint analysis of three registers: the individual, the collective and the organization, with a view, in particular, to corporate social responsibility (CSR). Has the productive enterprise of the 19th Century, which became a corporate citizen (d'Almeida 2001) at the end of the 20th Century, put aside the ethical question in the increasingly widespread use of predictive algorithms? The HR and internal communication functions have a considerable role to play in taking ownership of the subject and discussing it at all levels of the company in discussion spaces not only dedicated to strategic functions, but also open to all.

3.4. References

AFCI (2017). Parole au travail & parole sur le travail. White book. Association française de communication interne, Paris.

Andonova, Y. (2015). Approche critique des injonctions à la créativité : relations entre secteur culturel et monde du travail industriel. *Les Enjeux de l'information et de la communication*. Introduction au supplément 16/3B.

Andonova, Y. and Kogan, A.-F. (eds) (2017). *Questionner le tournant créatif : dispositifs, processus et représentations*. Available at: https://crea2s.hypotheses.org/files/2018/03/2017_ACTES-colloque-VARNA.pdf.

Andonova, Y. and Vacher, B. (eds) (2013). Nouvelles formes de visibilité des individus en entreprise : Technologie et temporalité. *Communication & Organisation*, 44. Available at: https://journals.openedition.org/communicationorganisation/4277.

Cardon, D. (2015). *À quoi rêvent les algorithmes. Nos vies à l'heure des Big Data*. Le Seuil, Paris.

Cousserand-Blin I. and Pinède N. (eds) (2018) Digitalisation et recrutement. Perspectives informationnelles et communicationnelles. *Communication & Organisation*, Bordeaux, (53), 9–16.

d'Almeida, N. (2001). *Les promesses de la communication*. Presses Universitaires de France, Paris.

d'Almeida, N. and Andonova, Y. (2006). La communication des organisations. In *Sciences de l'Information et de la Communication. Objets, savoirs, discipline*, Olivesi, S. (ed.). Presses Universitaires de Grenoble, Grenoble, 129–143.

d'Almeida, N. and Carayol, V. (2014). La communication organisationnelle, une question de communauté. *Revue française des sciences de l'information et de la communication*, 4. Available at: https://journals.openedition.org/rfsic/870.

Delcambre, P. (ed.) (2000). *Communications Organisationnelles, Objets, Pratiques, Dispositifs*. Presses universitaires de Rennes, Rennes.

Dujarier, M.-A. (2015). *Le management désincarné. Enquête sur les nouveaux cadres du travail*. La Découverte, Paris.

Georges, F. (2009). Représentation de soi et identité numérique. Une approche sémiotique et quantitative de l'emprise culturelle du Web 2.0. *Réseaux*, 154, 165–193.

Grosjean, S., and Bonneville, L. (2011). *La Communication Organisationnelle : Approches, Processus et Enjeux*. Chenelière Éducation, Montreal.

Klein, T. and Ratier, D. (2012). *L'impact des TIC sur les conditions de travail*. La Documentation française, Paris.

Lacroix, J.-G. and Tremblay, G. (1997). *The "Information Society" and the Cultural Industries Theory*. Sage Publications, London.

Larroche, V. (2013). Quelle visibilité professionnelle pour un salarié ambassadeur 2.0 auprès des recruteurs potentiels ? *Communication & Organisation*, 44, 53–64. Available at: https://journals.openedition.org/communicationorganisation/4309.

Mattelart, A. (2001). *Histoire de la société de l'information*. La Découverte, Paris.

Merzeau, L. (2013). Traces numériques et recrutement : du symptôme au cheminement. In *Traces numériques, de la production à l'interprétation*, Galinon-Mélénec, B. and Zlitni, S. (eds). CNRS Éditions, Paris, 35–53.

Miège, B. (ed.) (2000). Questionner la société de l'information. *Réseaux*, 18(101).

O'Neil, C. (2016). *Weapons of Math Destruction: How Big Data Increases Inequality and Threatens Democracy*. Crown Publishing Group, New York.

Peretti, J.-M. (2018). *Gestion des Ressources Humaines*. Vuibert, Paris.

Rouvroy, A. and Berns, T. (2013). Gouvernementalité algorithmique et perspectives d'émancipation. *Réseaux*, 177, 163–196.

Sadin, É. (2016). *La silicolonisation du monde. L'irrésistible expansion du libéralisme numérique*. L'échappée, Paris.

Stiegler, B. (2016). *Dans la disruption : comment ne pas devenir fou ?* Les Liens qui libèrent, Paris.

4

Nanotargeting and Automation of Political Discourse

This chapter seeks to detail what we call the "automation of political discourse", a concept developed from three main elements: first, nanotargeting, which constitutes the action of automated political discourse[1]; second, algorithmic governmentality, which constitutes its method; and third, the public space of "communicative capitalism" (Dean 2005), which constitutes its emerging context.

4.1. On nanotargeting

4.1.1. *Segmentation*

The notion of *target audiences* has been used for a long time and is common in marketing. However, this segmentation is accentuated by communication technologies. In terms of supply, the public has access to an exponential choice of media channels and opportunities for interaction with them. This fragmentation makes the planning of advertising campaigns more complex, while making it

Chapter written by Samuel COSSETTE.

1 The notion of *political discourse* is rather a large one: the two terms are polysemic. To discern what constitutes or does not constitute political discourse is an arduous task. In a literature review, Wilson (2008) notes that the notion sometimes refers to discourse that is explicitly political, and other times to any discourse related to a certain political context. It is important, however, Wilson notes, to avoid over-generalizing the notion as this could undermine the clarity of the analysis. In this sense, he proposes to offer, each time, a definition adapted to the objectives of the analysis (Wilson 2008, 398). In this chapter, much of which deals with the notion of nanotargeting, we will limit our understanding of the notion of political discourse to digital messages, although other elements of political discourse are affected, to varying degrees, by automation processes.

possible to select the audiences targeted by these same campaigns: it is the transition from broadcasting (broad) to narrowcasting (reduced) (Du Plessis 2012).

These new technological possibilities facilitate an extreme segmentation of the market, which thus becomes an alternative to product differentiation (Baines *et al.* 2003). In short, it is no longer necessary to offer a product – or a message – that stands out from the others: it becomes necessary to offer the message to the right person, when they are in a good state of mind to receive it. Segmentation mainly operates, in this sense, in what could be called a "transfer" of production. The role of the advertiser is no longer primarily to sell a product to a consumer, but rather to produce a consumer for a product: we identify exactly when, where and in what state of mind this consumer will be receptive to a certain message. This production is adjusted to market needs, constantly creating new groups of consumers, according to new specific characteristics in time and space (Zwick and Knott 2009). However, electoral politics is no longer very different from the market in its purely economic sense. The *political marketplace* is not very distinct from the market for products and services. Politicians present themselves as brands (Guzmán *et al.* 2015), and most of the scientific literature on segmentation includes the *political marketplace* (Baines *et al.* 2003). The place of segmentation in this market was highlighted by the unified field in 1990 (O'Shaughnessy 1993) and concerns about this segmentation soon followed: Elihu Katz was already concerned, in 1996, about the consequences of electoral segmentation in the democratic public space (Katz 1996).

The segmentation marketing dynamics described are therefore at work in the political sphere, more specifically in the electoral sphere. Such techniques became popular as early as the 19th Century, when firms kept lists of personal information with the collaboration of postal services and newspapers (Couldry and Turow 2014). The same principle has been applied to large-scale data collection and processing: different forms already existed, since the end of the 19th Century (Semetko and Tworzecki 2017). The novelty lies rather in the refinement. Magin *et al.* (2017) classify the types of traditional political campaigns, in terms of communication, into three categories: directed at supporters, directed at the general electorate or directed at groups. In addition, there is now a fourth type made possible by recent technical capabilities, namely "individual campaigns based on personal data offered by commercial companies" (Magin *et al.* 2017, p. 1701). These campaigns are effectively established on political microtargeting.

4.1.2. *Microtargeting*

Microtargeting, the act of sending a particular message to a specific and chosen group of individuals without their necessarily being aware of it (Faizullabhoy and Korolova 2018), is not a new technique and has been generating enthusiasm in the field of political communication for at least two decades (Milbank 1999). Microtargeting has been used in commercial advertising for a long time and its method has been devised by marketing researchers for even longer (Sivadas *et al.* 1998). Its use in political communication, on the other hand, has more fundamental implications than in a consumerist sales context. Although the use is similar, persuasion techniques are an integral part of the democratic process and, for this reason, they must be observed more closely (Bay 2017). The ethics of a targeted message or algorithm that seeks to influence the political process are not the same as those of an algorithm that seeks to sell a product (Bay 2017).

The increasing integration of microtargeting into political communication has therefore raised several concerns in the academic community, particularly with regard to the impact of voter segmentation on democratic regimes (Couldry and Turow 2014; Guzmán *et al.* 2015; Shorey and Howard 2016). The Cambridge Analytica case, in the spring of 2018, particularly exacerbated these concerns.

4.1.3. *Nanotargeting*

The term nanotargeting was first used in the field of political communication in 2009 by Josh Koster, campaign consultant and "new media" specialist (Harvey 2014). It is put forward with strong enthusiasm in marketing studies where we speak, with some reservation, of a "promised land" (Jovanovic 2014, p. 415). However, the concept of nanotargeting is still evolving. While Koster applied it to the segmentation of "niches", which concerned groups of individuals, it is now associated with microtargeting directed at a single individual or selected individuals rather than a group (Barbu 2014). Kerpen (2011) was the first to give it this meaning – at least in marketing – when he applied the term to his successful attempt to create a Facebook advert that only his spouse could see. Alexander Nix, CEO of Cambridge Analytica, also boasted that he was able to target specific individuals using the techniques developed by his company (Mavriki and Karyda 2017). In our opinion, nanotargeting differs from microtargeting in three main ways.

4.1.3.1. *Affects and psychometric analysis*

The notion of affects has been particularly prominent and developed in research in communication with the development of digital social networks. The concepts such as *affective networks* (Dean 2010), *affective economics* (Andrejevic 2011), *affective news* (Young and Soroka 2012) *and affective public* (Papacharissi 2014) have been designed to try to capture new communication dynamics. Dean and Paparachissi explain that digital communication networks are mainly built around the circulation of affects: affective networks that do not constitute real communities, but feelings of community (Dean 2010, p. 22), and public affective networks organized around structures of feelings (Papacharissi 2016, p. 320).

While microtargeting is mainly built on data that relate to purchasing habits, income, social class, location, employment or community membership, nanotargeting adds emotions, feelings and behaviors to this list. Massive data mining on the Internet introduces techniques of "sentiment analysis" and "opinion mining", terms that appeared in the academic field at the very beginning of the 21st Century (Pang and Lee 2008). These techniques are used to quickly identify a person's psychological state in order to offer the most appropriate message. It is the understanding of an individual's state of mind that allows advertisers to determine exactly what media should be used, what time and technique should be chosen and what message should be offered to not only receive the attention of the targeted individual, but, most importantly, be able to predict their reaction to the message (Du Plessis 2012). Psychometric analysis, based on data collected through *sentiment analysis* and *mood analysis*, is, in our opinion, a central feature of the automation of political discourse. First, because it marks a break with the types of data that could be collected before digital data mining; second, because it is part of this quest for immediacy that defines automation; and third, because it significantly changes the "classic" segmentation of markets. In short, psychometric analysis techniques offer added value to traditional market segmentation by integrating data that were previously difficult to obtain, particularly in real time, through *sentiment analysis* and *mood analysis*. It is the attempt by some digital communication actors to build electoral markets not only through the collection of demographic information, but also through "comprehensive, real-time, trustworthy databases of Internet users' behavior and conversations" (Andrejevic 2011, p. 604).

4.1.3.2. *Instantaneity*

The second main distinction of nanotargeting, in our view, is instantaneity: firstly, psychometric data, unlike demographic data, changes rapidly; secondly, generated message from collected data has to be sent at the precise moment when the targeted individual is in the best state of mind to receive the message. More so than ever, we are trying to anticipate a behavior that would be triggered by the reception of a certain message and, in fact, produce it.

4.1.3.3. *Individuality*

The last distinction, individuality, stems from the first two. Microtargeting was aimed at groups of people, sometimes quite small, but always groups. Nanotargeting, by adding sentiment building and real-time action possibilities carried by the Internet, reduces the message to the individual level. The targeted individual receives a specific message, built in part by the data they have produced themself, and sent at the moment when they are in a specific state of mind: in this sense, each message is unique.

4.2. On algorithmic governance

The concept of *algorithmic governance* broadly refers to "a certain type of (a)normative or (a)political rationality founded on the automated collection, aggregation and analysis of Big Data so as to model, anticipate and pre-emptively affect possible behaviors" (Rouvroy and Berns 2013).

Algorithmic governmentality takes place in three stages: first, the collection by data monitoring of huge amounts of data, otherwise known as Big Data. Big Data can be defined by the construction of large datasets from information that is collected on several people, by several devices, and that can be linked to each other to derive correlations and allow research (Shorey and Howard 2016). These data are generally anonymized and decontextualized, i.e. cut off from any relationship with the subject from whom they were produced. Second, these data are processed and knowledge is produced from them in an automated way: algorithms perform this task. Finally, thanks to this knowledge, we can take action on behavior (Rouvroy and Berns 2013).

Algorithmic governmentality introduces several notions. First of all, there is the capture of attention. Algorithmic governmentality is based on efficiency, instantaneity and real time. This capture takes place in an "attention economy", where we seek to capture affects rather than reasoning (Harsin 2015). Emanating in part from marketing and economic logic, we are witnessing a "systematic capture of any fragment of human attention available for the benefit of private interests (the economy of attention), rather than for the benefit of democratic debate and the general interest" (Rouvroy and Berns 2013, p. 167).

Then comes the action on the behavior. A call to deliberation and reason forms reflexivity; a call to affect causes a reaction. Algorithmic governmentality does not promote dialog, debate or even reflection: the injunction to efficiency rather imposes an action on the behavior. Actions are predicted, according to data, and a signal is sent to provoke a certain reaction. We want to act on what has not yet been done, but on what has been predicted, i.e. to build the real: the "target of algorithmic governmentality", explains Rouvroy, is "this unrealized part of the future" (Rouvroy and Stiegler 2015, p. 119).

These trends result in the disappearance of the subject. The algorithmic governmentality, in fact, "produces no subjectification, it bypasses and avoids reflexive human subjects" (Rouvroy and Berns 2013, p. 174). The capture of affects and then action on behaviors shapes models that are "supra-individual", i.e. there is never a call to the subject himself and to rationality. This leads to a depoliticization that "does not give rise to or take any active, consisting, reflexive statistical subject" (Rouvroy and Berns 2013, p. 180)[2].

Finally, there is a "disappearance of the common experience" (Rouvroy and Berns 2013, p. 167). A social space automated by algorithms, optimized, without reflexivity, simply without a subject, leads to a public space atrophied by its potentially subversive meaning. The emphasis on affects leads to a potential radicalization of opinions and the loss of common narratives and norms. Paradoxically, it is the constitution of a state of citizenship that is hyperindividualized, but deprived of its political capacity.

4.3. Public space and communicative capitalism

Political discourse, of course, is an integral part of the public space. In Habermas' work, Cossette (1987) explains that public space is above all a normative proposition: the theorist shares with us a "fiction" made possible by the conditions of the modern state, an unfinished reality. Habermas' model of public space is thus conceived "as the bearer of a utopian possibility [...] an ideal set in a critical context" (Cossette 1987, p. 11).

Habermas' public space is built on an institutional and liberal conception as well as on the fundamental role of free and rational deliberation (Goodsell 2003). For him, institutions must build a deliberative space that respects certain standards, including the equality of the people who take part and universal accessibility. For Castoriadis and Arendt, public space also deals with the issues of collective interest: this space is in fact the condition for the possibility of politics (*politique*)[3]

2 Analyses of new communication capabilities offered by objects such as algorithms or microtargeting methods often tend to limit the arrangement of subjects in their relationships with these objects. Some even put forward the idea of a return to a one-step flow of communication (Bennett and Manheim 2006; Neuman and Guggenheim 2011), where targeting and prediction methods would be so precise that they could go beyond the "decoding" step performed by the subject receiving the message. These hasty analyses risk recreating theoretical shifts from the past, the most famous being the "hypodermic syringe" theory, making the same epistemological error, that of considering an all-powerful device and ignoring the subject. Here, we analyze the tools of political discourse automation, the theoretical considerations it proposes and some of the risks we perceive in terms of political communication, but without denying its central place in these analyses: this will, however, need to be the subject of further research.

3 For Castoriadis and Arendt, the concept of *politics* is essential to the understanding of public space and its role. The two contrast *le politique*, which concerns rules, institutions, procedures and their applications, as well as the existence of a central power, and *la politique*, whose ultimate objective would be the infringement of freedom and the questioning of that power (Poirier 2009). It is "true politics" and "politics", for Castoriadis; genuine politics, authentic politics and politics proper, for Arendt (Straume 2012).

(Straume 2012). The public space is not maintained by institutions, but by political action: for Arendt, it is “active life” and for Castoriadis, it is the “ontology of being” (Straume 2012). The model of representative democracies, in this sense, is rejected by both authors, because it is based on a procedural vision of democracy in which there is no real participation, and therefore neither equality nor effective freedom (Poirier 2009). In this sense, the public space, according to Castoriadis (1997), is institutional in the sense of society and political action.

For the three authors, the notion of *public space* is also based on a tension with the private sphere. Different areas of life are classified, either in the public sphere, in the private sphere or somewhere in between. The economic sphere, in particular, is classified by Habermas outside the public sphere (Hohendahl 1992). Castoriadis and Arendt go in the same direction: Castoriadis (1997) separates society into three main spheres: the *oikos*, the family, the private sphere; the *agora*, the market place, the private/public sphere; and the *ekklēsia*, the public sphere, the place of political power. Arendt (1958), on the contrary, argues its distinction, particularly through the concept of *active living*, and presents the private sphere as the space of necessity and the public sphere as the space of the construction of freedom.

However, in the observation of each individual, there is a disappearance of these borders, a “colonization” of the public sphere by the private sphere. The capitalist dynamic aimed at always favoring the process of commodification, as Castoriadis explains (in Poirier 2009), leads to a process of privatization of the public space. For Arendt (in Goodsell 2003), the distinction between the public and private sphere is becoming blurred. This colonization of the public sphere, according to Arendt, has transformed it into a “pseudo-space” of interactions where individuals *no* longer *act* but *behave*, recalling the action of algorithmic governmentality described by Rouvroy and Berns.

The notion of public space allows us to highlight the criticism developed by Dean (2003) with the concept of *communicational capitalism*, which in several respects parallels that of algorithmic governmentality. These two concepts are, according to our understanding, closely linked within speech automation. These three elements mainly intersect.

First, the function of the message and its relationship to the individual. In Habermas’ model, explains Dean (2005), the message has a function based on its understanding, i.e. its “value” is measured according to whether it has been understood in the right way: the content of the message is essential for its use. This is not the case in communicative capitalism. The content of the message does not matter: its circulation, rather, verifies its success. “A contribution [message] need not be understood; it need only be repeated, reproduced, forwarded” (Dean 2005,

p. 59). At first glance, this definition may seem contradictory to the idea of microtargeting, where a message has very specific characteristics and does not necessarily have to circulate widely. The essential element is the *action* of the message. The content of the message, from a reflexive point of view, is also not important in a microtargeting campaign. Its success is confirmed by its action on behavior, as Rouvroy (Rouvroy and Berns 2013) explains, by the effectiveness of these signals. In this sense, the individual targeted is no more important either, than the importance of certain correlations previously plotted by the algorithm – such as his potentiality to react to a certain signal – and his ability, perhaps, to *circulate* the message in a certain network. We want to influence our behavior or even our place (Dean 2005).

Second, the central notion of communicational capitalism of *technological fetishism* refers to Rouvroy's thinking in several ways. For Dean, technological fetishism is the idea that complex political elements could be condensed into a single problem, and therefore a single solution, technological of course. This is what the algorithm actually claims to do: in a neutral and objective way, it absorbs huge amounts of data on complex subjects and derives correlations that make it possible to analyze them, but not to understand them. This is also a loss of reflexivity.

Third, the notion of *depoliticization*, essential to algorithmic governmentality, is also essential in the concept of communicative capitalism. Political fetishism, through its condensing action and technical "solution", depoliticizes problems. Algorithmic governmentality operates the same process, depoliticizing decisions: political reflection is useless in a context where data provide us with an accurate understanding of reality, where figures speak for themselves.

4.4. On the automation of political discourse

It is at the intersection of the theories presented that we find the global portrait of the automation of political discourse. Bernard Stiegler (in Rouvroy and Stiegler 2015) states that, unlike the process of reason, which is synthetic, automation is an analytical process. Automated speech occurs through data analysis, algorithmically processed and detached from any human reflexivity and arrangement. First, it creates elective "markets" (Harsin 2015), in which it instigates individuals not to appeal to their reason and deliberative capacities, but to capture their attention and try to influence their behavior, in real time: the technique operates both hyperindividualization and "desubjectivation" (Dufour 2008; Mondoux 2011; Rouvroy and Stiegler 2015). This entire process of capturing data and returning signals from the same data is circular and operates in fundamentally depoliticizing market logics, where the message, as long as it has the desired effect and becomes sufficiently large in a certain network, ultimately does not matter (Dean 2005). This same process, therefore, contributes to the formation of a reality that is not constructed, real, neutral and objective, but which in fact carries ideology and is constitutive: first of all, a political discourse that becomes *apolitical*, without reflexivity, personalized, but at the same time without subject; then a public space colonized by "an hypertrophied private sphere" (Rouvroy and Berns 2013, p. 167) where the common and democratic experience is disappearing.

4.5. References

Andrejevic, M. (2011). The work that affective economics does. *Cultural Studies*, 25(4–5), 604–620.

Arendt, H. (1958). *The Human Condition*. The University of Chicago Press, Chicago.

Baines, P.R., Worcester, R.M., Jarrett, D., and Mortimore, R. (2003). Market segmentation and product differentiation in political campaigns: A technical feature perspective. *Journal of Marketing Management*, 19(1–2), 225–249.

Barbu, O. (2014). Advertising, microtargeting and social media. *Procedia, Social and Behavioral Sciences*, 163, 44–49.

Bay, M. (2017). The Ethics of Psychometrics in Social Media: A Rawlsian Approach. Research Report. University of California, Los Angeles.

Bennett, W.L. and Manheim, J.B. (2006). The one-step flow of communication. *The Annals of the American Academy of Political and Social Science*, 608(1), 213–232.

Castoriadis, C. (1997). Democracy as procedure and democracy as regime. *Constellations*, 4(1), 1–18.

Cossette, J.-L. (1987). *L'espace public chez Habermas la légitimité à l'aune des raisons*. McGill-Queen's University Press, Montreal.

Couldry, N. and Turow, J. (2014). Advertising, big data and the clearance of the public realm: Marketers' new approaches to the content subsidy. *International Journal of Communication*, 8, 1710–1726.

Dean, J. (2005). Communicative capitalism: Circulation and the foreclosure of politics. *Cultural Politics*, 1(1), 51–74.

Dean, J. (2010). Affective Networks. *MediaTropes*, 2(2), 19–44.

Du Plessis, E. (2012). *2020, The Brand Feeling*. Wharton University of Pennsylvania, Philadelphia.

Dufour, D.-R. (2008). Vivre en troupeau en se pensant libres. *Le Monde Diplomatique*, 646, 20–21.

Faizullabhoy, I. and Korolova, A. (2018). Facebook's advertising platform: New attack vectors and the need for interventions. *Workshop on Technology and Consumer Protection*, 6.

Goodsell, C.T. (2003). The concept of public space and its democratic manifestations. *The American Review of Public Administration*, 33(4), 361–383.

Guzmán, F., Paswan, A.K., and Van Steenburg, E. (2015). Self-referencing and political candidate brands: A congruency perspective. *Journal of Political Marketing*, 14(1–2), 175–199.

Harsin, J. (2015). Regimes of posttruth, postpolitics, and attention economies. *Communication, Culture & Critique*, 8(2), 327–333.

Harvey, K. (2014), *Encyclopedia of Social Media and Politics*. Sage Publications, Thousand Oaks.

Hohendahl, P.U. (1992). The public sphere: Models and boundaries. In *Habermas and the Public Sphere*, Calhoun, C.J. (ed.). MIT Press, Cambridge, 73–98.

Jovanovic, D. (2014). Age of hyper, micro and nanotargeting. In *5th International Scientific Conference, Economic and Social Development*. Varaždin Development and Entrepreneurship Agency, Varaždin, 408–416.

Katz, E. (1996). And deliver us from segmentation. *The Annals of the American Academy of Political and Social Science*, 546(1), 22–33.

Kerpen, D. (2011). *Likeable Social Media: How to Delight Your Customers, Create an Irresistible Brand, and Be Generally Amazing on Facebook (& Other Social Networks)*. McGraw-Hill Professional, New York.

Magin, M., Podschuweit, N., Haßler, J., and Russmann, U. (2017). Campaigning in the fourth age of political communication. A multi-method study on the use of Facebook by German and Austrian parties in the 2013 national election campaigns. *Information, Communication & Society*, 20(11), 1698–1719.

Mavriki, P. and Karyda, M. (2017). Using personalization technologies for political purposes: Privacy implications. In *7th International Conference E-Democracy: Privacy-Preserving, Secure, Intelligent E-Government Services,* Katsikas, S. and Zorkadis, V. (eds). Springer, 33–46.

Milbank, D. (1999). Virtual politics. *The New Republic*. Available at: https://newrepublic.com/article/90746/virtual-politics.

Mondoux, A. (2011). Identité numérique et surveillance. *Les Cahiers du Numérique*, 7(1), 49–59.

Neuman, W.R. and Guggenheim, L. (2011). The evolution of media effects theory: A six-stage model of cumulative research. *Communication Theory*, 21(2), 169–196.

O'Shaughnessy, N.J. (1993). America's political market. *European Journal of Marketing*, 21(4), 60–66.

Pang, B. and Lee, L. (2008). Opinion mining and sentiment analysis. *Foundations and Trends in Information Retrieval*, 2(1–2), 1–135.

Papacharissi, Z. (2014). *Affective Publics: Sentiment, Technology, and Politics*. Oxford University Press, New York.

Papacharissi, Z. (2016). Affective publics and structures of storytelling: Sentiment, events and mediality. *Information Communication & Society*, 19(3), 307–324.

Poirier, N. (2009). Espace public et émancipation chez Castoriadis. *Revue du MAUSS*, 34, 368–384.

Rouvroy, A. and Berns, T. (2013). Gouvernementalité algorithmique et perspectives d'émancipation. *Réseaux*, 177, 163–196.

Rouvroy, A. and Stiegler, B. (2015). Le régime de vérité numérique. *Socio*, 4, 113–140.

Semetko, H.A. and Tworzecki, H. (2017). Campaign strategies, media, and voters: The fourth era of political communication. In *The Routledge Handbook of Elections, Voting Behavior and Public Opinion*, Fisher, J. *et al.* (eds). Routledge, New York.

Shorey, S. and Howard, P.N. (2016). Automation, algorithms, and politics. Automation, Big Data and politics: A research review. *International Journal of Communication*, 10, 5032–5055.

Sivadas, E., Grewal, R., and Kellaris, J. (1998). The internet as a micro marketing tool: Targeting consumers through preferences revealed in music newsgroup usage. *Journal of Business Research*, 41(3), 179–186.

Straume, I.S. (2012). A common world? Arendt, Castoriadis and political creation. *European Journal of Social Theory*, 15(3), 367–383.

Wilson, J. (2008). Political discourse. In *The Handbook of Discourse Analysis,* 2nd edition, Schiffrin, D., Tannen, D., and Hamilton, H.E. (eds). John Wiley & Sons, New York, 398–415.

Young, L. and Soroka, S. (2012). Affective news: the automated coding of sentiment in political texts. *Political Communication*, 29(2), 205–231.

Zwick, D. and Knott, J.D. (2009). Manufacturing customers: The database as new means of production. *Journal of Consumer Culture*, 9(2), 221–247.

5

Digital Practices, Cultural Practices, Under Surveillance

The omnipresent digital injunction concerns all sectors of activity. Data flows provided by networks, servers, cloud computing structures and terminals that are subject to intensive use no longer fall within the file paradigm, as they have been governed until now by the French Data Protection Act (CNIL 2018a). The European General Data Protection Regulation (GDPR) (CNIL 2018b) is now in force. In a context of data economy, algorithmic processing is for the most part oriented towards their exploitation for sales, positioning, recommendations and other marketing purposes. In fact, data monitoring in reticular territories is permanent and their users must deal with this new paradigm to such an extent that digital practices permeate all daily activities, whether informational, communicational or cultural. We propose to explore the hypothesis that cultural practices are diluted in digital practices. To verify this, we will discuss the conditions for the social acceptability of the injunction to permanent and invasive digital innovation and the deployment of digital monitoring devices, and then present empirical work conducted in the museum sector to identify the intertwining of digital and cultural practices.

5.1. Social acceptability of the digital injunction, monitoring devices and digital control

The intrusion of digital technology into all fields of social life is a major fact – although it varies greatly from one place to another – leading to a transformation of the ways of being together and even of making society. At first sight, the social appropriation of digital technology can lead to an increase in public and private freedoms, particularly of expression. However, the current expression

---

Chapter written by Robert PANICO and Geneviève VIDAL.

takes ephemeral forms and the political context is more a matter of governmentality (Foucault 1982) where relationships of domination are played out (Boucher-Bonnafous 2003). Power in liberalism is less and less repressive and is exercised over individuals whose lives must no longer be challenged, but instead managed, made productive, with the aim of keeping them valiant, healthy and ready to accept that their conduct be conducted according to biopolitics[1]. To achieve this orientation, it is necessary to make individuals visible so that they do not cease to express themselves, make themselves heard and show themselves to others (Foucault 1982).

In the disciplinary society, the important thing is to see, see everything, know everything, all the time. Visibility is essential for the ongoing monitoring of individuals who know they are under surveillance. It is applied in each of the places of confinement: prison, school, company, hospital, etc. In control societies, one passes from the confined and disciplinary space to the mobile checkpoint, circulating on the networks, which requires the individual to permanently display his/her identifier and password in order to be recognized. We are entering, for the most part, "societies of control, which no longer operate by confinement, but by continuous control and instant communication" (Deleuze 2003, p. 236). In other words, control is omnipresent.

Digital control is to be understood as a variation of control, with a view to managing conduct. It is based on the implementation of permanent automatic systems for the collection of personal data, the richness of which comes from the volume (Big Data) and the tacit agreement of the persons concerned. In return, the latter receive bonuses, in particular by allowing cookies and by accepting the general terms and conditions of use (T&Cs)[2], which are not widely read. Far from the idea of the police record (maintained), this digital social control (seen as repressive in the 1970s) can be considered as a *soft control*, a *soft* technology at the service of individuals, used in a diffuse way, especially during the individual's free, unconstrained use. A control continuum operates from the outside, at any time and in any place. The connected individual himself/herself produces the means and condition for this intrusive control. Tracking clues and traces (left unexpectedly by digital practices such as online cultural practices), sniffer programs maintain this control, which targets an increasingly informed individual who is tired of always having to decide on his/her own vigilance (check, set, accept, etc.). Thus, half-conscious, he/she

1 Thus, the medicalization of the different stages of life (gestation, birth, vaccination, etc.) can be read as an example of individuals' regular confrontation with the institutions that govern them.

2 Example of a GCU ad found on a public service radio site (April 13, 2018): "By continuing your browsing, you accept our GCU (general conditions of use) and the deposit of cookies that will allow the personalization of content, sharing on social networks, audience measurement and targeting of advertising…"

abandons, by negotiating, his/her most personal data to the profiling algorithms that exploit these megadata. Facebook, recently concerned about selling user profiles, will soon no longer need to justify – within the meaning of the 1978 law on the protection of personal data – the collection of behavioral information, which it monetizes for its customers, partners and advertisers at a high price (*Le Point* 2018). With the rapid increase in computing power and the size of clouds, user profiles say more than names (protected personal data) – especially since a behavioral profile is measured, but is not evaluated as a use. From the sociology of use to the calculation of a behavior, profiling, in the digital age, is indeed the new El Dorado of control.

Thus, Foucault's (1982) analysis still seems to be relevant to determine the normative nature of the new power in order to understand in return the consent of Internet users to the traceability of their behaviors and the profiling of their uses. The transparency of the monitored data reflects the opacity of the institutions, which exploit large amounts of data collected online and promise to personalize tailor-made and frequently offered services. Exit the alleged net neutrality flouted by the GAFAM and other major digital players, in a dynamic of tacit transfer of embedded data, uninterrupted collection of traces. Consequently, the role of algorithms is increasing in decision-making, based on the convergence of media and content, in the age of the Web of data and the Internet of Things. Would it be a regression towards a conception of the social considered as a simple collection of individuals, of aggregates whose behaviors can consequently be oriented?

This brief portrait of social control reveals the paradoxical idea that more freedom can lead to more control and surveillance. However, this paradox ceases to be one if we place ourselves in the Foucauldian perspective of normative power that intends to "*manage* conduct" (Foucault 1982). Therefore, the coercive force that acted on the bodies has *been gradually* replaced by a force of conviction to coerce minds and subordinate individuals to express themselves. We would have reached a stage where it becomes imperative for power that the individual collaborates, that he/she speaks about himself/herself, his/her practices, his/her digital social networks (DSN), his/her ways of consuming and of communicating, etc., all these *contemporary* characteristics of a society that has oscillated for half a century between a police record and a chosen self-display (Carré and Panico 2014). In addition, the individual must feel the need for the services he/she is visiting, that he/she feels confident and in control of the situation.

Considering the control of digital practices, granted up to a threshold of acceptability that marks an ability to develop a critical posture, albeit limited, in the face of powerful economic actors, we will initiate a reflection on monitoring and control mechanisms in the context of cultural practices.

5.2. Dilution of cultural practices in digital technology

Controlled digital use is concerned with cultural practices (Donnat 2008) in a context of social appropriation of the network technologies omnipresent in society. However, this appropriation does not allow control of the data captured on platforms offering goods and services. Even the most sophisticated users circumventing instructions, or even hiding their activities on the darknet (Gayard 2018), are the object of surveillance. The use of the authorized functionalities are part of a free or low-cost market. For a social acceptability of these restrictive and liberticidal conditions, strategies consist of valuing interactivity, the adequacy of the supply and demand calculated by algorithms, and creativity, in a process of intensive commodification of social activities. The vast majority of them still have to put in place tactics to be renewed as programmed obsolescence progresses in the interests of economic actors.

Cultural institutions, implementing their strategies to pursue their missions and aiming to increase the number of visitors and increase the loyalty of their audiences, are subject to this obsolescence and must deal with the technologies at their disposal until they find themselves actors in the digital injunction and traceability. They offer interactive and participatory activities (Vidal 2015) to audiences, who experience a sense of freedom with digital interfaces that facilitate multimedia consultations (Vidal 2014) and make the data tracking system invisible. However, these conditions of access to cultural content, the circulation of which is part of social emancipation (Arnaud 2015), can reduce it to a freedom to consume goods and services within the framework of "technological control of the symbolic" (Freitag 2009, p. 93)[3]. This situation seems to feed the confusion between cultural and digital practices, as online cultural consumption and confusion with digital leisure are spreading[4]. Internet users then continue to make their expressions public in a few settings via so-called "intuitive" interfaces. Interactivity is experienced as a delight, socially valued, meaningful, supporting a tendency to negotiate uses in exchange for a waiver of data protection. Users' reflexive posture circulates on digital social networks, the content of which, including critical content, is exploited. The bypasses and profits of the networks under surveillance are thus part of negotiations on the territory of renunciation (Vidal 2010). The processes of technological sophistication, aimed at controlling cultural consumption, do not prevent users from being identified under the influence of the utopia of empowerment, thanks to their participation in mediation, without guaranteeing the possibility of extricating

3 We also refer to Michel Freitag's (2006) work, in particular the section "3. Sur le plan culturel": "The main problem is the one resulting from the ever closer integration of the cultural-symbolic universe into technological and economic logic" (online).

4 See details about teenagers (Mercklé and Octobre 2012).

themselves from this situation of domination. Conducts continue to be subject to the requirements built into profiling devices, falling under the "incontestable" expansion of the concentration (George 2006) of offers from the communication and culture industries, as well as the economic exploitation of connection data and online activities.

Based on the empirical work conducted by us in the museum sector, which disseminates digital content and resources, we continue to explore the hypothesis of a tangle of cultural and digital practices, which leads, in so doing, to a possible dissolution of the former within the latter, which are treated in the same way in digital networks under surveillance and control.

Since the second half of the 1990s, the analysis of the use of digital museum mediations has made it possible to envisage this sector through the prism of a constant professional appropriation of digital technologies, contributing to the transformation of the heritage environment. The cultural Internet is the subject of economic and political exploitation to enhance the value of territories and digitalized heritage content. The strategies implemented are part of a globalization of cultural heritage and concern its influence in society. Indeed, the Web of data based on the semantization of patrimonial data (Bermès 2011) opens new reports on interconnected and traceable content. This Web 3.0 requires partnership agreements between institutions and with research centers[5], by pursuing the involvement of audiences while keeping them at a distance – which places them in an ambivalent position – as part of a renewal of cultural dissemination (Vidal 2018).

Museums are thus developing innovative experiments that inspire beyond this cultural sector (Museomix (n.d.)). They diversify mediations (Falk 2012; Montpetit 2011) and cultural prescription by relying on the craze for mobile applications (UDPN 2016), augmented reality, 3D-immersion and the participatory Web. Institutions, such as economic actors, want to control the flow of content and communication. The human–machine dialog establishes new relationships with audiences and digital communication strategies, within the framework of hyperconnectivity (Carré and Vidal 2018).

The legacy data then join the flows orchestrated by the IT[6] and telecommunications industries. These circulate on networks which are becoming the

5 See, for example, the partnership between the Ministry of Culture-France, Wikimedia and Inria (*Institut national de recherché dédié aux sciences du numérique*) (Ministère de la Culture et de la Communication, 2012a) and the partnership between the Musée d'histoire de Nantes, the University of Nantes and the École centrale de Nantes, Polytech Nantes (Château des Ducs de Bretagne, n.d.).

6 We do not discuss the significant case of the "Google Art Project" launched in 2011, now "Google Arts & Culture". Available at: https://artsandculture.google.com.

dominant communication model, without being able to avoid geolocation technologies. Nevertheless, it should be remembered that audiences negotiate, albeit without privacy protection, with these technologies to achieve services that serve their informational, communicational and cultural objectives through interactions of practices. During the time of the negotiated renunciation (Vidal 2010), the structuring and semantization of data (Vidal 2009) punctuate the flows controlled by economic and cultural actors to allow access to resources. However, even though Internet users make their way through the networks under surveillance, develop their technical and ergonomic skills, and exercise "informational self-determination"[7], inequalities persist in a context of "fatal illusion of autonomy" (Rancière 2008, p. 21). This digital experience infiltrates all social activities taken in the whirlwind of pervasive networks, in an invisibility of algorithms and their processing power.

5.3. Conclusion

New forms of control and monitoring of cultural activities are part of digital transformations that open up relationships with culture that increasingly resemble those with all other activities. This does not mean that the digital attempt at cultural democratization should be abandoned (Ministère de la Culture et de la Communication 2012b); it is a question of measuring the exploitation of all behavioral data irremediably subjected to predictive algorithms. Predicting cultural practices in the same way as all other practices and consumptions raises the question of the reification (Honneth 2007) of digital cultural resources, indexed according to an ambivalence between access and exploitation.

The first period of computerization with the creation of large interconnected administrative files gave rise to a regulatory framework, first French ("*Informatique, fichiers et libertés*"), then European, with the GDPR, leading to the transition from a centralized conception of data to a decentralized but no less restrictive conception (Carré and Vétois 2016; Vitalis 2016). In addition, the study of data processing has evolved, requiring methodologies that are themselves evolving, to capture the socio-political issues of data exploitation by economic and political actors. Digital data monitoring is spreading to all social fields, with the museum sector being no exception. Cultural data are part of reticular flows subject to generalized traceability, in a context of interactions between cultural and digital practices. Indeed, cultural practices tend to be subject to the same digital exploitations in Big Data and reopen the dialectic of freedom/control, which we have seen is the effect of a governmentality where power is exercised over free subjects in a context of social

7 The right for all citizens to control information about themselves (Humanrights.ch 2017).

acceptability from the injunction to permanent and invasive digital innovation, based on monitoring and control mechanisms.

5.4. References

Arnaud, L. (2015). Action culturelle et émancipation par la culture. Un éclairage socio-historique. *Informations sociales*, 190(4), 46–56. Available at: https://www.cairn.info/revue-informations-sociales-2015-4-page-46.htm.

Bermès, E. (2011). Bibliothèques, archives et musées : l'enjeu de la convergence des données du patrimoine culturel. *Documentaliste sciences de l'information*, 48(4), 45–47.

Boucher-Bonnafous, M. (2003). *Un libéralisme sans libertés. Du terme "libéralisme" dans la pensée de Michel Foucault*. L'Harmattan, Paris.

Carré, D. and Panico, R. (2014). Puissance d'agir à l'ère du Websocial. In *Réseaux socionumériques et médiations humaines : le social est-il soluble dans le Web ?*, Rojas, E. (ed.). Hermès-Lavoisier, Paris, 177–197.

Carré, D. and Vétois, J. (2016). Contrôle social et techniques numériques. *tic&société*, 10(1).

Carré, D. and Vidal, G. (2018). *Hyperconnectivity: Economical, Social and Environmetal Challenges*. ISTE Ltd, London, and John Wiley & Sons, New York.

Château des ducs de Bretagne (n.d.). Nantes 1900. Available at: http://www.chateaunantes.fr/fr/nantes-1900.

CNIL (2018a). Loi no. 78-17 du 6 janvier 1978 relative à l'informatique, aux fichiers et aux libertés, 22 June 2018. Available at: https://www.cnil.fr/fr/loi-78-17-du-6-janvier-1978-modifiee.

CNIL (2018b). RGPD : se préparer en 6 étapes. Available at: https://www.cnil.fr/fr/principes-cles/rgpd-se-preparer-en-6-etapes.

Deleuze, G. (2003). *Pourparlers*. Éditions de Minuit, Paris.

Donnat, O. (2008). Les pratiques culturelles des Français à l'ère numérique. Enquête 2008. Available at: http://www.pratiquesculturelles.culture.gouv.fr/index.php.

Falk, J. (2012). Expérience de visite, identités et self-aspects. *La lettre de l'OCIM*, 141, 5–14.

Foucault, M. (1982). Le sujet et le pouvoir. In *Dits et Écrits, Tome II*. Édition Quarto Gallimard, Paris, 1041–1062.

Freitag, M. (2006). Combien de temps le développement peut-il encore durer ? *Les ateliers de l'éthique, la revue du CRÉUM*, 1(2), 114–133. Available at: http://classiques.uqac.ca/contemporains/freitag_michel/combien_de_temps_devel/combien_de_temps.html.

Freitag, M. (2009). L'émancipation. Réflexions sur la liberté et le progrès moderne. In *L'émancipation hier et aujourd'hui*, Tremblay, G. (ed.). Presses de l'Université du Québec, Quebec, 89–107.

Gayard, L. (2018). *Darknet: Geopolitics and Uses*. ISTE Ltd, London and John Wiley & Sons, New York.

George, É. (2006). De la concentration du capital à la production d'information et de culture : bilan critique des écrits. *Colloque international "Mutations des industries de la culture, de l'information et de la communication"*. Available at: http://www.observatoire-omic.org/colloque-icic/pdf/GeorgeTR1.pdf.

Honneth, A. (2007). *La réification. Petit traité de théorie critique*. Gallimard, Paris.

Humanrights.ch (2017). L'autodétermination informationnelle : le nouveau défi des droits humains ? Available at: https://www.humanrights.ch/fr/droits-humains-suisse/interieure/protection/protection/autodetermination-informationnelle.

Le Point (2018). Facebook – Zuckerberg : le mea culpa permanent. *Le Point Tech&Net*, 22 March. Available at: https://www.lepoint.fr/high-tech-Internet/facebook-zuckerberg-le-mea-culpa-permanent-22-03-2018-2204737_47.php.

Mercklé, P. and Octobre, S. (2012). La stratification sociale des pratiques numériques des adolescents. *RESET*, 1. Available at: http://journals.openedition.org/reset/129.

Ministère de la Culture et de la Communication, France (2012a). Lancement DBpédia en français et inauguration de Sémanticpédia. Speech given 19 November 2012. Available at: http://www.culture.gouv.fr/Presse/Archives-Presse/Archives-Discours-2012-2018/Annee-2012/Lancement-DBpedia-en-francais-et-inauguration-de-Semanticpedia.

Ministère de la Culture et de la Communication, France (2012b). Histoire des politiques de "démocratisation culturelle". Document created by Pierre Moulinier, Comité d'Histoire, CH/GT Hist. dém. cult./DT. 12 – revised 28 April 2011 – revised July 2012. Available at: http://www.culture.gouv.fr/content/download/44026/350480/version/1/file/Ecrits+sur+la+democratisation+cult.pdf.

Montpetit, R. (2011). Médiation. In *Dictionnaire encyclopédique de muséologie*, Desvallées, A. and Mairesse, F. (eds). Armand Colin, Paris, 215–233.

Museomix (n.d.). Comment fonctionne Museomix ? Available at: https://www.museomix.org/comment-fonctionne-museomix/.

Rancière, J. (2008). *Le spectateur émancipé*. La fabrique éditions, Paris.

Usage des patrimoines numérisés (UDPN) (2016). Politique numérique et applications "durables" des institutions patrimoniales : usages et modélisation. Available at: http://udpn.fr/spip.php?article159.

Vidal, G. (2009). Le Web 3.0, pour en finir avec le Web 2.0 ? *Documentation et bibliothèques*, 55(4), 201–207.

Vidal, G. (2010). Le renoncement négocié. Pour une analyse dialectique des usages des technologies interactives. HDR in Information Sciences and Communication, Université Bordeaux 3, Bordeaux.

Vidal, G. (2014). Critique et plaisir au cœur des usages des médiations numériques muséales. *Interfaces numériques*, 3(1), 163–177.

Vidal, G. (2015). La médiation numérique, formes renouvelées de participation des publics aux activités des musées. In *Expressions et pratiques créatives numériques en réseaux*, Chapelain, B. (ed.). Éditions Hermann, Paris, 139–157.

Vidal, G. (2018). *La médiation numérique muséale : un renouvellement de la diffusion culturelle*. Presses universitaires de Bordeaux, Bordeaux.

Vitalis, A. (2016). *The Uncertain Digital Revolution*. ISTE Ltd, London, and John Wiley & Sons, New York.

6

The Hypothesis of the Privacy of Ancients and Moderns

"The Internet is a threat to privacy". This sentence expresses a conclusion, a generally shared feeling, whether in the press, in militant and political speeches, or in academic literature. In this academic literature, there is a regular reference to the "privacy paradox". In a nutshell, this paradox results from the observation of the contradiction between the expression of a strong attachment to "privacy" and the observed behaviors of hyper-displaying oneself (Carré and Panico 2012) which, in practice, transgress the border between public and private space and contribute to one's own surveillance (Carré and Panico 2011; Lyon 2015). The behavior of Facebook users is regularly mentioned to illustrate this famous paradox (Acquisti and Gross 2006; Estienne 2011). These are often referred to as "naïve" and "attentive" (Walczak 2014, p. 504) and some online behaviors as "pathological" (Granjon 2011; Sziklay 2016), partly because of this paradox. According to Anita Allen (1999), we should even go so far as to "coerce", in some cases, privacy behaviors.

Studies that have analyzed this "privacy paradox" have shown the existence of a market failure for the exploitation of personal data and, if we share the assumption that privacy is conceived as a market, of the privacy market (Rochelandet 2010). In such a context, the behavior of digital content consumers who claim to be concerned about protecting their privacy while endangering it is irrational, economically speaking, given the preferences they claim to have.

Chapter written by Julien ROSSI.

Nevertheless, the first studies on the privacy paradox (Acquisti and Gross 2006; Norberg *et al.* 2007), however convincing they may be, mainly suffer from the following flaw: if, in the empirical survey system on which they are based, the respondents have indeed been questioned about the importance they attach to "*privacy*", the notion itself is not really questioned. However, it is a notion that is "essentially contested" (Mulligan *et al.* 2016) and, in reality, controversial.

So, in what sense is the "paradox of privacy" a paradox?

6.1. Privacy under discussion

According to a definition by Bénédicte Rey (2012), which is based on that of Irwin Altman (1977), "privacy is in fact a behavior rather than a state" (Rey 2012, para. 20), caused by a reaction to a feeling of intrusion, which serves to operate a "selective control of access to oneself" (Altman 1977, p. 67). Another, more traditional definition, the oldest recorded expression which dates back to Aristotle (Jaulin 2014), consists, as popularized by Jürgen Habermas, of opposing private space to public space and drawing a line between the two (Habermas 1988). But what exactly is a matter for the public and private spheres? As with some research, one way to answer this question is to try to identify the object protected by privacy law. Bert-Jaap Koops *et al.* (2016) have thus carried out important comparative law work to propose a typology of what the privacy laws protect, ranging from controlling access to the physical space of the body to protecting personal data.

There is a whole fringe of feminist literature that criticizes the concept of privacy. According to Anita Allen (1988, 2000), this privacy that is subject to legal protection can become bad when it leads to confining women to the domestic space without allowing them to make autonomous choices, which is, for her, a good form of privacy. Catharine MacKinnon (1989) argues that the notion of the right to privacy should be "exploded", as it would ultimately only serve to mask the political dominance that takes place behind the legal barrier built around privacy. While Judith DeCew (2015) points out that this position is not unanimously accepted among feminists interested in the notion of privacy, this criticism has the merit of reminding us that, until 1992, in France, the argument of privacy could be invoked to prevent a court from adjuciating a case of marital rape[1]. The fact that this is no longer the case today, at least in France, shows that the subject matter of the

1 *Cour de cassation*, Ch. Crim. of June 11, 1992. In 1984 (C. Cass. Ch. Crim., July 17, 1984), the *Cour de cassation* (French Court of Cassation) had already opened the possibility of filing a complaint of rape against a spouse, but only if they were in the process of divorce.

protection of the right *to* privacy (the fundamental right) and privacy law (the corpus of positive law texts that translate this fundamental right into concrete provisions) is evolving, reminding us that these subjects are historically and culturally embedded (Altman 1977; Ariès and Duby 1985; Moore 2003).

The evolution of the material and technical environment plays a significant role in the development of the notion of privacy and its conditions of exercise. Between the end of the 19th Century and the beginning of the 20th Century, the widespread use of the single bedroom in Europe profoundly transformed the social relationship to privacy (Guerrand 1987; Mumford 1938; Prost 1987). For the Italian constitutionalist Stefano Rodotà (1974), there are material prerequisites for the possibility of exercising a right to privacy. Today, the conclusion that digital transformation is changing the *relationship with* privacy seems generally accepted (see, in particular, Carré and Panico 2011; Galinon-Mélénec 2011; Kessous and Rey 2009; Rey 2012; Vitalis 1988). What does digital transformation do to privacy *rights*?

Despite what Irvin Altman's definition may suggest to his reader, the right to privacy has not always been the right to (individual) control of access to oneself. We will see, indeed, after studying the progressive emergence of the right to privacy as it was traditionally understood, how the emergence of computer technology was the trigger for the legal emergence of a right to self-determination that would individualize the right to privacy.

6.2. The invention of the right to privacy

Unlike freedom of the press, the right to privacy is not part of the Declaration of the Rights of Man and of the Citizen or the Bill of Rights of the Constitution of the United States of America. In France, it was only in 1970 that the right to privacy was enshrined in the Civil Code by Act No. 70-643 of July 17, 1970, aimed at strengthening the guarantee of the individual rights of citizens. But this does not mean that the guarantee of this right then became constitutional. It began with the ratification of international instruments, such as the 1948 Universal Declaration of Human Rights, which no court is responsible for enforcing, and the 1950 European Convention on Human Rights, which has a European Court of Human Rights to ensure its compliance. However, it should be recalled that this last convention was only ratified by Alain Poher, the Acting President of the French Republic, on May 3, 1974. The Constitutional Council's recognition of a right to privacy did not finally take place, in stages, until the second half of the 1990s (Mazeaud 2015). As it has been carried out under the influence of international legal instruments, it is towards rights other than French law that we must turn to in order to understand its genealogy.

American lawyers Samuel Warren and Louis Brandeis, in an article published in 1890 in the *Harvard Law Review* (Warren and Brandeis 1890), are generally credited with having invented, in doctrine, the notion of a "right to privacy", which, in its most succinct definition, is a "right to be let alone". The technical and organizational upheavals that affected the media of the time are no strangers to their thinking:

> "Recent inventions and business methods call attention to the next step which must be taken for the protection of the person, and for securing to the individual what Judge Cooley calls the right 'to be let alone'. Instantaneous photographs and newspaper enterprise have invaded the sacred precincts of private and domestic life; and numerous mechanical devices threaten to make good the prediction that 'what is whispered in the closet shall be proclaimed from the house tops'" (Warren and Brandeis 1890, p. 195).

From that date, several attempts to have a constitutional right to privacy recognized by the United States Supreme Court failed. It was not until 1965 that the Court censored a Connecticut law prohibiting access to contraception even for married couples on the grounds of the existence, that it revealed on that occasion, a constitutional right to the protection of privacy[2]. The conception then enshrined by a Supreme Court of the right to privacy thus protects a group (the family, the married couple, the home, etc.) from public scrutiny and State intervention. More than a protection of the individual, it is, in an ideal way, a legal protection of a sacred barrier between what is a public space and what is a private space, which was strongly mentioned in the founding article of Samuel Warren and Louis Brandeis:

> "Even gossip apparently harmless, when widely and persistently circulated, is potent for evil. It both belittles and perverts. It belittles by inverting the relative importance of things, thus dwarfing the thoughts and aspirations of a people. When personal gossip attains the dignity of print, and crowds the space available for matters of real interest to the community, is there any wonder that the ignorant and thoughtless mistake its relative importance?" (Warren and Brandeis 1890, p. 196).

2 Supreme Court of the United States of America, June 7, 1965, "Griswold v. Connecticut", 381 US 479.

6.3. The emergence of informational self-determination and the privacy of the Modern

When computer technology first appeared in the 1950s and 1960s in the United States, it was not unanimously accepted. As Fred Turner (2008) points out in the introductory part of his book on Silicon Valley utopias, the dominant imagination of computer science at that time was closely linked to that of the military–industrial complex that gave rise to it. The computer's ability to store information on individuals, to find them quickly and to cross-reference databases that were previously compartmentalized gave rise to concern among the elected officials in the United States House of Representatives, who set up a commission of inquiry in 1966 to study the issue. This is how the notion of the *right to be forgotten* arises: "The possible future storage and regrouping of […] personal information also strikes at the core of our Judeo-Christian concept of 'forgive and forget', because the computer neither forgives nor forgets" (US House of Representatives 1966, p. 4).

In 1967, a conference was organized in Stockholm by the International Commission of Jurists on the Right to Privacy. In 1968, a resolution of the Parliamentary Assembly of the Council of Europe called for the opening of discussions to strengthen the legal protection of privacy in the face of new intrusion technologies, in particular telephone tapping (recommendation 509 of 1968). In the same year, the Committee of Ministers entrusted the discussion to the European Committee on Legal Co-operation (CDCJ), which decided, at a meeting from 11 to 13 October 1971 (Council of Europe 1971), to focus on the question of information technology and to set up a group of experts on the protection of privacy with regard to electronic data banks (Council of Europe 1972), whose work would lead to the adoption in 1981 of Convention 108 of the Council of Europe.

In the meantime, a law adopted by the State of Hesse in 1970[3] enshrined the invention of the term *data protection* (from the German *Datenschutz*). Then, in 1973, the first national law on the protection of personal data, the Swedish *Datalag* of 1973[4], gave rise to the first legal definition of the concept of *personal data.* This definition, which has remained stable until now, covers any data directly or indirectly related to an identified or identifiable natural person and therefore extends well beyond the simple domain of data relating to the privacy of the person.

For those who took part in the discussions of the time, who quickly structured themselves into a network of civil servants and activist academics, to whom Charles Raab and Colin Bennett (2003) refer to as the "*privacy community*", and who were

3 *Datenschutzgesetz vom October 7, 1970 (Hessen)* (Data Protection Act of 7 October 1970 (Hesse)).

4 *Datalag* (Data Act) (1973:289).

inspired by John Stuart Mill's (1989) liberal philosophy, it is impossible for public authorities, by virtue of the principle of individual autonomy, to provide a definition for the domain of public or private communication *a priori* for everyone and for the future.

This concept was reinforced by a decision of the Federal Constitutional Court of the Federal Republic of Germany in 1983[5], which revealed the existence of a "right to informational self-determination" (*informationelle Selbstbestimmung*) based on the principle of the dignity of the human person enshrined in the country's basic law.

The new right to the protection of personal data, which appeared in the 1970s in Europe, no longer serves to defend a sacrosanct border between the public and private sectors. It is the right of the individual, and not the collective, to negotiate independently what they want or do not want to reveal about themselves. It no longer protects the public space from unworthy comments, but seeks to give individuals the tools to manage the risks of the information society (Rossi 2018).

Computerization has therefore prompted discussions at the institutional level, which have led to the emergence of a new fundamental right, which now takes its place in the Charter of Fundamental Rights of the European Union in an article (Article 8) separate from that on the right to privacy (Article 7) (González Fuster 2014).

6.4. Conclusion

In 1819, Benjamin Constant (2010) noted that a "Modern" form of freedom, a freedom to act individually and autonomously, was gaining in importance in the face of a conception he called "Ancient", which consisted of taking part in collective decisions. Similarly, in many countries, the right to privacy has evolved from a traditional concept of legal protection of the border between public and private space to one that is centered on the individual, who is given a role in determining how to access themselves and their personal information.

This gives people the opportunity to express in public things that social conventions conceive as private or intimate. This is particularly what happened during the #MeToo movement. This form of political extimacy (Tisseron 2011) allows new political issues to be put on the agenda by pooling stories that, at the origin of individual intimacy, acquire the status of common experiences through collective awareness, thus achieving the status of a political problem (Cefaï 1996).

5 Decision of the German Federal Constitutional Court: BVerfG Urteil vom 15 Dezember 1983 (Judgment of December 15th) Az. 1 BvR 209/83, 1 BvR 484/83, 1 BvR 420/83, 1 BvR 362/83, 1 BvR 269/83, 1 BvR 440/83 (*Volkszählungsurteil* – Census Judgment).

The existence of a *de jure* evolution, from a right to privacy of Ancients to a right to privacy of Moderns, does not mean that it is translated everywhere in the field into concrete practices. Some studies, such as those by danah michele boyd (2012; Donath and boyd 2004), seem to us to be moving in this direction, but they were not specifically designed to test this hypothesis, so further empirical research will be required. If it were to be demonstrated, it could explain part of the privacy paradox by the fact that the expressed attachment to "privacy" would then reflect the desire to control the flow of information circulating about oneself in specific contexts (Nissenbaum 2010), and not the desire to defend an impassable and frozen barrier between private and public.

6.5. References

Acquisti, A. and Gross, R. (2006). Imagined communities: Awareness, information sharing, and privacy on the Facebook. In *Proceedings of the 6th International Conference on Privacy Enhancing Technologies*, 36–58.

Allen, A. (1988). *Uneasy Access: Privacy for Women in a Free Society*. Rowman & Littlefield, Lanham.

Allen, A. (1999). Coercing privacy. *William and Mary Law Review*, 40(3), 723–757.

Allen, A. (2000). Gender and privacy in cyberspace. *Stanford Law Review*, 52(5), 1175–1200.

Altman, I. (1977). Privacy regulation: Culturally universal or culturally specific? *Journal of Social Issues*, 33(3), 66–84.

Ariès, P. and Duby, G. (eds) (1985). *Histoire de la vie privée*. Le Seuil, Paris.

Bennett, C.J. and Raab, C.D. (2003). *The Governance of Privacy. Policy Instruments in Global Perspective*. Ashgate, Aldershot.

boyd, d.m. (2012). Taken out of context: American teen sociality in networked publics. PhD thesis, University of California, Berkeley.

Carré, D. and Panico, R. (2011). Le contrôle social à l'heure des technologies de mobilité et de connectivité. Du fichage ciblé des individus au traçage continu des agissements. *Terminal. Technologie de l'information, culture & société*, 108–109, 17–31.

Carré, D. and Panico, R. (2012). L' "affichage de soi" comme "puissance d'agir". Contrôle social et enjeux éthiques à l'heure de l'hyperconnectivité. In *Médias sociaux : enjeux pour la communication*, Proulx, S., Millette, M., and Heaton, L. (eds). Presses de l'Université du Québec, Quebec, 61–79.

Cefaï, D. (1996). La construction des problèmes publics. Définitions de situations dans des arènes publiques. *Réseaux*, 14(75), 43–66.

Council of Europe and Parliamentary Assembly (1968a). Recommandation 509.

Council of Europe and Committee of Ministers (1968b). Memorandum "Right to privacy". Document OM [60] 53 from 27 March 1968.

Council of Europe and European Committee on Legal co-operation (1971). Sub-committee to study the civil law aspects of the protection of the right to privacy, report on meeting held at Strasbourg from 11–13 October 1971. Document CCJ [71] 66 from 18 October 1971.

Council of Europe, Comité sur la protection de la vie privée vis-à-vis des banques de données électroniques (1972). Report on the first session held in Strasbourg from 13–15 March.

Constant, B. (2010). *De la liberté des anciens comparée à celle des modernes*. Mille et une nuits, Paris.

DeCew, J.W. (2015). The feminist critique of privacy: Past arguments and new social understandings. In *Social Dimensions of Privacy*, Roessler, B. and Mokrosinska, D. (eds). Cambridge University Press, Cambridge, 85–103.

Donath, J. and boyd, d.m. (2004). Public displays of connection. *BT Technology Journal*, 22(4), 71–82.

Estienne, Y. (2011). Un monde de verre : Facebook ou les paradoxes de la vie privée (sur)exposée. *Terminal. Technologie de l'information, culture & société*, 108–109, 65–84.

Galinon-Mélénec, B. (2011). L'universalité de la trace. Le XXIème siècle, siècle de la trace ? In *L'homme-trace : perspectives anthropologiques des traces contemporaines*, Galinon-Mélénec, B. (ed.). CNRS Éditions, Paris, 31–58.

González Fuster, G. (2014). Fighting for your right to what exactly? The convoluted case law of the EU Court of Justice on privacy and/or personal data protection. *Birkbeck Law Review*, 2(2), 263–278.

Granjon, F. (2011). De quelques pathologies sociales de l'individualité numérique. *Réseaux*, 167, 75–103.

Guerrand, R.-H. (1987). Espaces privés. In *Histoire de la vie privée. Tome 4. De la Révolution à la Grande Guerre*, Ariès, P. and Duby, G. (eds). Le Seuil, Paris, 325–411.

Habermas, J. (1988). *L'espace public : archéologie de la publicité comme dimension constitutive de la société bourgeoise*. Payot, Paris.

Jaulin, A. (2014). L'espace public dans l'Athènes classique. *Philonsorbonne*, 8, 155–165.

Kessous, E. and Rey, B. (2009). Économie numérique et vie privée. *Hermès, La Revue*, 53, 49–54.

Koops, B.-J., Newell, B.C., Timan, T., Škorvánek, I., Chokrevski, T., and Galič, M. (2016). A typology of privacy. *University of Pennsylvania Journal of International Law*, 38(2), 483–575.

Lyon, D. (2015). *Surveillance After Snowden*. Polity Press, Cambridge.

MacKinnon, C.A. (1989). *Toward a Feminist Theory of the State*. Harvard University Press, Cambridge.

Mazeaud, V. (2015). La constitutionnalisation du droit au respect de la vie privée. *Nouveaux Cahiers du Conseil constitutionnel*, 48, 7–20.

Mill, J.S. (1989). *On Liberty, with the Subjection of Women, and Chapters on Socialism*, Collini, S. (ed.). Cambridge University Press, Cambridge.

Moore, A.D. (2003). Privacy: Its meaning and value. *American Philosophical Quarterly*, 40(3), 215–227.

Mulligan, D.K., Koopman, C., and Doty, N. (2016). Privacy is an essentially contested concept: A multi-dimensional analytic for mapping privacy. *Philosophical Transactions of the Royal Society A: Mathematical, Physical and Engineering Sciences*, 374(2083). Available at: https://www.ncbi.nlm.nih.gov/pmc/articles/PMC5124066/.

Mumford, L. (1938). *The Culture of Cities*. Harcourt, Brace and Company, New York.

Nissenbaum, H.F. (2010). *Privacy in Context: Technology, Policy, and the Integrity of Social Life*. Stanford Law Books, Stanford.

Norberg, P.A., Home, D.R., and Home, D.A. (2007). The privacy paradox: Personal information disclosure intentions and behaviors. *Journal of Consumer Affairs*, 41, 100–126.

Prost, A. (1987). Frontières et espaces du privé. In *Histoire de la vie privée. Tome 5. De la Première Guerre mondiale à nos jours*, Ariès, P. and Duby, G. (eds). Le Seuil, Paris, 13–154.

Rey, B. (2012). La privacy à l'ère du numérique. *Terminal. Technologie de l'information, culture & société*, 110, 91–103.

Rochelandet, F. (2010). *Économie des données personnelles et de la vie privée*. La Découverte, Paris.

Rodotà, S. (1974). Protection de la vie privée et contrôle de l'information : deux sujets d'inquiétude croissante pour l'opinion publique. In *Questions d'ordre politique soulevées par la protection des données et des libertés individuelles, principes et perspectives. Compte-rendu du séminaire*. OCDE, Paris.

Rossi, J. (2018). Qu'est-ce que le droit à la protection des données à caractère personnel ? Chaire de géopolitique du risque de l'École normale supérieure, Paris, France. Available at: http://geopolitics-of-risk.ens.fr/en/vie-privee-donnees-personnelles-et-risques-quels-parametres-pour-leur-cohabitation-venir-0.

Sziklay, J. (ed.) (2016). *KULCS A NET VILÁGÁHOZ! A gyermekek biztonságos és jogtudatos internethasználatáról (a gyermekek (jog)tudatos internethasználatának elősegítése az alapjogi jogvédelem eszközeivel)*. NAIH, Budapest, Hungary. Available at: http://www.naih.hu/files/Kulcs_anv_v2.pdf.

Tisseron, S. (2011). Intimité et extimité. *Communications*, 88, 83–91.

Turner, F. (2008). *From Counterculture to Cyberculture: Stewart Brand, the Whole Earth Network, and the Rise of Digital Utopianism*. University of Chicago Press, Chicago.

US House of Representatives (1966). *The Computer and Invasion of Privacy. Hearings before a Subcommittee of the Committee on Government Operations*. House of Representatives, 89th Congress, Second Session, 26 July. Available at: https://archive.org/details/U.S.House1966TheComputerAndInvasionOfPrivacy.

Vitalis, A. (1988). *Informatique, pouvoir et libertés*, 2nd edition. Economica, Paris.

Walczak, N. (2014). La protection des données personnelles sur l'Internet. Analyse des discours et des enjeux sociopolitiques. PhD thesis, Université Lyon 2, Lyon.

Warren, S.D., Brandeis, L.D. (1890). The right to privacy. *Harvard Law Review*, 4(5), 193–220.

7

Very Precious Memories: Digital Memories and Data Valorization

"We have more 'old' photos and content than ever before, yet most of the Internet focuses on the 'new'"[1]. By introducing its application in this way, Timehop company disseminates something that was previously lacking and Internet users can organize and promote the ever-increasing mass of content of a dynamic. First, there is a lack of tools made available to Internet users to organize and value the ever-increasing mass of archived content. Second, there is a dynamic that claims to respond to this lack and of which Timehop would like to be the precursor: that of the development by the digital industry of a large number of tools to meet a need that it has largely contributed to producing.

This contribution is part of my doctoral research work in which I questioned how these "digital memories" reflect a certain conception of individual memory and the role that the digitalization of user history plays in an environment often described as the present and the "instantaneous". In recent years, however, we have seen an increase in the number of applications and functionalities that allow users to centralize, sort and organize their data in order to suggest the creation of "digital memories" (Figure 7.1). As early as 2010, Foursquare introduced the connection history of its users and Momento, a "smart diary", but it was Timehop which, in 2011, popularized the principle of algorithmic suggestion of old content in the form of memories. Every day, the application offers its users the opportunity to rediscover content produced or published on the same day in previous years. In 2013, Memoir adopted this feature, completing an ambitious project of suggestions for sharing memories according to a place, a person associated with certain content or even annotations and indexing of content. Nevertheless, Memoir closed in 2017.

Chapter written by Rémi ROUGE.

1 www.timehop.com/about.

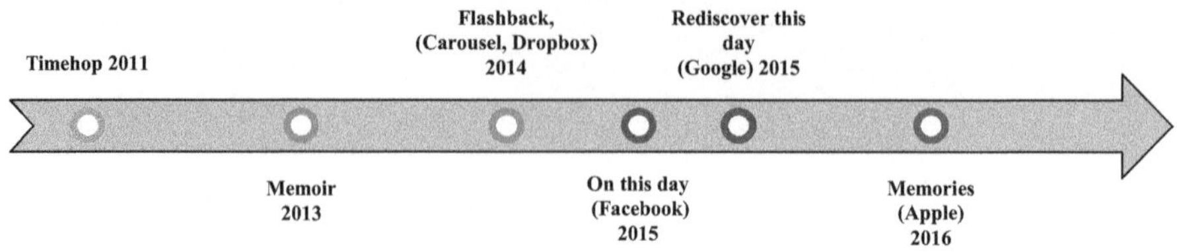

Figure 7.1. *Timeline of the launch of the main applications and features for suggesting digital memories*

This principle has been adopted by major players in the digital economy. At the end of 2014, Carousel (Dropbox's photo application) included "Flashback", its memory suggestion feature. Facebook's launch of "On This Day" in 2015 was part of a series of features and changes to the interface, producing a temporal ordering of digital identities. Among these, as early as 2010, there was the "Photo memories" sidebar, followed in 2012 by the Timeline and the "Life Events", which began the digitalization of the biographical elements preceding the very existence of the network. More recently, in 2018, the "Memories" sidebar was unveiled, bringing together most of the content (re)produced by these different features. For its part, in 2015 Google Photos proposed "Rediscover This Day" and, in 2016, Apple introduced its "Memories" feature.

There are of course different explanatory factors that can explain the adoption of these mechanisms of digital memory suggestion. While the strength of the conventions (Alloing and Pierre 2017) and the personalizing effect[2] have probably had an important role in the development of these functionalities, it is above all the economic stake relating to the control of data flows that interests me here. Indeed, the decompartmentalization and access to pre-used data by platforms[3] such as Facebook or Google by new players (applications such as Timehop and Memoir) are key issues to which all stakeholders have had to respond. By choosing to direct my investigation towards the practices of the actors who produce and promote these tools, it is a question of reporting on how their positions partly determine their conceptions of "digital memories" and, consequently, of memory. Among the determinations that work on the practices of the actors, economic stakes are of

2 "The irruption of photo memories wants to invite us to inject subjectivity again", Laurence Allard explained to Annabelle Laurent (2016).

3 I use the term *platform* here to refer to Google, Facebook and Apple, which, with their dominant position in the digital data economy, have undertaken to develop their own memory suggestion services. The term *platform* refers more generally to the digital spaces where the various actors brought together by the intermediation services offered by these companies converge. GAFA can also be described as "multi-platforms", as they connect consumers with a variety of content (see Casado and Miguel (2016)).

course at the forefront and therefore play a significant role in our daily practices of reminiscence: there is a majority view of memory and the value of memories that is played out in the economic competition that opposes, for example, Google to Facebook. It is also all the more legitimate to question the economic value of digital memories as the resurgence of old content relaunches the competition for the appropriation of user data. Indeed, the production of "digital memories", and especially their algorithmic suggestion, involves a new circulation of data that has remained "dormant"[4]. These are therefore likely to escape the company that owns them. If we agree with the idea that "value comes not so much from data as from their circulation and combination in algorithms and mediation processes" (Henri 2018, p. 80), questioning the "path" that these digital memories take is particularly revealing of the economic stakes that mobilize the different actors involved. Therefore, in support of the interviews conducted in the United States with the employees of Timehop, Memoir, Facebook and Google Photos, I inquired about the types of channels used by the suggested content. These flows differ according to the companies that convert archived content into memories, which means that these data use different channels and this invites us to consider the various economic issues they respond to. In other words, it means asking where the content converted into memory comes from, where it goes according to the actors who grasp it and how they will, according to their divergent interests, try to influence these flows.

In this chapter, I will briefly report on the emergence of "digital memories" and the actors who produce them (section 7.1). This inventory is essential to understand how the trajectories initiated by the start-ups behind these tools (section 7.2) have generated a response from dominant players in the digital economy, consisting of limiting these trajectories to an internal circulation (section 7.3).

7.1. The high dependency of start-ups

Start-ups that create applications that offer memory suggestions are highly dependent on dominant platforms. This obvious dependence was expressed several times during my investigation. An employee occupying a high position in the hierarchy of one of these start-ups explained to me that its growth "depends on the other networks". This dependence is mainly expressed in terms of content

4 The expression "dormant material" is used by Jérôme Denis (2018) in a critical perspective: "the data exist. Or rather, they are already there, 'dormant' material, hidden in public administrations and companies, that would simply have to be moved outside the boundaries of the institutions that house them to unleash their potential" (p. 154). Denis refers here to the assumptions of some calls for data opening. Although in digital memories, data are not usually presented as "immediately available", content that can be converted into digital memories is nevertheless regularly presented by actors as "dormant materials" whose resurgence would reveal their potential.

circulation, as these applications operate partly on content from "outside" (from platforms such as Facebook, Google and Dropbox) and, once converted into memories, enhance their distribution by or on these platforms (Facebook wall, Twitter, Google+, Gmail, etc.).

7.1.1. *Capturing dormant content*

Indeed, in order to work, these applications require a significant amount of data that can be regularly converted into memories: "Basically everything that your memory does, we can do if we have enough data being captured", Memoir director Lee Hoffman told the press (quoted in Fiegerman 2013). The volume of data needed to suggest memories is indeed an aspect highlighted by a large number of actors I have met. Only if the application has allowed access to a large volume of data can it fulfill the promise made to the user to provide him/her with his/her regular stream of memories. However, a large part of this data is held by dominant players in the digital economy (Fabernovel, cited in Casado and Miguel 2016), who act as intermediaries between advertisers and users[5]. It is therefore with regard to data collection that this dependence of start-ups on these dominant actors is first established.

This dependence is also based on the acquisition of users that enables platforms to dominate. Indeed, one of the keys to the success of an application, according to the several stakeholders interviewed, consists of the rapid growth in the number of users, which makes it possible to engage with public revenues as soon as possible. The difficulties encountered following the reduction in the scope of "pages" on Facebook[6] reflect the role that Facebook played in the visibility and acquisition of the users of these applications. Timehop and Memoir have therefore developed alternative strategies to win new users. Developing application-specific communication systems was one of these strategies. Hence, in 2014, Timehop proposed a system of sharing by email or SMS which, thanks to a widget, allowed the recipient to see the shared memory, accompanied by the company logo. Memoir also offered exchanges by email and internally through the application itself.

A true social network of memories, Memoir encouraged sharing by informing its users of the memories of their friends that might interest them. Developing "new forms of sociability based on the logic of monitoring" (Merzeau 2009, p. 76) was a

5 On this subject, see, for example, Acquisti *et al.* (2016).

6 Unlike profiles, Facebook "pages" are public profiles for companies, organizations and celebrities, and allow for a lucrative use of the platform. The scope corresponds to the number of users to whom the publication was distributed. For several years, the "organic" (i.e. free) reach of these pages gradually decreased.

strong response for the company to the obstacles posed by the dominant players in the digital economy.

7.1.2. *Confirming their value*

Each of these applications offers a simplified way to share content on digital social networks. Content originally published by a user on Facebook, once converted into a memory by Timehop, can be republished on Facebook. The trajectory of content is therefore not one-way (from a dominant platform to the application), but circular (from a dominant platform to the application, then to one of these platforms), because the return in the form of memory of the initial content on a platform, from which it is often derived, is a guarantee of value. It is indeed an important signal in terms of quality: "the strongest metric [of the quality of the suggested memory] is when they share it again", explained a manager of one of these applications. The dominant platforms are therefore spaces where the value of these memories is negotiated and confirmed.

The publication of a memory in these spaces is also part of the company's growth strategy. A user sharing a memory there offers an opportunity to acquire new users (personal pages that have, for example, a different scope from corporate pages on Facebook). Start-ups' dependence on dominant players is therefore established both in terms of access to content and in terms of the visibility of their production. The trajectory that these contents processed by the applications follow is, therefore, circular and exogenous, with start-ups – and Timehop in particular, which does not offer any "social" function or profile page accessible to the user where memories could be saved – acting as "conversion" tools (converting various content into memories) that have not necessarily been produced to stay there.

Although they benefit from the activity and exchanges generated by applications, it is, therefore, the dominant platforms and their policies towards other stakeholders in their business ecosystems that determine attack strategies for application growth and monetization.

7.2. Tagging traffic: the response of dominant platforms

7.2.1. *Limiting external traffic*

This dependence on applications has resulted in a frontal difficulty: from 2014, the dominant platforms have produced similar functionalities, limiting the circulation of their data to the outside and thus avoiding their possible leakage to other important platforms. Indeed, Facebook content suggested as a memory by Timehop can for example be easily published on Twitter or shared by Gmail. Start-up actors seem to have experienced these limitations as barriers imposed by multinationals, with which they had sometimes been able to maintain collaborative relationships while contributing to their development. The development of such functionalities by players such as Facebook or Google has had the dual effect of strengthening their activities while limiting competition from applications seeking to monetize this data through the sale of advertising space.

This limitation of data flow to applications has proven to be very effective: Timehop, which had reached 6 million daily users at the end of 2014, had about 38% fewer downloads in the United States one year after the arrival of "On this day" which, during the same period, had reached 60 million daily users (Lunden 2017). There is no need, moreover, to offer similar services in their entirety. Benefiting from what Alloing and Pierre (2017) call "cognitive impregnation" (p. 38), and considering that this type of service was already known to a large number of users, these dominant platforms were able to settle for less-complete products that were sufficient to make the applications that were developed by independent companies (start-ups) less attractive. One respondent testified to this point, explaining that Facebook's launch of "On this day", although based on a limited amount of user information, had stopped the growth of her own application.

These dominant actors will in turn try to strengthen exchanges within their platform (Hutchinson 2017). However, these shares take different forms and the development of memory suggestion features seems above all to reflect the competition between the dominant players in the digital economy. Regarding Google Photos, where the sharing function is presented as one of the essential pillars of the service, the focus is on the different types of content: sharing a photo, an album or the entire library, or automatically sharing content filtered according to places, dates, faces, etc. Following the failure of Google+, it is a question of the company competing with Facebook in the field of digital social networks and, more particularly, in the field of content sharing. To achieve this, Google Photos intends to distinguish itself by the mode of relationships to which the proposed shares respond. Indeed, the actors of Google Photos are pleased to value relationships of proximity, with people "truly" close to themselves, suggesting the fictitious nature of relationships promoted by competitors like Facebook.

While this collaboration/competition relationship (Kelly, cited in Casado and Miguel 2016) is the hallmark of these ecosystems (between them and with all the actors that compose them (Casado and Miguel 2016)), the astonishment aroused by the rapid transition from collaboration to competition, mentioned by the actors of the start-ups I met[7], seems to suggest that the adoption of these functionalities is driven by particular economic challenges. These issues relate to the object of "digital memory", the initiator of a new type of data flow.

7.2.2. *Introducing new types of data circulation*

Indeed, unlike start-ups, mobilizing dormant content consists, for platforms such as Facebook and Google, of creating additional value from data that are already economically valued by making them use new channels.

First, it involves adding additional layers of information to pre-existing content on the platform, for example to features that were not available at the time of the first publication. This includes, as I have been told, taking advantage of technological developments on the platform to enrich content, for example by using "reactions", "moods", "stickers", etc. or simply by adding information that we could not or did not bother to specify. The publication of a suggested memory is therefore an opportunity to obtain new data that can enrich the information companies have about their users. By "bringing content to the surface", they recirculate the data that constitute them at new costs and generate new data.

"On this day" is sometimes presented by Facebook employees as a response to a large volume of information that is not sufficiently accurate. Paradoxically, it is by presenting their functionalities as functional solutions in relation to the surplus content that would affect users (overwhelmed by the amount of photos, videos and archived documents) that companies are encouraging them to divest themselves of an ever-increasing volume of data. It appears that, in return, this consideration of the temporal depth of digital content opens a new field of application of algorithmic power. It seems to offer an opportunity to work on new ways to "make the masses of data that make up user profiles speak" by closely identifying what, over time, constitutes them. This internal circulation becomes, when it comes to suggestions of memories, longitudinal and diachronic. Content flows through the same user at two points in his or her life, thus providing feedback through the data layers. Precise and increased, all the data constituting the memory, therefore, makes it possible to increase the income from the sale of advertising space.

7 According to one of these managers, Memoir had a privileged relationship with Apple, benefiting greatly from the success of the applications available on its online store, as Cecere *et al.* (2015) have shown. Apple has developed "Memories" without any proposal to buy the start-up.

7.3. Conclusion

The external circulation of personal content, necessary for the operation of applications, is limited by dominant platforms seeking to preserve and increase their databases. While the emotion and "personalization" produced by these applications and features are one of the recurring arguments of their promoters – to the point of designating "On this day" on Facebook as a "gift" (Weinberger 2017) – they play an important role in the challenges related to data flow and the appropriation of personal content. As such, they also refer to the issues described by Alloing and Pierre (2017) regarding "the production of value and [the] circulation of affects by digital devices" (p. 11). As it comes to the surface, the content of this personal and moving "gift" becomes, for dominant platforms, a valuable tool to specify profiles made up of an ever-increasing volume of data.

Thus, dominant platforms may have, at the same time, found a way to respond to the temporal break between the logic of the flow and that of the archive described by Coutant and Stenger (2010). In a new way, they involve users who are registered in a flow logic in their own archive logic and, consequently, in this strategy of diachronic profile enrichment.

7.4. References

Acquisti, A., Taylor, C.R., and Wagman, L. (2016). The economics of privacy. *Journal of Economic Literature*, 52(2), 442–492.

Alloing, C. and Pierre, J. (2017). *Le Web affectif, une économie numérique des émotions*. INA Éditions, Paris.

Casado, M.Á. and Miguel, J.C. (2016). GAFAnomy (Google, Amazon, Facebook and Apple): The Big Four and the b-Ecosystem. In *Dynamics of Big Internet Industry Groups and Future Trends*, Gómez-Uranga, M., Zabala-Iturriagagoitia, J., and Barrutia, J. (eds). Springer, Berlin, 127–148.

Cecere, G., Le Guel, F., and Rochelandet, F. (2015). Les modèles d'affaires numériques sont-ils trop indiscrets ? Une analyse empirique. *Réseaux*, 189(1), 77–101.

Coutant, A. and Stenger, T. (2010). Pratiques et temporalités des réseaux socionumériques : logique de flux et logique d'archive. *MEI – Médiation et Information*, 32, 125–136.

Denis, J. (2018). *Le travail invisible des données : éléments pour une sociologie des infrastructures scripturales*. Presses des Mines, Paris.

Fabernovel (2014). GAFAnomics: new economy, new rules. Available at: https://en.fabernovel.com/insights/economy/gafanomics-new-economy-new-rules.

Fiegerman, S. (2013). Memoir app aims to give everyone a perfect memory. *Mashable*, 18 September. Available at: https://mashable.com/2013/09/18/memoirapp/?europe=true#tfeuRRHICPqC.

Henri, I. (2018). La donnée numérique, bien public ou instrument de profit. *Pouvoirs*, 164(1), 75–86.

Hutchinson, A. (2017). Here's how Facebook is automatically telling your good memories from your bad ones. *SocialMediaToday*, 26 August. Available at: https://www.socialmediatoday.com/social-networks/facebooks-adding-new-memories-reminders-prompt-more-sharing.

Laurent, A. (2016). Facebook, Apple, Google : mais qu'ont-ils tous avec nos souvenirs ? *20 minutes*, 17 June. Available at: https://www.20minutes.fr/culture/1867291-20160617-facebook-apple-google-tous-souvenirs.

Lunden, I. (2017). Timehop founder Jon Wegener replaced as CEO by design lead Matt Raoul. *Techcrunch*, 14 January. Available at: https://techcrunch.com/2017/01/14/timehop-founder-jon-wegener-replaced-as-ceo-by-design-lead-matt-raoul/.

Merzeau, L. (2009). De la surveillance à la veille. *Cités*, 39(3), 67–80.

Weinberger, A. (2017). Here's how Facebook is automatically telling your good memories from your bad ones. *Business Insider*, 25 August. Available at: http://www.businessinsider.fr/us/facebooks-updated-on-this-day-memory-feature-how-it-works-2017-8.

Part 2

Digital Technology and Changes in Cultural and Communication Industries

8

Capital as Power: Facebook and the Symbolic Monopoly Rent

The purpose of this chapter is to contribute to the debates on the question of economic valorization in the context of digital capitalism. My central argument is that the main approaches dealing with digital labor as a source of value within digital media are not able to propose an adequate critique of capitalism in the digital age. Based on a synthesis between the reexamination of Marx proposed by the value criticism current, the institutionalist political economy of advanced capitalism initiated by Thorstein Veblen as well as the Innisian theory of communication media in the constitution of knowledge monopolies, I will challenge the hypotheses stemming from the theories on *digital labor*, which postulate that value in digital capitalism would increasingly come from users' unpaid work (Arvidsson and Colleoni 2012; Fuchs 2010, 2012).

Against these approaches, which are inspired in particular by the theorists of cognitive capitalism, I will first show that Marx does not seek to produce a positive theory of labor value, but that his approach consists rather of a critique of the categories of political economy, including commodities, value, labor and capital. In a second step, I will show the limits of traditional Marxist analysis to capture the institutional changes of advanced capitalism from the Veblenian institutionalist political economy approach. I would argue that the traditional Marxist approaches that digital labor theorists rely on do not generally take into account the institutional changes that have taken place within advanced capitalism since the late 19th Century. In this context, I will use the case of Facebook to demonstrate that accumulation within advanced capitalism is based on the ability of corporations to accumulate from a "symbolic monopoly rent". In this sense, the process of capital

---

Chapter written by Maxime OUELLET.

accumulation does not consist so much in the accumulation of material wealth as in extra-economic mechanisms of "symbolic quantification of power".

8.1. The debate on value production in social media: digital labor versus affective labor

The concept of digital labor is based on the assumptions of what could be called "traditional Marxism" (Kurz 2002; Postone 2009). This political economy ignores the Marxian approach, which consists of a real critique of political economy. The intention of Marx's critique of political economy is to criticize the central categories of political economy – labor, commodity, value, capital – which, in his view, are not natural or economic categories, but social and cultural categories that belong only to a specific socio-historical period. These categories are not so much false as they are fetishized (Marx 1993), i.e. Marx, like Harold Innis (2009), as we will see below, proposes a materialist theory of the forms of human consciousness to the extent that the categories of political economy consist of mediations that are constitutive of forms of social objectivity and subjectivity. This means that Marx is not Ricardian in the sense that he is trying to produce a positive theory of value. Rather, it is intended to criticize the fact that work products have value. In this sense, the concept of *digital labor* is often based on a confusion between the Marxian categories of concrete labor and abstract labor, which is also confused with immaterial labor. Productive labor and unproductive labor are also confused, as are the concepts of wealth and value. The theory therefore unduly forces Marx's categories of analysis when it is argued that value in digital social media would come from unpaid labor or user affects (Arvidsson and Coleoni 2012; Fuchs 2010). Value, according to Marx, can only come from the abstraction of social activity that allows the quantification of labor and its exchangeability for a salary. Unpaid work cannot produce value as defined by Marx; it is unproductive work since it does not produce surplus value. The exploitation of unpaid labor in digital social media is more in line with the rent category, i.e. it produces a commodity that has a price but no value. In this sense, digital capitalism is part of a fetishized dynamic, where concrete labor is carried out by algorithms and user data is reified so that it can be used as natural resources extracted through data mining techniques (Foley 2013).

Marxian analysis therefore aims to capture a fundamental contradiction within capitalist societies, since, if human labor solely produces value, replacing workers with machines or algorithms leads to a decrease in the unitary value of produced goods, hence the need to produce ever more goods in the same time unit in order to compensate for the tendency of the profit rate to fall (Postone 2009). In this logic of automating capitalism, the process of valorization becomes more and more difficult, or even impossible – since living labor is increasingly excluded – since it requires the institution of credit mediation as a condition of possibility to allow the reproduction of labor. Nevertheless, the Marxian hypothesis is set in the context of a liberal capitalism specific to the 19th Century. It is therefore necessary to take into account the nature of the institutional transformations that took place within capitalism at the turn of the 20th Century, in a context that some Marxists have called "monopoly capitalism".

8.2. Capital as power: accumulation through symbolic monopoly rent

The contemporary deployment of what some call a "surveillance capitalism" (Bellamy Foster and McChesney 2014) fueled by megadata (Big Data) has its origins in the fundamental transformation of capitalism at the end of the 19th Century according to Thorstein Veblen (1932), namely the institutionalization of the corporation as the central figure of advanced capitalism. In advanced capitalism, the corporation replaces the classic figure of the bourgeois owner of the means of production as the central institution within this mode of production.

On the economic level, this institutional transformation has not been taken into account by Marxist economists and requires a reformulation of the analytical framework that was initially formulated by Marx in the context of liberal capitalism where price competition is the predominant form of constraint that is required, both on capitalists and proletarians. In a monopoly context, according to Marxist economists Baran and Sweezy (1968), it is necessary to take into account the contribution of institutionalist economists such as Veblen in the analysis of capitalism, since the tendency of the profit rate to fall is replaced by the all the more complicated problem of overaccumulation induced by oligopolistic competition.

In this context, capital accumulation is no longer achieved through price competition, but rather through what Veblen calls "differential accumulation strategies", i.e. intellectual property rights, patents, trademarks and strategic alliances with other companies, or through formal and informal agreements with governments (Veblen 1932). In other words, in monopoly capitalism, the mediation of social relations through the market is replaced by planning within corporations whose power is based on their ability to capitalize on future income flows in the financial markets (Nitzan and Bichler 2012). The advent of the corporation induces a profound transformation of capitalism in that the whole economic process, from production to consumption, is based on the anticipation of future incomes through access to a credit currency produced by the financial system. It is a liquefaction of ownership – in short, an intangible or informational capitalism before the letter[1] –

1 It is necessary to specify that capitalism is in its very nature immaterial since it is a social relationship and not a thing. In this sense, current theses on the intangible nature of so-called "informational" or "cognitive" capitalism are heuristically problematic. If capital is a "real abstraction", it can be said that what is called informational capitalism results from a process of abstraction and quantification that is in the very nature of capitalist dynamics. It is therefore not a break with this logic.

insofar as it aims to generate liquidity based on a right regarding the company's future income that takes the form of exchangeable financial securities (Nitzan and Bichler 2012). In this context, the function of mass culture disseminated by cultural industries is to ensure, particularly through advertising, that it produces an awareness adapted to the logic of overproduction of monopoly capitalism. The captain of the liberal capitalism industry thus became "captain of conscience" (Ewen 1983) whose role was to produce audiences that would be sold to advertisers (Smythe 1977), in order to link the logic of overproduction to that of overconsumption.

8.3. The institutional transformations of advanced capitalism: the financialization of the economy and the commodification of knowledge

It is in this context that it is possible to understand that digital capitalism is based on a capitalization process, i.e. the discounting of future profits at current value. To put it in Innissian terms, it is a control of historicity based on a presentist temporal regime made possible by the mediation of digital technologies (Innis 2009). The power of capital is thus characterized by its ability to institute a social imaginary (Castoriadis 1975). It is a power that is therefore based on the ability to quantify the unquantifiable through different political, technical and legal means, thus making it possible to transform the whole of social life into future income flows that can be captured. As Facebook shows, the process of capital accumulation is not so much based on the exploitation of users' unpaid labor as on its ability to "symbolically quantify power" (Nitzan and Bichler 2012, p. 26)[2].

In this context, Facebook uses various extra-economic strategies to produce a differential accumulation that consists of transferring surplus value from other sectors of productive activity into a rentier dynamic (Rigi and Prey 2015) and restricting access to income flows to other subordinate capitalists in order to exceed the normal financial rate of return.

In the case of Facebook, these means are: 1) an accumulation on intangible assets (patents); 2) control of communication risks; and 3) a strategy of imperial expansion of the knowledge monopoly through investment in education and research.

2 In other words, in advanced capitalism, the process of capital appreciation is mainly carried out by the ability of corporations to make quantifiable what is not quantifiable by various extra-economic means. As we will try to show with the Facebook case study, capital appreciation results from a dynamic of political accumulation.

8.3.1. *Accumulation on intangible assets and patents*

The analysis of Facebook shows how differential accumulation strategies are part of a dynamic specific to financialized capitalism. First, it should be recalled that its initial public offering, which was described as a catastrophic disaster by financial analysts, was marked by rumors of insider trading fomented by Goldman Sachs (Ugueux 2011). Its value fell by US$19 billion in four days, mainly due to investors' fears about the ability of the social network to monetize audiences who use mobile technologies such as tablets and smartphones. In response to this market pressure, Facebook will intensify the extractive activity of its users' data in order to make its operations more profitable and meet its financial commitments.

Facebook's differential accumulation strategy is based on extra-economic factors that have been made possible by the institutional complementarity between the new privatized knowledge production regime and the deregulation of the financial system (Orsi and Coriat 2006). Indeed, these two sectors complement each other institutionally insofar as stock market mechanisms are considered more reliable than bank financing, because they would make it possible to anticipate and assess the value of a company's intangible assets (Mouhoud and Plihon 2009). According to public databases (Justia Patents 2008), Facebook has approved more than 8,000 patents on algorithms, which creates barriers to market entry for potential competitors. In addition, since its inception, Facebook has made more than 50 business acquisitions, the best known of which are Instagram, WhatsApp and Oculus. According to Mark Zuckerberg, Facebook's acquisition strategy consists mainly of talent acquisition, i.e. the acquisition of patents that are held by competitors in order to ensure its monopoly on knowledge, patents that are mainly filed in Ireland, the number one tax haven for new technology companies (Colin and Colin 2013).

In this context, Facebook also contributes to the logic of the financialization of the daily lives of its users (Martin 2002). Indeed, in a context where the salary of the majority of the population has not increased for more than 30 years, they must finance their overconsumption by increasing the value of their financial assets (Toporowski 2009). Social reproduction no longer depends solely on the relationship of wage domination, but largely on the ability of households to obtain credit. This does not mean that labor as a central form of social mediation – and domination – has disappeared, but rather that its role has changed. The main function of employment is now to obtain a minimum wage salary in order to acquire sufficient financial credibility to access credit and repay part of one's debts. In this sense, credit as a form of social mediation becomes a condition of possibility to allow the reproduction of labor. It is therefore an accumulation of capital in a completely fictitious futurized time, which is at the root of the crises in contemporary capitalism. To the extent that financial capital is based on the mediation of financial information, the informational traces left by users of digital social media are used to assess the financial credibility of consumers, locking them in a virtual debt prison (Manzerolle 2010). It is in this context that we can understand the agreement that Facebook signed in 2013 with the main data brokers such as Axciom, Datalogix and Epsilon. Facebook has also recently obtained a patent for an algorithm to authenticate and authorize users for a bank loan based on the financial credibility of their Facebook friends (Christl 2017).

8.3.2. *Control of communication risks*

In an increasingly volatile financial environment due to financial deregulation, risk management has become the main activity of a firm like Facebook. In a financialized economy, the value of companies' assets is not so much about the products and services they produce as it is about their ability to control risks (LiPuma and Lee 2005). For Facebook, the risks are mainly based on potential privacy and tax evasion regulations, as well as reputational risks related to users' loss of trust in the digital social network. Indeed, since the physical production of goods is no longer the main source of profits for companies – in fact Facebook produces nothing – it relies instead on the control of information, knowledge and image. In this sense, the main source of profit in digital capitalism is based less on the creative capacity and communicative exchanges of users, as argued by cognitive capitalism theorists, or on consumer affects (Arvidson and Coleoni 2012), than on the ability of corporations to accumulate from a "symbolic monopoly rent" (Mouhoud and Plihon 2009, p. 127). Hence, following the Cambridge Analytica scandal, in two days, $60 billion of Facebook's market capitalization evaporated, as investors feared that any regulation on the use of personal data could harm their business model. "Stock market bubbles explode due to regulation", investor Jeffrey Gundlach pointed out. "Nothing new is happening in the field of speculation", Gundlach added, quoting famed 1920s investor Jesse Livermore. "What happened in the past will happen again and again" (Pressman 2018). Then, immediately after Mark Zuckerberg's intervention in Congress, Facebook's stock price rose by 4.5% after the poor representation of Congress members. The "philistine" questions asked by its members can be explained by the fact that lobbyists hired by Facebook have donated US$600,000 since 2013 to the parliamentarians who questioned it (West 2018). Facebook's total spending on lobbying reached US$11 million in 2017 (Open Secret 2018).

We also learned from the newspapers that Kevin Chan, Director of Public Policy at Facebook Canada, had privileged access to several federal cabinet ministers, including the Minister of Finance, but did not register as a lobbyist. During his appearance before the Privacy Committee in Ottawa, Conservative MP Peter Kent said threats were allegedly made by Facebook representatives during a meeting with

Canadian elected officials in Washington "regarding possible Canadian regulations to further protect Canadians' private data online". Mr. Kent noted: "During our visit, we were told that any new regulations could hurt Facebook's investments in Canada, such as the artificial intelligence project in Montreal" (Baillargeon 2018).

8.3.3. *Facebook and the imperial expansion logic of the knowledge monopoly*

Facebook's investment in artificial intelligence (AI) in Montreal is part of an imperial expansion strategy of a new knowledge monopoly. The new Quebec Research and Innovation Strategy (QRIS), and the latest budget of the Government of Quebec, which reserves 100 million Canadian dollars every five years for research, support for start-ups and even the creation of an industrial cluster dedicated to AI, expresses this submission to the imperial strategy of digital giants. The investments of Facebook, Google, Microsoft and Thales in Montreal, as well as the partnerships between the giants of GAFAM and the Universities of Montreal and McGill, are also part of this strategy (Sanfaçon 2018). For companies like Facebook, it is essentially a matter of outsourcing its research and development costs to publicly funded research, and then privatizing it in the form of a patent. According to researcher Joëlle Pineault, who heads the Facebook-funded laboratory in Montreal, "[t]he purpose of all this is not to improve Facebook products, but to do fundamental research on machine learning" (Lortie 2017).

From an Innissian perspective, this strategy can be said to endorse the submission of Canada's (and Quebec's) economic, political and cultural sovereignty to the American Empire. In other words, AI feeds on two things: computing power and a mountain of data. However, it is the GAFAMs that have the most gigantic computers to process large amounts of information. In this sense, the federal government's attitude towards digital companies reflects an abdication of the very principle of sovereignty that was at the root of political modernity.

Hence, we could talk, following Harold Innis, about the emergence of a new knowledge monopoly that is being established with the domination of digital giants. Their domination is exercised through the mediation of cybernetic technologies that contribute to the reproduction of hegemonic categories of thought based on a form of quantifying abstraction. This new monopoly of knowledge is based on a form of symbolic quantification of power. The automated systems developed by Facebook have therefore transformed knowledge into digital data, and therefore into operational knowledge that produces mechanical knowledge that makes any critical and synthetic dimension that was at the root of scientific knowledge unnecessary (Andersen 2008).

This strategy of knowledge monopolization is also reflected in the Chan–Zuckerberg initiative, an organization set up to develop forms of personalized learning in American public schools:

> "Our hope over the next decade is to help upgrade a majority of these schools to personalized learning and then start working globally as well, Mr. Zuckerberg told the audience. Giving a billion students a personalized education is a great thing to do" (Singer 2017).

Facebook's Internet.org project to provide free access to the Internet, Facebook and a few other partner sites in developing countries is also part of an imperial expansion strategy of knowledge monopolization. This "voluntary" strategy mainly aims to capture the personal data of populations that are considered "unprofitable" in terms of advertising, mainly in order to capture their data to improve algorithms and thus create an entry barrier for potential competitors in this market (Cario 2016).

8.4. Conclusion: Facebook and the contradictions of capitalism in the digital age

In conclusion, it can be argued that Facebook condenses all the contradictions of capitalism in itself, contradictions that are well summarized by the title formula of the latest book co-written by media theorist Robert McChesney: *People Get Ready: The Fight Against a Jobless Economy and a Citizenless Democracy* (McChesney and Nichols 2016).

A "citizenless democracy" on the one hand, because the algorithms developed by Facebook make it possible to model social regulation in a personalized way by anticipating the actions of individuals before they occur (Rouvroy and Berns 2013). The ability of citizens to deliberate in a reflective way on the normative orientations that life in society takes is then destroyed, or rather privatized (Stiegler 2015). The new technologies of personalization of consumption lead to a fragmentation and depoliticization of the old political communities articulated around the nation-state, which are composed into depoliticized virtual communities, gathered around particular lifestyles[3]. "Citizenless democracy", on the other hand, because with the technological and scientific advances based on the cybernetic capacity for predictability, of which Big Data is an integral part, it is now possible to individualize the risk that had once been socialized within the framework of

3 It is this depoliticized vision of society that the theorist and Web 2.0 guru Henry Jenkins defends in *Convergence Culture* (2006) and which is echoed by Mark Zuckerberg of Facebook in his manifesto entitled *Building Global Community* (2017). On this subject, see (Ouellet 2017).

post-war democratic capitalism and that had allowed the construction of a middle class. It is therefore the end of the common world, which is a condition for the possibility of politics. In this sense, the fundamental political question in the digital age is to rebuild the common against the technological fetishism that locks us into "tautistic" bubbles (Sfez 1992).

This disaffection with policies leads correspondingly to its "consumerization", since the same computerized data mining tools are used by politicians to collect detailed information on voters/consumers and to adjust their message according to the preferences of each specific group (Groshek and Al-Rawim 2013). In the era of digital social media, the common political culture is tending to dissolve in favor of particularist issues (Giroux 2011) and the production of "fake news".

Moreover, McChesney and Nichols' book refers to a "jobless economy" since the main corporations at the heart of digital capitalism – Google, Apple, Facebook, Amazon and Microsoft (GAFAM) – are accumulating value through rentier practices. This logic of rentier accumulation risks accentuating the extreme polarization of wealth between an extremely rich minority and a mass of precarious or even obsolete workers. As Paul Krugman (2012) argues:

> "Smart machines may make higher GDP possible, but also reduce the demand for people – including smart people. So we could be looking at a society that grows ever richer, but in which all the gains in wealth accrue to whoever owns the robots".

8.5. References

Andersen, C. (2008). The end of theory: The data deluge makes the scientific method obsolete. *Wired*. Available at: http://www.wired.com/2008/06/pb-theory/.

Arvidsson, A. and Colleoni, E. (2012). Value in informational capitalism and on the Internet. *The Information Society*, 28(3), 135–150.

Baillargeon, S. (2018). À Ottawa, des députés outragés ont affronté des dirigeants de Facebook. *Le Devoir*. Available at: https://www.ledevoir.com/culture/medias/525624/facebook-a-livre-un-peu-ouvert-au-parlement-d-ottawa.

Baran, P.A. and Sweezy, P.M. (1968). *Le capitalisme monopoliste : un essai sur la société industrielle américaine*. Maspéro, Paris.

Bellamy Foster, J. and McChesney, R.W. (2014). Surveillance capitalism monopoly-finance capital, the military-industrial complex, and the digital age. *Monthly Review*, 66(3). Available at: https://monthlyreview.org/2014/07/01/surveillance-capitalism/.

Cario, E. (2016). Le club sélect des milliards d'utilisateurs inscrits. *Le Devoir*. Available at: https://www.ledevoir.com/monde/462294/Internet-le-club-select-des-milliards-d-utilisateurs-inscrit.

Castoriadis, C. (1975). *L'institution imaginaire de la société*. Le Seuil, Paris.

Christl, W. (2017). Corporate surveillance in everyday life. How companies collect, combine, analyze, trade, and use personal data on billions. *Cracked Labs*. Available at: https://crackedlabs.org/en/corporate-surveillance.

Collin, P. and Colin, N. (2013). Mission d'expertise sur la fiscalité de l'économie numérique. Report, Ministère de l'économie et des finances. Available at: https://www.economie.gouv.fr/files/rapport-fiscalite-du-numerique_2013.pdf.

Ewen, S. (1983). *Conscience sous influence*. Aubier Montaigne, Paris.

Foley, D. (2013). Rethinking financial Capitalism and the information economy. *Review of Radical Political Economy*, 45(3), 257–268.

Fuchs, C. (2010). Labor in informational capitalism and on the Internet. *The Information Society*, 26(3), 179–196.

Fuchs, C. (2012). With or without Marx? With or Without capitalism? A rejoinder to Adam Arvidsson and Eleanor Colleoni. *tripleC*, 10(2), 633–645.

Giroux, H.A. (2011). The crisis of public values in the age of the new media. *Media, Critical Studies in Media Communication*, 28(1), 8–29.

Groshek, J. and Al-Rawim, A. (2013). Public sentiment and critical framing in social media content during the 2012 U.S. presidential campaign. *Social Science Computer Review*, 31(5), 563–674.

Innis, H. (2009). *The Bias of Communication*. University of Toronto Press, Toronto.

Jenkins, H. (2006). *Convergence Culture*. New York University Press, New York.

Justia Parents (2018). *Facebook Patents*. Available at: https://patents.justia.com/company/facebook [Accessed 13 May 2018].

Krugman, P. (2012). Is growth over? *The New York Times*. Available at: http://krugman.blogs.nytimes.com/2012/12/26/is-growth-over/?r=0.

Kurz, R. (2002). *Lire Marx. Les Textes les Plus Importants de Karl Marx pour le XXIème siècle. Choisis et commentés par Robert Kurz*. La Balustrade, Paris.

LiPuma, E. and Lee, B. (2005). Financial derivatives and the rise of circulation. *Economy and Society*, 34(3), 404–427.

Lortie, M.-C. (2017). Joëlle Pineau, personnalité de la semaine. *La Presse*. Available at: http://www.lapresse.ca/actualites/personnalite-de-la-semaine/201709/24/01-5136157-joelle-pineau-personnalite-de-la-semaine.php.

Manzerolle, V.R. (2010). The virtual debt factory: Towards an analysis of debt and abstraction in the American credit crisis. *tripleC*, 8(2), 221–236.

Martin, R. (2002). *The Financialization of Daily Life*. Temple University Press, Philadelphia.

Marx, K. (1993). *Le capital, Livre 1*. Presses universitaires de France, Paris.

McChesney, R.W. and Nichols, J. (2016). *People Get Ready: The Fight Against a Jobless Economy and a Citizenless Democracy*. Nation books, New York.

Mouhoud, E.M. and Plihon, D. (2009). *Le savoir et la finance*. La Découverte, Paris.

Nitzan, J. and Bichler, S. (2012). *Le capital comme pouvoir : une étude de l'ordre et du créordre*. Max Milo, Paris.

Open Secret.org (2018). *Annual lobbying by Facebook inc*. Available at: https://www.opensecrets.org/lobby/clientsum.php?id=D000033563&year=2017.

Orsi, F. and Coriat, B. (2006). The new role and status of intellectual property rights in contemporary capitalism. *Competition and Change*, 10(2), 162–179.

Ouellet, M. (2017). L'empire de la communication. *Liberté*, 318, 25–27.

Postone, M. (2009). *Temps, travail et domination sociale*. Mille et une nuits, Paris.

Pressman, A. (2018). Facebook stock is a bubble about to be popped, famed fund manager says. *Fortune*. Available at: http://fortune.com/2018/04/23/facebook-bubble-gundlach/.

Rigi, J. and Prey, R. (2015). Value, rent and the political economy of social media. *The Information Society*, 31(5), 392–406.

Rouvroy, A. and Berns, T. (2013). Gouvernementalité algorithmique et perspectives d'émancipation. *Réseaux*, 177, 163–196.

Sanfaçon, J.-R. (2018). Intelligence artificielle : la mondialisation 3.0. *Le Devoir*. Available at: https://www.ledevoir.com/opinion/editoriaux/519416/intelligence-artificielle-la-mondialisation-3-0.

Sfez, L. (1992). *Critique de la communication*. Le Seuil, Paris.

Singer, N. (2017). The Silicon Valley billionaires remaking america's schools. *The New York Times*. Available at: https://www.nytimes.com/2017/06/06/technology/tech-billionaires-education-zuckerberg-facebook-hastings.html.

Smythe, D.W. (1977). Communications: Blindspot of Western Marxism. *Canadian Journal of Political and Social Theory*, 1(3), 1–28.

Stiegler, B. (2015). *La société automatique 1 : l'avenir du travail*. Fayard, Paris.

Toporowski, J. (2009). The economics and culture of financial inflation. *Competition and Change*, 13(2), 145–156.

Ugueux, G. (2011). Facebook et Goldman Sachs : un bel imbroglio. *Le blog de George Ugueux*. Available at: http://finance.blog.lemonde.fr/2011/01/21/facebook-et-goldman-sachs-un-bel-imbroglio/.

Veblen, T. (1932). *The Theory of the Business Enterprise*. The New American Library, New York.

West, G. (2018). Facebook lobbyists donated $600 K to lawmakers interrogating Zuckerberg. *Open Secrets Blog*. Available at: https://www.opensecrets.org/news/2018/04/fbook-lobbyists-gave-600k-zuckerbergs-congres sional/.

Zuckerberg, M. (2017). Building global community. *Facebook*. Available at: https://www.facebook.com/notes/mark-zuckerberg/building-global-community/10154544292806634/.

9

On the "Platformization" of the Culture and Communication Industries

This chapter continues my critical analyses of the extension of web and mobile platforms in – or "above" – extremely diverse fields of human activity, in particular towards a large number of areas historically located outside the field of culture and communication: sexual and romantic encounters, tourism and accommodation, engineering and manufacturing, transport, "personal services" or energy supply. This list is obviously not exhaustive.

A first question that can be asked is whether the multiplication of these actors is in itself a novelty, and it is probably necessary to recognize that the intermediation model is not fundamentally new. The importance of intermediation apparatuses can be illustrated with the development of Minitel in the late 1980s and early 1990s. Similarly, the intermediation model (and multifaceted markets) was undoubtedly already at work with television and broadcasting in the 1950s and 1960s, particularly with the launch of the first private channels and the increase in their interdependence with the advertising industry. These are well-documented elements in the political economy of culture and communication, which Bernard Miège (2017) summarizes very well. If the emergence of the web continues and reinforces this trend, my purpose is not to retrace this historical evolution.

This chapter merely presents three points, which are also research hypotheses that I submitted to the participants of the conference *Generalized Digitalization of Society* (2018), and which cover both theoretical and practical (or empirical)

Chapter written by Jacob MATTHEWS.

questions. It also offers some examples of how specific intermediation processes carried out by different web platforms can be observed today at work, and how their supposedly "collaborative" nature can be questioned.

9.1. Towards a dilution of the specificities of the culture and communication industries?

My first point explicitly refers to reflections made more than 20 years ago now, by Jean-Guy Lacroix and Gaëtan Tremblay (1997), among others, who mentioned the risks of diluting the specific characteristics of the culture and communication industries and, at the same time, of extending the characteristics of these industries in many socio-economic fields. It should be noted here that we are referring in particular to the function of the cultural and communication industries as bodies for the production of symbolic goods, "texts", to use the notion put forward by David Hesmondhalgh (2007), as a fundamental characteristic of these industries. However, it is also a question of the conditions of production: which production relationships dominate in this specific sector of culture and communication? How is work historically organized there and what specificities of work in the cultural and communication industries extend to other socio-economic sectors? Indeed, one of the hypotheses I defend is that web platforms have two fundamental socio-economic functions. On the one hand, they are institutions of ideological production; on the other hand, they are instruments of labor organization, tools for managing living labor and dead labor (capital). These two functions are closely linked, as I will try to illustrate below.

With regard to the hypothesis of diluting the specific characteristics of the culture and communication industries, research on digital intermediation platforms is quite telling: these are companies where the labor force has almost completely disappeared, whether it is the internal labor force or what can be referred to as an external labor force, composed of, among others, consumer–users (Matthews and Rouzé 2018). A significant part of the value – or rent – captured by the holders of these means of communication and work organization depends on the work of users in their various forms, including in the basic form of data producers, and in what Brice Nixon (2014) calls *audience labor*. This brings me to my second point, which is more of a questioning of some of the concepts used to account for productive activities on and by the platforms, which I think deserve to be reconsidered.

9.2. The notion of uses of digital intermediation platforms

This second point deals with the notion of usage of digital intermediation platforms. As we know, for a long time, particularly because of the influence of functionalist approaches, it was generally considered that there were, on the one hand, media strategies (or, more precisely, the strategies of media owners and managers) and, on the other hand, usage or receptions that were sometimes more or less compliant, hegemonic, and sometimes oppositional or alternative. These uses were in reaction to the media, to the device. The notion of *audience labor* (Nixon 2014) and the importance of the production of culture by the supposed "receivers" or "consumers" confirm the heuristic weakness of this vision. However, the nuance I wish to bring to this sense of the notion of *usage* does not simply refer to the practices of "receivers", even though they fall under the hijacking or hacking of web platforms.

I propose that we consider the usage of those who are part of the internal workforce of the platforms, who work in what is called the "back office", and even the most senior managers hierarchically. Vincent Rouzé and I (Matthews and Rouzé 2018) suggest that we take a step back and consider as users of these platforms all their "agents" – trainees, freelance "collaborators" and even more broadly all the commercial and financial partners' agents who rely on these platforms (who use or instrumentalize them) in their own productive activity. Without wishing in any way to portray them as naive martyrs, the co-founders and platform managers can also be analyzed as users of the same socio-technical apparatuses that they have helped to shape. The latest surveys to which I have contributed, for example on crowdfunding platforms, highlight characteristics shared throughout the chain, from the smallest sponsors of the projects to the managers of these sites. From one end to the other, there is a deep uncertainty due to social and economic insecurity, a very high degree of versatility and, in particular, the need to acquire or develop key skills such as the production of "pedagogical" speeches and intermediation at its most practical level: research and management of partnerships, and connection of socio-economic actors (in order to obtain direct or indirect monetary benefits).

A significant proportion of the activity of managers, whether they are the founders of the platforms, in the early stages of their development, employees or even the numerous trainees, is thus dedicated to the managerial and psychological/ideological support of project leaders (Matthews and Rouzé 2018). The internal usage of these platforms make it possible to deploy work organization and optimization methods, while these tools often do not (or no longer) belong to these managers. Even when the founders still hold, for example, shares in these companies, they operate in accordance with the wishes of their financial sponsors. Relations between managers and project leaders are fundamentally asymmetrical, insofar as the ideological production of the former serves objectively to train and supervise the latter (Bihr 1989). However, it can hardly be assumed that platform managers would be agents, free subjects. It is clear that a significant part of their "work" corresponds to ideological production in its own right.

It is in this respect that I ask the question of digital intermediation, as the continuation or end of the cultural and communication industries. Are these actors, like the information or entertainment "media", specialized ideological producers? The function of producing "texts" that Hesmondhalgh (2007) sees as a fundamental characteristic of the cultural and communication industries is evident in these actors. Similarly, their activity, reflected all the way down to the seduction efforts of small cultural project promoters, is fully integrated into the system of the culture industry described by Max Horkheimer and Theodor Adorno in the 1940s. Isn't this precisely the "core business" of digital intermediation platforms such as crowdsourcing and cultural crowdfunding sites? In this case, are they not producers of cultural and ideological forms, in the same way as project carriers themselves? In conclusion to this second point, platform managers appear to be *other users* of tools that, in many respects, surpass them and alienate them themselves.

9.3. Strategies of digital intermediation platforms

My third point concerns the question of the strategies of digital intermediation platforms. I deal with this issue by offering several concrete examples. One question that can obviously arise following the reading of my proposals concerning the notion of use is the following: what about strategies where the activities of managers are themselves to be considered as uses of platforms? I would propose to reserve the notion of *strategy* for the major socio-economic guidelines, involving the cumulative and correlated (but not necessarily concerted) actions of the various agents linked together by the web platforms. What we perceive with the all-out development of these apparatuses are indeed attacks by financial capital in order to secure an ever-increasing share of the value produced, and in these specific cases, this is done – moreover – in the name of a supposed "collaborative economy".

Here are some recent illustrations, based on events that took place in France in the spring of 2018, around the offensives of political and economic power against the public rail service, on the one hand, and against the occupants of the Notre-Dame-des-Landes ZAD, on the other hand. Two categories of so-called "collaborative" platforms have played an interesting role in these struggles and, more particularly, in relation to the railway workers' strike. The crowdfunding platforms Leetchi (Figure 9.1) and Lepotcommun (Figure 9.2) both hosted campaigns in support of striking railway workers, based on the model that was initiated in 2016 to support workers fighting against the El Khomri law, seemingly offering a digital version of the strike fund.

Figure 9.1. *Screenshot from the Leetchi website*[1] *(taken on April 30, 2018)*

Figure 9.2. *Screenshot from the Lepotcommun website*[2] *(taken on April 30, 2018)*

1 www.leetchi.com.

2 www.lepotcommun.fr.

These solidarity actions may at first seem very encouraging, but it should be pointed out that in both cases, the platforms collect 2.9% of the amounts, i.e. in the first case, more than €36,000 at the time of writing (end of June 2018) and, in the second case, a total amount of more than €16,000. These are in effect bank charges levied on the strike fund. Let us consider the identity of the entities that hide behind the welcoming brands of Lepotcommun and Leetchi. The first was acquired on October 20, 2015 by the Banque Populaire Caisse d'Épargne banking group, through its subsidiary S-money 3, in which it held an 85% stake. As for the second platform, launched thanks to investments by Xavier Niel, 360 Capital Partners and IDInvest, it was recently bought by the Crédit Mutuel bank, which recently acquired 86% of shares.

Another so-called "collaborative" platform whose activity has been strongly sustained as a result of the strike, is Blablacar – which had already been officially recommended by Ségolène Royal when she was French Minister of the Environment, as a solution both against railway strikes and to reduce air pollution (Figure 9.3).

Figure 9.3. *Screenshot from the Blablacar website*[3] *(taken on April 9, 2018)*

3 www.blablacar.fr.

Indeed, in the face of the railway workers' strike in spring 2018, the Blablacar community was present. As the April 5, 2018 issue of the French newspaper *Le Monde* teaches us, "overwhelmed by demand, Blablacar has begun offer coach trips. The experiment begins on Friday 6 April for Paris–Lille, and will then be extended to Paris–Rennes and Paris–Rouen. The idea could be a long-term one". The next day, *Challenges* magazine's website told us that "the company, ten years after its launch, still does not earn any money", but sees "a threefold increase in the supply of seats, i.e. 184,000 seats offered" during railway strike days.

Travelers who used French motorways in the spring of 2018 (and in particular the 8,886 kilometers of roads managed by Vinci Autoroutes) could not miss this small "educational" message encouraging car-sharing (Figure 9.4).

Figure 9.4. *Screenshot (detail) from the Vinci Autoroutes website*[4] *(taken on April 29, 2018). The sign says "SNCF strike: think carpooling"*

Probing a little deeper on Vinci's website, we find the following information presented in Figure 9.5.

4 www.vinci-autoroutes.com.

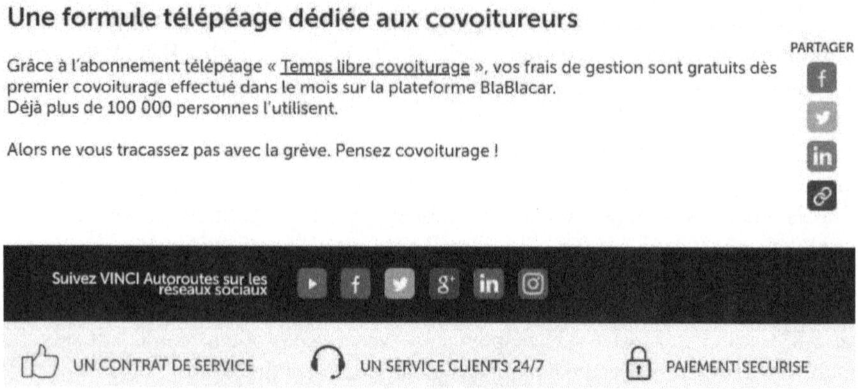

Figure 9.5. *Screenshot (detail) from the Vinci Autoroutes website*[5] *(taken on April 29, 2018)*[6]

This is a specific example of the forms of intermediation that result from the *combined use* of these platforms by their managers, drivers and passengers, as well as by commercial partners – in this case, the Vinci group. Faced with the railway workers' strike in spring 2018, many other initiatives of the same kind have emerged, bringing together platforms such as Waze and Facebook, the SNCF, as well as a number of public players such as the Île-de-France region, the city of Paris, the *Groupement des autorités responsables de transport*, the *Assemblée des communautés de France*, the *Fédération nationale des agences d'urbanisme*, etc. The Blablaca–Vinci-State alliance against the railway strike is neither isolated nor insignificant. It is part of a more general *strategic objective*, which also includes the attacks on the ZADists of Notre-Dame-des-Landes. As the Vinci group's slogan states: "Real success stories are the ones we share".

As is commonly known, the Notre-Dame-des-Landes airport project was withdrawn in 2018. Admittedly, this political decision led to the loss of a lucrative contract for Vinci group – however, in the meantime, the company has taken over entire parts of the French motorway and air transport network – and has already begun to position itself in the rail sector (with the Paris–Bordeaux high-speed line)

5 *Ibidem*.

6 "An electronic toll payment formula dedicated to carpoolers.
Thanks to 'free time rideshare'electronic toll payment subscription, your management fees are free with your first carpool during the month on the BlaBlacar platform.
100,000 people already use it.
So don't worry about the strike. Think carpooling.

pending the privatization and dismantling of the SNCF network. The Minister of the Economy, Bruno Lemaire, announced that the State would compensate Vinci for the loss of the Notre-Dame-des-Landes contract, and the group will probably also be largely indemnified for this "loss of profit" when the shares still held by the State in Aéroports de Paris are soon sold. This makes it easier to understand why Vinci Autoroutes can afford to offer Blablacar users the cost of managing their motorway passes, as the message says: "Don't worry about the strike. Think carpooling!"

Although the airport project has been withdrawn, the embodiment of a genuine form of "collaborative economy" (if these two terms can be juxtaposed) – the embodiment of the commons that the ZAD represents – remains quite intolerable for political and economic powers. This makes it easier to understand why hundreds of thousands of euros have been spent every day to restore order and private property in this enclave of commons (Figure 9.6).

Figure 9.6. *Screenshot (detail) from the Planetes360 website[7] (taken on June 22, 2018)*

7 www.planetes360.fr.

9.4. Conclusion

In conclusion, this mention of specific intermediation processes carried out through web platforms makes it possible to put forward at least four proposals.

First, the platforms are discourse production bodies, mainly monopolized by their managers who defend the interests of their financial holders (GAFAM, investment funds, etc.), as well as those of their various private and public partners. In this respect, they place themselves "next to" or "above" the traditional culture and communication industries, competing with them in this ideological function, without intrinsically threatening them. Second, the different forms of use (by their various types of users, including commercial partners and the platforms' own management) may be locally or temporarily contradictory. However, and third, they combine or correlate objectively to participate in more general strategic movements, in every respect in line with the ideological agenda of contemporary capitalism: justification for the intensification of the exploitation of labor, imperative assertion of private ownership of the means of production, defense of the international financial system against any potential interference or challenge to its private appropriation, etc. Fourth, this extension of web and mobile platforms into – or "above" – extremely diverse fields of human activity is carried out in the name of a "sharing" economy, of "collaboration", and many of the discourses accompanying or driving the different uses borrow from this register and that of the commons. However, it can be observed that their combinations contribute in fact to strategic aims that by no means challenge private property, alienation and material relations of production specific to capitalism, quite the contrary.

To conclude my remarks, I would like to reproduce these two quotes from Toni Negri, who replied in these terms, during an interview conducted by the union journal *Cheminots en lutte* in France, in April 2018:

> "This struggle – which we all want to see transformed into a 'social strike', which is, moreover, the condition for its victory – attacks privatization, a fundamental instrument of the system of governance of neoliberalism and the transfer of income to financial capital.
>
> There is a deeper ideological element in the attempt to take away the status of railway workers: this status has been and remains a collective conquest. And that's what the bosses are up against. They are ready to grant individual privileges but they refuse any 'common' conquest".

9.5. References

Bihr, R. (1989). *Entre bourgeoisie et prolétariat : l’encadrement capitaliste*. L’Harmattan, Paris.

Hesmondhalgh, D. (2007). *The Cultural Industries*. Sage Publications, London.

Lacroix, J.-G. and Tremblay, G. (eds) (1997). The information society and the cultural industries theory. *Current Sociology*, 4(45).

Matthews, J. and Rouzé, V. (2018). Les plateformes de *crowdfunding* culturel : entre figures de l’artiste entrepreneur et entrepreneurs polymorphes. *Les enjeux de l’information et de la communication*, 19(1). Available at: https://lesenjeux.univ-grenoble-alpes.fr/2018/03-Rouze-Matthews/.

Miège, B. (2017). *Les industries culturelles et créatives face à l’ordre de l’information et de la communication*, 2nd edition. Presses universitaires de Grenoble, Grenoble.

Nixon, B. (2014). Toward a political economy of ‘audience labour’ in the digital era. TripleC: Communication, Capitalism & Critique. *Open Access Journal for a Global Sustainable Information Society*, 12(2), 713–734.

10

Digital Audiovisual Platforms, Between Transnational Flows and National Frameworks

A preliminary observation can easily be made: digital platforms now play a central role in the economy of cultural industries. They are a central vehicle for dissemination, monetization and promotion, particularly through recommendation and fund-raising mechanisms (especially participatory financing) as well as creation and production (especially for the discovery of new artistic and creative talent, production renewals or ticket sales, etc.).

In the audiovisual sector – which is of interest to us here and which we will define as the television, film and video sectors – the deployment of digital platforms is not a new phenomenon. Nevertheless, with the so-called "Over-The-Top" (OTT) offers, it would seem that these players are playing a growing role and are now at the center of audiovisual change. In particular, these digital platforms have become an essential vector for the transnationalization of the audiovisual sector. This is the proposal at the heart of this chapter.

This presents the questions and the first results of ongoing research on the deployment of digital platforms in the audiovisual sector in France and India conducted within the LabEx "*Industries culturelles et création artistique*" (ICCA – Cultural industries and artistic creation). These two national situations are of course very different in terms of market size, consumer creditworthiness, number of consumers and growth prospects. Similarly, the Indian markets are also distinguished from the French markets by a strong fragmentation into various linguistic basins, by the weight of foreign capitalism in the ownership of the major

Chapter written by Philippe BOUQUILLION.

players in the television industries and by the importance of mobile phones in online video consumption. Nevertheless, the perspective of two very different national situations makes it possible to verify whether digital platforms present the same structuring challenges or whether national particularities prevail. Indeed, various studies, particularly in economics, (those of Hagiu 2007 and Hagiu and Wright 2015), stress the structuring dimension that digital platforms, and especially those known as “multi-purpose” platforms, which are based on dynamics of externalities between suppliers and consumers, would have – whatever the socio-economic framework and the history of the geographical areas where they are deployed.

This research involves various participants and partners, including, for India, Christine Ithurbide, postdoctoral fellow at the ICCA LabEx, and colleagues from the Center for Internet Studies in Delhi. Exploratory field surveys, including interviews with decision-makers from key industrial actors, public officials, lobbyists, independent creators, etc., were conducted in February 2018. In France, surveys are currently being carried out with public or regulatory authorities as well as with actors in the audiovisual industries cooperating with OTT’s main platforms.

The first part is devoted to industrial strategies, and the second part is devoted to public policy and regulatory issues.

10.1. Industrial strategies: a trend towards the weakening of national historical audiovisual actors

In France and even more so in India, the deployment of OTT platforms has led to the development of a generous offer, partly from “new entrants” in these markets. On the one hand, these are national players in the telecommunications industries (Orange and SFR in France, Airtel and Reliance Jio in India) or transnational digital players, including Amazon (in both countries) and Alibaba. These actors share lower tariffs because they consider the supply of cultural products less as a direct source of income than as a set of joint products that distinguish their offer from that of their competitors or collect data on consumers, data that is necessary to add value to their main offer (connection services or e-commerce). As a result, they may agree to record losses. Orange as well as SFR (Discovery and NBCUniversal) expenses with major American studios for ensuring content exclusivity are very high (US$30 million for Orange alone with HBO[1])). On the other hand, these new offers come from transnational actors in the cultural industries, including Netflix, as well as, and more

1 Picard, A. (March 23, 2017). Pourquoi Orange rafle le contrat des séries HBO. *Le Monde*. Available at: https://www.lemonde.fr/actualite-medias/article/2017/03/22/pourquoi-orange-rafle-le-contrat-des-series-hbo_5098910_3236.html.

significantly in India than in France, from historical audiovisual actors. Disney is one of the most important players in Indian television. Its importance has increased further since the acquisition of major Indian chains owned until 2017 by News Corporation. Other US players, including Viacom, are present in India, but there are also Chinese and Japanese interests (Sony, in particular).

Historical national audiovisual actors are also present, but with more "defensive" strategies. In France, Canal+ has long tried to minimize the place of its subscription-based video-on-demand channel Canal Play (Bouquillion *et al.* 2011), because these forms of broadcasting are less profitable. In doing so, a boulevard was offered at Netflix's entry into the French market, which took place in 2014. Overall, the deployment of the OTT helps to challenge and weaken the positions that the dominant players had acquired. Three important trends are underway.

First, there is a relative loss of autonomy of the content economy as the logic of joint products increases. The monetarization of this content is seen more indirectly than in other offers. Telecommunications operators are seeking to improve sales of their subscription offerings by integrating content into their network connection services, while Amazon is clearly seeking to direct consumers to its e-commerce offerings. As a result, the incumbent national players may suffer from a decrease in their resources due to increased competition and lower subscription prices. This is the situation of Canal+, the main historical player in pay-TV in France:

> "From 5.4 million direct subscribers as of September 30, 2016, Canal+ had fallen to 5.25 million at the end of 2016 and below the 5 million mark at the end of June 2017, as a result of competition from beIn Sports or SFR regarding sport or Netflix regarding cinema and series"[2].

OTT platforms tend to lower the profitability of pay-TV and, in particular, to accentuate a decline in the video market already underway before the OTT boom, at least in France. Thus, during the period 2008–2015, the global video market fell by nearly 29% (LIFO 2017). The deployment of digital offers has made up for the market decline even less, as it has been carried out at low rates initiated by Netflix. At the same time, there has been a rapid and profound transformation of the market structure. Subscription accounted for 49.5% of the video market in 2017 compared to only 10.4% in 2012 (CNC 2017).

---

2 *Le Parisien* and AFP (November 16, 2017). Canal+ gagne des abonnés pour la première fois depuis 3 ans. *Le Parisien*. Available at: http://www.leparisien.fr/culture-loisirs/tv/canal-gagne-des-abonnes-pour-la-premiere-fois-depuis-trois-ans-16-11-2017-7397496.php.

Second, complex interplay between transnational and national content is at work. National content is not eliminated, but is offered according to specific strategies. Indeed, the dominant players within OTT rely both on the offer of foreign content, which can be particularly attractive, and on the production of national content. In the case of India, they rely on content in Hindi and major regional languages. In both countries, different strategies are at work depending on the actors. They can seek to make content profitable on an international scale, including some "directly", i.e. without using the former relays of the major national channels when they bought retransmission rights on their territory for foreign, especially American, films or series. This practice still exists, but Netflix tries to hinder it by buying the rights for the world of productions from the major studios.

Similarly, Netflix is committed to enhancing the value of its original content offering on a global scale. OTT actors may also seek to hold exclusive rights to transnational content in order to attract subscribers while preventing competitors from benefiting from it. These players may also seek to "nationalize" or regionalize part of the content offer to better penetrate markets. Most of them also try to build an image of their company as a more "creative" actor than others, particularly by contributing to the discovery of new talent through partnerships with local actors and by developing offers on YouTube. Such a strategy goes hand in hand with a desire to conquer urban and youth markets. This is especially true in India, where the expression on major television channels with advertising funding is particularly restricted, notably in the name of the protection of moral values. Similarly, actors can then plead all the more easily with regulatory authorities because they do not have to submit to public policies aimed at defending creation and diversity since their "ecosystem" would "naturally" be an element in promoting creation.

These games between transnational and national content allow the segmentation of the offer in order to provide not only costly content that justifies subscription to "premium" packages, but also content produced at a low cost, which in turn presents a large number of "short" content that is quickly renewed and is intended for mobile media with a value mainly through advertising. This strategy is very important in India, where some of the players are thinking about the continuity of their offer on different media and with different methods of valuation.

Third, the strong influence of financial actors benefits transnational actors and puts national actors at a disadvantage. Admittedly, it is not new for financial actors to support companies in the culture and communication industries with transnational ambitions. Amazon's history at the time of the so-called "new economy" in the 1990s is an example of this trend which continues even today. It can also be noted that the level of development achieved by Netflix today is largely due to the support of financial players. Without significant fund-raising, Netflix would not have been able to finance its very costly international expansion strategy or its ambitious spending program in the production of original content. Netflix has spent US$17 billion on content in recent years. A quarter of the expenses go to original productions with exclusive rights[3]. It should also be noted that this international expansion has been quite largely accompanied by a decline in average income per user (ARPU).

In other words, this costly development could not be self-financed. Compared to other competing industrial players, Netflix[4] has a clear advantage, while these competitors are less able to raise funds. For example, at the end of 2017, Netflix's revenues were US$11.6 billion and their earnings were US$0.6 billion, which is lower than those of Vivendi (owner of Canal+), respectively €11.4 billion and €1.2 billion. On the contrary, Netflix's market capitalization, measured on May 3, 2018, was US$133 billion, while Vivendi's was only €28.8 billion. Netflix's market value is therefore more than 11.4 times its turnover, while Vivendi's is only 2.5 times its turnover. The disproportion would be even greater if it were calculated in relation to profit.

One of these two groups, Netflix, is a speculative stock, and thus has all the financial facilities to develop, while the other, Vivendi, is considered unlikely to grow and, as a result, cannot raise significant funds. On the one hand, there is a virtuous circle between the financing and growth of the company and, on the other hand, a vicious circle. Similarly, Disney benefits from positive expectations from financial circles without which it could not finance its expansion policy, including in India. However, Disney is not considered a speculative value, unlike Netflix, as evidenced by the proportions of its market valuation, US$147.6 billion (May 3, 2018), with sales of US$55 billion and profits of US$8.9 billion in the fiscal year 2017.

Overall, it has to be said that the financial weights of the competing players in the OTT market are very different. The main transnational players, particularly American ones, benefit from very high financial weights compared to the others. For example, on May 3, 2018, the stock market valuation of the two major OTT players other than Canal+ was relatively low. Altice's was €11.6 billion and Orange's was €40.1 billion. One of the players in OTT that far exceeds all the others, including Netflix, is Amazon, which is both a transnational company and a

3 Netflix (October 16, 2017). Q3_17_Shareholder_Letter_COMBINED. Available at: http://files.shareholder.com/downloads/NFLX/5562135392x0x959841/8E7F87AB-2E5C-41DB-862B-E872EF39B039/Q3_17_Shareholder_Letter_COMBINED.pdf.

4 All financial data below, unless otherwise stated, are from Yahoo Finance's website. Available at: https://fr.finance.yahoo.com/.

communications industry. On July 13, 2018, its market capitalization was US$871.7 billion (with sales of US$177.8 billion and profits of US$3 billion in 2017). Amazon's financial size gives Amazon Prime Video a very wide margin of flexibility.

10.2. Public policies: between transnational logic and national policy development

In both France and India, the deployment of OTT has increased tensions around public policy issues with complex interplay between transnational logic and its national dimension.

In France, with the arrival of transnational players, particularly Netflix, there are increasing demands from national players to reduce regulatory obligations. National broadcasters are challenging obligations to finance film production (calculated as a percentage of their turnover) and broadcasting quotas. There are three reasons for this. First, new foreign entrants refuse to submit to it, which creates a distortion of competition. Second, broadcasters are not entitled to acquire co-production shares through the sums thus spent. They only have broadcasting rights and cannot therefore compile catalogues of rights. Finally, they point out that these obligations are becoming unbearable given the decline in their turnover. This questioning of the public system is not new. Canal+ had already made such a request in the very early 2000s, when Jean-Marie Messier, its then leader, praised the merits of cultural diversity against the cultural exception.

Similarly, media chronology is also a sensitive issue. While a large majority of producers still support this system, broadcasters are asking for it to be made more flexible. For digital platform players, these rules can be obstacles to their strategies. For example, for Orange, it is more interesting to be able to quickly broadcast new films in order to promote its Triple-Play offer. This operator therefore requested a shortening of the deadlines. Netflix wants to win more and more subscribers, thanks in particular to the films produced by the company. Netflix has thus announced its intention not to respect the chronology and, even more radically, its intention not to release films in cinemas. Canal+ has a more intermediate position, in that the chronology allows the group to reserve recent films for the channel and the satellite bouquet, and not for its OTT Canal Play service, whose promotional model is less interesting for the group.

Faced with these pressures, the French government seems to want to maintain the regulatory framework in place and extend it to the various forms of nonlinear television, including OTT offers and foreign players. The French Minister of Culture and Communication in office in 2017 and 2018, Françoise Nyssen, relied on the plans to revise the European Audiovisual Media Services (AVMS) Directive presented in May 2017, which provided the possibility for Member States to impose, in particular, quotas for the broadcasting of European and national products, and extended creative financing mechanisms to broadcasters whose offer covers their territory, but whose head office is located in another Member State of the European Union.

In India, the situation is very different. The audiovisual sector is not considered as part of the culture, but only as an economic activity like any other, a "business". As a result, there is no support policy in its favor. Neither the economic actors nor the authorities seem to want its development. On the contrary, the audiovisual sector raises political issues that require regulation. These issues are related to respect for tradition and religions, in particular Hinduism, as well as, for other social groups, freedom of expression. At the same time, other regulatory issues, more directly economic, are raised. In concrete terms, there are currently lively debates on four themes with closely intertwined economic and political implications: censorship, broadcasters' retransfers to broadcasting network operators, net neutrality and intellectual property rights (IPR).

Censorship and self-censorship are commonly practiced in the case of *broadcasting*, cinema and even the Internet. Citizens can file an application with the courts if they consider that a content violates religious, moral or national values. As a result, professionals have developed a strong self-censorship in order to avoid disastrous economic consequences. Similarly, terrestrial channels must pay heavy retransfers to the operators of broadcasting networks. The amounts are set by the Telecom Regulatory Authority of India (TRAI).

On the contrary, OTT offers are not subject to the same regulations. They are less censored, because it is considered that viewing this content requires a voluntary and thoughtful approach on the part of users, unlike viewers of flow television, who have to deal with channel programming. Freedom of expression, therefore, is greater among OTT offers, which gives them a greater comparative advantage, making them very attractive to young and less conservative people. In addition, the absence of repayment in the name of net neutrality rules is another advantage that limits the cost of offering these services. Regulators, under pressure from leaders of religious and political movements, leaders of terrestrial channels and telecommunication operators, have tried to increase the censorship of nonlinear pay-TV offers and impose fees on network operators by sacrificing net neutrality. Nevertheless, in 2017, these attempts triggered a major citizen protest movement, which was widely covered by the media and which, for the time being, has stopped these political wills.

In addition, IPR regulations have been adopted and India has signed various international agreements, notably under pressure from the United States. Artists have also been explicitly granted rights. However, in practice, these regulations mainly benefit the industrial actors who take control of the law, grant almost no *royalties*, except to the most recognized creators, or even never pay the main remuneration promised to creators. Relations between sponsors and the least recognized creators take place outside written contracts, in a logic of the informal economy that is very important in India. Working for a sponsor acting on behalf of a prestigious company such as Amazon or Netflix can confer a prestige that can be earned elsewhere. This is one of the interests of industrial players in presenting themselves as "creative". In any case, the deployment of OTT as well as mobile advertising financing offers leads artists to mobilize and refer to international standards or what appears to be international standards.

10.3. Conclusion

By way of conclusion, still provisional at this stage of the research, some elements of the answer to the question initially asked can be put forward. The transformations linked to the deployment of digital platforms, particularly OTT offers, are indeed important. They accompany a progression of globalization with a redistribution of cards between actors to the benefit of transnational as well as national actors, mainly telecom operators. They revive regulatory issues with tensions between, on the one hand, the desire to maintain economic or moral and political regulations in place at the national level and, on the other hand, calls for developments that claim to be due to globalization or international standards. While it is clear that industrial and regulatory frameworks are being disrupted, the challenges for content and in particular the production of national content are still difficult to grasp. When the situation is more stable, the analysis of offers by socio-economic models will certainly provide a better understanding of current trends.

10.4. References

Bouquillion, P., Brigaud-Robert, N., and Combès, Y. (2011). Les mutations des filières cinématographiques et audiovisuelles. Quels enjeux pour la diversité ? In *Diversité et industries culturelles*, Bouquillion, P. and Combès, Y. (eds). L'Harmattan, Paris, 203–242.

Conseil national de la cinématographie et de l'image animée (2017). *Observatoire de la VàD*. Available at: http://www.cnc.fr/web/fr/publications/-/ressources/13491027.

Hagiu, A. (2007). Merchant or two-sided platform. *Review of Network Economics*, 6(2), 115–133.

Hagiu A. and Wright, J. (2015). *Multi-Sided Platforms*. Available at: http://www.hbs.edu/faculty/Publication%20Files/15-037cb5afe51-6150-4be9-ace2-39c6a8ace6d4.pdf.

Ministère de la Culture et de la Communication (2017). Chiffres clés, statistiques de la culture et de la communication 2017. *Ministère de la Culture – DEPS*, Paris, France.

11

Scientific Publishing: Coexistence Between New Entrants and Traditional Players

Our research is carried out in the context of the digitalization of publishing. In fact, publishing, as a sector of the cultural industries, has long been affected by a phenomenon of "generalized digitalization". For Christian Robin (2016), in the past 40 years, all of the phases of publishing, from writing to selling books, have gradually been digitalized. Digitalization also affects the organization of activity in the sector – with the introduction of information technology in management, for example.

From this perspective, at least since the beginning of the 2010s, the production of so-called "digital" books has been developing. Behind this generic term is a multitude of forms and formats – such as PDF files, EPUBs, HTML documents, "enriched" books (i.e. multimedia files) as well as printed or digital works linked to "companion sites". These heterogeneous productions are not yet stabilized, either in terms of form or in terms of economic models. Their development is attracting the interest of "new entrants" who are investing in the sector.

These new players with very variable dimensions come from various sectors, for example IT. They are often linked to cultural industries or network industries (Miège 2017). Their investment in publishing raises the question of a possible redefinition of the sector and its borders. These "new entrants" are not the only ones to take a position on digital publishing. The "traditional" players are also taking advantage of these new forms of publishing.

Chapter written by Édith LAVIEC.

In this context, the publication of scientific books is a particular sector. By scientific works we mean specialized works produced by players from the world of research, all disciplines combined. This is a particular area in the sense that publishers, who publish books as well as journals and sometimes other types of documents, have been addressing the issue of producing "digital" documents for a number of years.

11.1. Questioning, hypotheses and methodology

This chapter's objective is to better understand the articulation of the logics of the so called "traditional" players (scientific publishers) with those of "new entrants", who remain to be qualified. This underlies a series of questions: do "new entrants" exist in the scientific publishing sector and, if so, how can they be characterized? Is there a meeting between these different players? Why and how does it work?

Two hypotheses guide this work. First, "new entrants" are not strictly speaking publishers. In particular, they do not have certain attributes specific to the editorial function. Second, "new entrants" must show specific signs of legitimacy in order to enter the field of scientific publishing.

In short, the objective is to situate the position of "new entrants" in the sector based on their relationships with "traditional" publishers. This study allows us to question the evolution of the central function of the editor within the sector (Miège 2000).

This work is based on research conducted as part of our thesis. It concerns the challenges of publishing scientific works at the territorial level, based on the Rhône-Alpes region of France. In France, the region is the largest echelon of local administrative territory. In 2016, a regrouping of regions was carried out throughout the country, from 25 to 16. The Rhône-Alpes region merged with Auvergne, becoming Auvergne-Rhône-Alpes. Since our research began before this merger, it is geographically limited to the former Rhône-Alpes region.

Our research concentrates on the years following the development of publishing formats and "digital" reading materials with regards to which all stakeholders are positioned, namely the 2000s and early 2010s.

We conducted a series of interviews with scientific publishers in the Rhône-Alpes region (11 editorial structures) in order to find out, among other things, about their investment in new forms and formats of publishing as well as the relationships they had with possible new players in relation to these forms.

We also met with some of the "new entrants" identified in the region in order to find out the reasons and forms of their investment in publishing, as well as their possible relationships with "traditional" players. There are four structures, which were created after 2000: BeeBuzziness, Épisciences, Hal and Persée.

We will start by focusing on the new entrants and try to qualify them in light of the preliminary results of our field study. Then, we will see to what extent these new entrants are positioning themselves within the scientific publishing sector and in relation to their stakeholders.

11.2. Scientific publishing and new entrants in the Rhône-Alpes region

11.2.1. *Elements of definition*

The traditional definition of a publisher in France covers a set of distinctive characteristics that differ from the English-language definitions of *editor* and *publisher*. First of all, they fulfill a dual role, both as a trader and an intellectual with the ability to design and manage an intellectual property fund (Mollier 2005).

Three criteria, taken up by Sophie Noël (2012) in her work on independent critical publishing, seem to constitute the publisher's criteria. First of all, the *gatekeeper* role or filter role: the publisher makes choices regarding the manuscript proposals that they receive. They develop a recognizable editorial line, even though it is generalist. Then, there is the *editor* role: the editor does an editing job – in the sense of modification – of the text, both in content and form. Finally, the role of *publisher* or visibility: this is the publisher's commitment to a nationwide distribution of works (Noël 2012).

These definitions are not neutral in that they reject other forms of publishing. For example, Guylaine Beaudry (2011), a book historian who has worked on scientific communication and digital technology, points out that it is possible to publish a text without necessarily having edited it. In addition, vanity publishing is excluded from these conceptions of the editorial function.

Finally, in the theories of cultural industries, within the book trade, the publisher is a central industrial player, generally located "at the interface of artistic, technical, financial, reproductive, promotional and commercial activities" (Miège 2000, p. 26). Beyond this interface dimension, the publisher is a central player, because it participates, in one way or another, in each of the activities mentioned, at least where it can exercise responsibility (Miège 2000).

In general, the term "new entrant" refers to any player outside a given sector who chooses to establish itself in that sector. This term is linked to economic analyses and corporate strategy. It is particularly used in Porter's five forces analysis which was developed in 1979. It is also used in the context of research on cultural industries, in particular analyses of the publishing sector and its developments (Bouquillion 2008; Rouet 2013).

11.2.2. *About new entrants*

In Rhône-Alpes, 18 scientific editorial structures were identified as part of our field survey. They are all more than 10 years old and were created between 1972 and 2002, and a large part of them were established in the 1970s (seven structures). None of them was created in the context of the production of new forms of publications. They are therefore not new entrants, but rather traditional players in publishing.

A search of the profession's directories, in particular the annual supplements to the professional journal *Livres Hebdo* in recent years[1], does not reveal the creation of new structures of this type in Rhône-Alpes. The same is true for the directory proposed by the regional book structure in Rhône-Alpes, the Arald[2].

However, other structures involved throughout the creative process have emerged in the region. In addition, the heads of editorial structures we met mentioned the players with whom they had recently collaborated (or who had recently approached them) as part of the development of their digital offer. These elements, although not exhaustive, are the first indicators that make it possible to detect some examples of new entrants to scientific publishing.

11.2.3. *Some examples of new entrants*

Not all of these new entrants are located in Rhône-Alpes. They were identified by looking at professional information and through interviews with publishers in Rhône-Alpes. In the next section, we will see how they interact with publishers in our field.

1 *Livres Hebdo* magazine offers annual supplements, including directories listing publishers and book service providers present in France. See the 2016 Yearbook of the *Livres Hebdo* edition, supplement to No. 1051 of August 28, 2015, and the 2016 Yearbook of *Livres Hebdo* service providers, supplement to No. 1061 of November 6, 2015.

2 Auvergne-Rhône-Alpes Livre et Lecture (n. d.). *Annuaire éditeurs*. Available at: https://auvergnerhonealpes-livre-lecture.org/annuaires/editeurs (accessed July 6, 2018).

First, digitalization or digital publishing service providers have been developing for several years, in France and abroad. They work on collections that have already been funded by the publisher (in retrospect), from printed copies or printer files, or support the publication of future titles in order to propose a digital version. It is marketed either by the publisher through their chosen channels or directly by the service provider, who makes it available on their own website. The development of assistance for digitalization by a service provider, proposed by the National Book Centre for several years[3], has undoubtedly contributed to the emergence of this type of player.

Second, with the marketing of books in "digital" formats, a whole series of websites have appeared in different countries. The players behind these sites have different positions within the book industry, although they seem to be more downstream at first sight. Some of these players position themselves on the equivalence of traditional functions of the sector. For example, the Eden books platform distributes digital books to resellers. Others, such as Cairn.info, handle several or even all of the downstream activities of the sector, namely distribution and sales. Finally, some have a more global position, taking on a set of tasks from the creation of a digital file to its availability to final audiences. This is the case, for example, with the Persée portal.

Finally, some players are positioning themselves in parallel with – or even as an alternative to – traditional publishers, without performing all the functions of a publisher. These include open archive platforms, of which Hal is an emblematic example in France. These platforms allow for varying degrees of editorialization of content and the emergence of "epi-newspapers", i.e. journals composed of articles deposited in open archives. Scientific blogging platforms, such as Hypotheses.org, although far from the formal book, represent to some extent an alternative to book publishing.

Generally speaking, the perception of these players as "new entrants" in the scientific publishing sector remains delicate. First, the analysis of the presentation of their activities indicates that they do not assume all the characteristics of the editor function as we have defined. This partly explains why they are not listed in professional directories as publishers.

Second, the positioning of these players is multifold and sometimes unclear regarding the activities they undertake. This makes the attempt to categorize them more difficult and irrelevant, especially if the typology is based on the traditional functions of the book trade. This difficulty seems revealing, as does the status

---

3 This material was implemented in part to provide an alternative to Google's digitalization project (Robin 2016).

of these players, who are not publishers in the "traditional" sense of the term. On the one hand, the apprehension of new entrants questions the operationality of the analysis criteria based on the traditional vision of the sector. On the other hand, it undoubtedly shows a potential restructuring of the players and the roles they assign to themselves within the sector.

Third, many of these players (such as Lekti, a digital publishing service provider) do not only position themselves in scientific publishing, but also cover a multitude of editorial fields. Others, on the contrary, are specialized in this sector, such as the Persée portal, or even in certain fields such as the human and social sciences, which is the case for OpenEdition.

Finally, the positioning of these new entrants in relation to the traditional players in the sector, in particular publishers, is also very variable. Some (such as Lekti) wish to become service providers or partners of publishers, while others (such as Hal) represent a possible "threat of substitute products or services", as Michael Porter (1979) refers to them in his model. These are closer to the definition of new entrants, without being publishers in the traditional sense of the word.

The diversity of the positions of these new entrants also raises the question of their relationship with the more traditional players in scientific publishing.

11.3. Legitimacy and interactions with traditional players in Rhône-Alpes

11.3.1. *Tendency to circumvent new entrants*

Traditional scientific publishers have also taken up the issues related to digital publishing themselves, for both the digitalization of printed material and the marketing of "natively digital" files. Thus, all publishers offering digital books indicated that they carry out these activities internally. Some use conversion software, such as EBK's Ebook-LR; others have reorganized their publishing chain by adding tools to it to implement structured publishing, as is the case for two structures that have set up the "XML chain" developed within the Caen University Press.

In addition, out of five publishers who digitalized their collections retrospectively, three used external service providers. These were structures specialized in tasks related to digital publishing and the digitalization of holdings such as Lekti and Persée.

Finally, of the 11 structures offering digital works in various forms, five have delegated the distribution and sale of their production to one or more external players. These may be their distributor-retailer for printed works, which also supports digital works (e.g. Harmonia Mundi), or players specialized in this type of product (e.g. OpenEdition Books).

Therefore, in a way, there is a circumvention of new entrants by the identified scientific publishers. These publishers are aware of the existence of many structures that regularly approach them. Beyond the budgetary issues that reduce the possibility of using external service providers, a certain mistrust regarding new entrants emerges in the interviews with these scientific publishers; new entrants sometimes seem unknown and appear to be a confused group.

11.3.2. *Legitimacy and collaboration*

However, various structures have initiated collaboration with these scientific publishers, including Numédif and its Métopes structure (structure under the University of Caen that offer a structured publishing chain TEI-XML), OpenEdition Books (offering the distribution and marketing of works on their portal, in various ways), Amazon and Google.

The identification and choice of these structures by publishers seems to be based on various forms of legitimacy linked to common values or skills, sometimes mentioned by our interlocutors. We have identified two types, which are not exclusive.

First, a form of legitimacy linked to the positioning of new entrants appears in our interview analyses. Some of the new entrants have engaged in *open access* logic, in particular Persée and OpenEdition Books. The distribution modalities and business models differ between these two portals, but this commitment is a value shared by several academic publishers.

Then, we have identified a certain legitimacy in the experience and knowledge of traditional book trades. Indeed, a private publisher from our group has chosen to work with Lekti for a retrospective digitalization operation. This publisher did not fully indicate the reasons for this choice, but was satisfied with it. They even continue to solicit this player for technical questions related to digital publishing, but not related to service monitoring or even to the digitalization of collection. To justify this relationship, the publisher insisted on the knowledge that the person in charge of Lekti had of the publishing profession, based on the fact that he came from this profession and he had practiced it for many years.

Finally, we assume another form of legitimacy, which remains to be verified: namely public institutional legitimacy at the national or regional level. Indeed, most of the new entrants mentioned in the interviews receive support or guidance from public institutions: Metopes, OpenEdition and Persée are all national research infrastructures. EBK also seems to have deployed its software in partnership with its Regional Council and its regional book structure, then Languedoc-Roussillon Livre et Lecture (LR2L). The digitalization activity carried out by Lekti was implemented with funding from the CNL; Lekti was probably an approved service provider under this grant. Without being able to conclude definitively on this point, it should be noted that the new entrants that we have interviewed all have close relations with and even come from the publishing or higher education and research worlds.

This trend is also found in almost all of the new entrants interviewed: Persée, whom we mentioned, as well as Hal and Episciences. The latter two are affiliated with the Center for Direct Scientific Communication (CCSD), a joint service unit under the supervision of the CNRS, Inria, the University of Lyon and INRA. Hal and the CCSD are considered as research infrastructures and are taken into account in the national strategy for higher education and research. Hal is not intended to work directly with publishers and is more oriented towards researchers. It represents a way that is parallel with or alternative to traditional publishing. In this sense, this new entrant has succeeded in entering the scientific publishing sector. The Episciences platform seems less developed. It is currently being restructured and hosts 11 journal titles.

A contrary case is particularly evocative. Among the managers of "potential new entrants" with whom we met was someone from Bee Buzziness, who offered dematerialization and rematerialization solutions for documentation. This player has not succeeded in penetrating the scientific publishing sector or other publishing sectors. The reasons given are primarily budgetary. Bee Buzziness does not yet have an economic model adapted to the funding possibilities of higher education and research players, as the cost is still too high. The manager also mentioned a method of designing an editorial production chain that is too different from what is traditionally implemented by publishers. It seems that this player does not have any legitimacy, either in terms of positioning in the book trade or knowledge of the publishing industry. Its managers, including its founder, have no experience in publishing. These are people from the IT and business sectors. The products and services they offer are based on business models that do not take a specific position on open publishing and the dissemination of research results. Finally, this structure has no particular affiliation with a cultural or higher education and research institution.

11.3.3. *Particularity of GAFA*

Some players that we have not yet mentioned represent a special case in our analysis. Often referred to as GAFA or GAFAM (Smyrnaios 2016), they represent important players in the cultural industry sectors. They have more or less close links with the publishing sector (Robin 2016).

From the point of view of the editors interviewed, eight of them spontaneously mentioned Google, Amazon and, to a lesser extent, Apple. Three publishers consider these companies mainly as "platforms" on which they market their works directly. In addition, these players were mentioned when we discussed the current developments in publishing in our interviews. Google and Amazon are considered both as key players and as threats. On the one hand, these players have such a significant weight that avoiding them is too much of a loss of income, or even impossible. On the other hand, they represent a threat as competitors – in terms of market share – and as partners – due to a possible infringement of publishers' autonomy.

These cases show that it is, however, possible for some players to enter the scientific publishing sector without showing any sign of particular legitimacy. Access to this sector is based on other strengths, particularly human and financial, which have enabled these companies to take a particular lead on technical developments in publishing and to position themselves ahead of the others. Amazon is also a particular newcomer, since its entry into the publishing industry dates back to the 1990s, before the creation of some of the traditional publishers in our group. At the time, this company was not specifically related to the commercialization of digital works.

11.4. Conclusion

In short, an analysis of activity in the Rhône-Alpes region shows that scientific publishing is a sector that has not seen any new entrants take up residence and perform all the traditional functions of publishing. The new entrants who have been best able to integrate into the sector work in collaboration with traditional publishers. They come from fields close to these publishers and base their legitimacy on common values and knowledge of traditional professions and their challenges. Other players have benefited from their dominant status at the international level to enter this sector.

The selection of publishers is limited to the Rhône-Alpes region. This particularity raises questions about the generalization of the results. However, there are a few leads that seem to confirm the trends identified in our survey. For example, the OpenEdition Books and Persée portals have an increasingly wide range of digital documents and work with a growing number of public and private publishers. Métopes also deploys its structured publishing chain to an increasing number of university publishers in France and abroad (particularly in Latin America).

Our results apply primarily to small publishers, although we are dealing with a sector that also contains the most important editorial structures in the world. For example, new entrants are emerging at the international level, namely "predatory editorial structures" such as the European University Editions. They are outside the scope of our work, but are interesting to take into account as new entrants. To this end, it would be appropriate to extend the field survey to the national level, in order to take into account a wider variety of publishers and interactions with new entrants.

Finally, it would be interesting to extend the characterization of new entrants to publishing and to compare it with possible changes in the publishing profession. It would make it possible to see to what extent the arrival of new entrants into the sector is changing the attributes defining the publishing profession within the book sector.

11.5. References

Beaudry, G. (2008). *La communication scientifique et le numérique*. Hermès-Lavoisier, Paris.

Bouquillion, P. (2008). *Les industries de la culture et de la communication : les stratégies du capitalisme*. Presses universitaires de Grenoble, Grenoble.

Miège, B. (2000). *Les industries de contenu face à l'ordre informationnel*. Presses Universitaires de Grenoble, Grenoble.

Miège, B. (2017). *Les industries culturelles et créatives face à l'ordre de l'information et de la communication*. Presses Universitaires de Grenoble, Grenoble.

Mollier, J.-Y. (2005). Naissance de la figure de l'éditeur. In *Figures de l'éditeur*, Legendre, B. and Robin, C. (eds). Nouveau Monde Éditions, Paris, 13–24.

Noël, S. (2012). *L'édition critique indépendante : engagements politiques et intellectuels*. Presses de l'Enssib, Villeurbanne.

Porter, M. (1979). How competitive forces shape strategy. *Harvard Business Review*, March–April, 137–145. Available at: https://hbr.org/1979/03/how-competitive-forces-shape-strategy.

Robin, C. (2016). *Les livres dans l'univers numérique,* 2nd edition. La Documentation française, Paris.

Rouet, F. (2013). *Le livre : une filière en danger ?*, 4th edition. La Documentation française, Paris.

Smyrnaios, N. (2017). *Les GAFAM contre l'Internet : une économie politique du numérique*. Ina, Paris.

12

A Digital Redefinition of the Pornography Industries

The "generalized digitalization of society" movement has some of its roots in the progressive development of the Web and public access to the Internet since the early 1990s, which has been the starting point – or more certainly the acceleration – of many transformations in the media, culture and communication markets and industries. The so-called digital economy contributes to profound changes in their environment, in the context in which they develop, and in the financing structures established for nearly a century by several movements for the industrialization and commodification of culture and information. Within these transformations, many dimensions are frequently mobilized and studied, such as economic strategies, organizational changes or discursive practices.

It is in this context that this text will address the space of pornography markets and industries whose contents, which have become mass consumer products (Cronin and Davenport 2001), do not yet seem to be fully studied as such, in light of repeated findings in the scientific literature. Their contemporary places and transformations in the digital context will be examined here, while keeping in mind the similarities with and distinctions from the other components of culture and communication, particularly in the mechanisms of production, publishing and distribution (Jacobs 2007). Pornography can sometimes be considered as an "illegitimate" object both in research spaces and in public spaces (Landais 2014), being affected by forms of normative relegation (Damian-Gaillard 2014), linked in particular to certain representations, gender issues or exploitation phenomena. How is this opposition built between on the one hand, relegation, and markets and mass

Chapter written by Arnaud ANCIAUX. This chapter is in part the result of a collaborative effort with Nathalie Bissonnette (Université Laval), Éric George (Université du Québec à Montréal) and Julie Alice Gramaccia (Université Laval).

consumption products, on the other hand? What are the strategies in place to resolve this tension? Could they be considered as more than just simple answers and tactics, by participating in the shaping and framing of the concerned markets? Who are the actors – and possibly the "beneficiaries" – of this resolution?

In the end, these different questions should allow us to analyze what pornography tells us about all the cultural industries and vice versa. In order to develop possible answers, this chapter will first provide a very brief overview of the scientific literature on pornography before presenting certain problems and research questions on the basis of a socio-economic approach and, finally, proposing to deploy them in analyzing the sexcam sector, a particular component of pornography markets and industries.

12.1. Socio-economics of pornography markets and industries: a brief review of the scientific literature

Pornographies and their contents can be placed in a long history (Vörös 2015a), extending beyond cinematography. As Rea (2001) points out, the boundaries of pornographic content sometimes appear blurred, whether the content is affected by nature, intent or effect, or if there is a demarcation between eroticism and pornography (D'Orlando 2011), for example. These qualifications, although complex, may appear critical to some institutions. Within pornography itself, many distinctions are made. Particularly, we can think of the tempered discussion between *netporn* and *porn on the net* by Paasonen (2010) that are respectively designated as a redefinition of content, notably under the influence of amateurs and certain dynamics of resistance against commercial pornography, and a recycling of content and formats by industries (Paasonen 2010). With Paasonen, it is possible to underline that one of the main challenges of these dynamics lies not in clear distinctions (mainstream/alternative, professional/amateur, etc.), but rather in the study of continuities between poles – opportunely – opposed, contributing both to a digitalization of the existing (continuity of industries, formats, sexual scripts, etc.) and to "new" developments (involvement of amateurs, alternative or protest scripts, etc.).

In the digital context, some of the literature has sought to describe the presence and contributions of amateurs in creation and production, as well as in new modes of content distribution. It is possible to note that the involvement of amateurs and unpaid production, although it is in genres partly distinct from those initially offered by the commercial pornography industries, has been partly built in the form of competition (Gomez-Mejia 2014; Paasonen 2010; Ruberg 2016). The implications of these amateurs can give way to forms of commercial reuse (D'Orlando 2011), whether in their presence on video platforms that mobilize amateur and consumer producers (Keilty 2017) or in being showcased on dedicated platforms and devices, such as sexcams (Bleakley 2014; Preudhomme 2016; van Doorn and Velthuis 2018). Some digital platforms have thus been able to promote a massive and free distribution of content in an ambivalent relationship with existing industry players (Fayner 2010) and an antagonistic relationship with consumers (Johnson 2011). Several have pointed out that pornography seems to have acquired the status of a mass consumer product (Arnberg 2012; Coopersmith 2006; Cronin and Davenport 2001; D'Orlando 2011; McKee 2016; Paasonen 2010). Its revenues are often assessed to be very significant, with some of the biggest estimates amounting to \$15 billion in the US market and \$100 billion worldwide (Szymanski and Stewart-Richardson 2014). However, those clearly remain uncertain – not to say sometimes risky – indicating how much uncertainty still surrounds these industries (Tarrant 2016).

Beyond this uncertainty, these questions are partly found within the public space and in social and cultural representations (Attwood 2014; Brents and Hausbeck 2007; Coopersmith 2006; Edelman 2009; Hardy 2008; Paasonen 2006, 2009; Sarracino and Scott 2008). They have become subjects of analysis in the "general public" as well as in media directed towards a specialized public interested in economic issues. A particular tension can thus be observed around visibility in the public space, which can be described as an attempt at "rehabilitation" and "rhetorical reframing" by the industry (Cronin and Davenport 2001, p. 42).

However, this industrial and economic questioning is still somewhat underdeveloped in academic work, particularly in approaches to pornography:

> "We might expect to find that this persistent and prevailing category of goods would feature in scholarly critiques of e-commerce. […] However, in the literature on the information society and information economy the subject of sex, and, by extension, pornography, has been undertheorized" (Cronin and Davenport 2001, p. 34).

This gap, although deplored by many authors, is frequently still confirmed (Berg 2014; Coopersmith 2006; Voss 2012) and can be found in the call, particularly formulated around porn studies (Dubois 2014; Paveau and François 2014; Vörös 2015a), for a "materialistic turn":

> "Initially focused on representation issues, the research agenda of porn studies is now shifting towards reception issues on the one hand and production issues on the other, through the study of socio-economic models and forms of social division of labor in the cultural and creative industries specialized in the production of sexual goods and services" (Vörös 2015b, p. 22).

This proposal is in line with Paasonen's call (2010, p. 1309):

> "I suggest that thinking about amateur and user production as forms of labor that feed the Internet economy, online porn industry included, enables seeing different fields of activity as interconnected and interdependent. Ultimately, the category of pornography needs to be reconsidered in terms of esthetics, media economy and agency as a diverse field of practice involving affective investments, forms of labor and exchange."

It is in this direction, mentioned but still not very active, that the possibility of jointly studying socio-economic structures, transformation strategies and legitimization discourses around pornography markets and industries is particularly relevant.

12.2. Mobilizing discourse analysis and socio-economic analysis to understand markets and industries

12.2.1. *Cross-questioning to be carried out*

The research project briefly presented here aims to study the transformation of socio-economic strategies and structures surrounding pornography markets and industries in the digital context. It follows the hypothesis that these, like other spaces, are based as much on a socio-economic construction as on a discourse-based formation. Two objects can then be followed jointly. First, it is possible to focus on the metadiscourse of pornography as a tool for the manufacture and shaping of pornography products and markets, among consumers and, more generally, among all the actors concerned. Evoked in particular by Kunert (2014) – before she focused her analysis on feminist pornography – it is a heterogeneous field, which is "defined by the presence of pornography in a discourse, as the *object of that discourse* (object that the metadiscourse criticizes, comments, defends, attacks, etc.)" (p. 139), and whose various forms can be identified in different spaces. It is then possible to understand those discourses as contributing to the creation of a *field of presence* in the sense of Foucault's work (1969). As the latter subsequently proposed, this will particularly involve:

> "to start from these positive mechanisms, producers of knowledge, multipliers of speech, inducers of pleasure, and generators of power, [to] follow them in their conditions of appearance and functioning, and [to] seek how the facts of prohibition or occultation related to them are distributed in relation to them. In short, it is a question of defining the power strategies that are immanent to this will to knowledge. In the specific case of sexuality, constituting the 'political economy' of a will to knowledge" (Foucault 1976, pp. 97–98).

Second, the identification of the pornography market and industry players should make it possible to map their respective positions and offers, as well as the articulation between them and the networks they can form. A networked mapping will make it possible to go beyond looking only at the final products presented to consumers and to approach the relationships between all the actors as a complex whole, at the source of actual sectors or ecosystems. It therefore seems possible to establish a detailed understanding of business models and to better understand socio-economic structures and interrelationships as well as existing networks and strategies for the transformation or development of new markets and products. In particular, the cross-analysis will help to understand how market and industry metadiscourses affect the identified stakeholders, who may seek to mobilize, deploy or bypass them. The project will thus make it possible to pursue Damian-Gaillard's (2014) perspective of a "political economy of desire" (p. 53), while avoiding the trap of "moralist rhetoric on 'the commodification of the body' (which makes sexuality exceptional and isolates it from the rest of the capitalist economy) [which has] long hindered the emergence of research on the economic aspects of pornography" (Vörös 2015b, pp. 22–23).

12.2.2. *An example of deployment: the erased construction of a sexcam industry*

Although they can only be mentioned briefly in this chapter, the digital context has been an opportunity for some actors to develop alternatives – claimed in part as such – to the mainstream pornographic industries with, for example, the increasing visibility of queer or feminist pornographic creations. The case of sexcam platforms can be an example of the possible and potentially fruitful cross-analysis to understand the structuring of a market and an industry. These digital platforms offer central access to live performances, mainly of a sexual nature, to the public. They generally present a separation of performances into gendered categories, then according to other characteristics (language, country, practices, etc.) and following an order related to popularity.

While these platforms vary from and compete against each other, they strongly emphasize the "amateur" character of the models and a stated distance from the pornographic industries. Whether it is the presentation of the system itself, statements within and around it, or presentations in other discourse spaces (including public and journalistic spaces, specialized or not), an important discourse is formed and reproduced by various actors. This discourse participates in a distinction with the industry and highlights the platforms and practices that they present under the banner of the alternative, a certain authenticity and sometimes even forms of sociability between user-consumers and user-models. Amateurism (both in the sense of it being a pleasure to do and the absence of a professional status) then coexists with the freedom claimed around the models. At the same time, these platforms achieve an assumed, visible and sometimes claimed commodification as well as an erased industrialization. First, they use a trading tool, or "token", which are purchased by consumers, spent on the models and traded on the platform (the selling price of these tokens to consumers is always higher – but in degrees that can vary widely – than the "buy-back" price from the models). These tokens are often centrally visible around visual performance, with, for example, the display of the number received by the models, or the objectives set by them. Far from being erased, they can be the subject of interaction and discussion and – depending on the models on the platform – be prerequisites for access to a performance, thresholds for certain practices in public performances, tips not directly linked to a request, etc.

Second, however, and beyond the mechanism proposed by the platform, it is possible to observe a strong network organization and outsourcing around the platforms following an organization of an actual and structured industrial sector. Particularly, it should be noted that, upstream of the platforms, many intermediaries can, in exchange for different forms of remuneration, interact with the models in order to organize their presence and performance on the platforms ("Studios", agencies, councils, etc.) and even take on important organizational roles for them (Supply of production equipment, proposal of a "professional working environment", etc.). On the other side of the supply chain, many platforms aim to distribute the produced content as efficiently as possible (e.g. by hosting and reproducing the platform device) or attract more consumers to the platform (e.g. affiliation networks).

As such, the existence of an organized sector and a clear commodification corresponds to a relatively erased industrialization, the recognition of which could be in conflict with some of the speeches and statements made about or by these platforms. These aim to or contribute to creating a distinction and differentiation – in whole or in part – with the mainstream pornographic industries and to justify, in the eyes of some consumers, paying for content in an environment marked by a high level of free access (particularly under the influence of large portals). A similar tension can be observed around the activity of the models, which is a productive, widely prescribed and organized activity, and which is a source of value for platforms, seemingly covering the characteristics of the work formulated by Dujarier (2008). However, and although platforms often present this activity of models as potentially lucrative, sometimes giving "career" advice, the explicit recognition of a job – and especially of job status that could be linked – is not, or very little, present on platforms.

12.3. Conclusion

In the long term and together, this cross-analysis will make it possible to understand the strategies and discourses surrounding and transforming pornography markets, products and industries. Based on the elements highlighted in the scientific literature, it seems desirable to better understand and analyze the socio-economic models at work in pornography markets and industries, as a direct follow-up to studies such as Trachman's (2012) central study.

By mobilizing both meso and macro approaches, it seems possible to better understand the intertwining of different dynamics that come to participate in the creation, shaping and framing of new markets and renewed models. Thus, when part of the production and publishing of pornographic content is digitalized, it is possible to observe and analyze a transformation of models, structures and commodification modalities. While industries and sectors may be partially erased, particularly in the report proposed to consumers and in the speeches accompanying and manufacturing markets, their organizational and managerial capacities seem to remain very present. It is therefore possible to critically question this dynamic in formats and markets that are being built as alternatives, but are also participating in the renewal of outsourcing and – possibly – digital exploitations.

12.4. References

Arnberg, K. (2012). Under the counter, under the radar? The business and regulation of the pornographic press in Sweden 1950–1971. *Enterprise and Society*, 13(2), 350–377.

Attwood, F. (2014). Immersion: "Extreme" texts, animated bodies and the media. *Media, Culture and Society*, 36(8), 1186–1195.

Berg, H. (2014). Labouring porn studies. *Porn Studies*, 1(1–2), 75–79.

Boyle, K. (2011). Producing abuse: Selling the harms of pornography. *Women's Studies International Forum*, 34(6), 593–602.

Brents, B.G. and Hausbeck, K. (2007). Marketing sex: US legal brothels and late capitalist consumption. *Sexualities*, 10(4), 425–439.

Coopersmith, J. (2006). Does your mother know what you really do? The changing nature and image of computer-based pornography. *History and Technology*, 22(1), 1–25.

Cronin, B. and Davenport, E. (2001). E-rogenous zones: Positioning pornography in the digital economy. *The Information Society*, 17(1), 33–48.

D'Orlando, F. (2011). The demand for pornography. *Journal of Happiness Studies*, 12(1), 51–75.

Damian-Gaillard, B. (2014). L'économie politique du désir dans la presse pornographique hétérosexuelle masculine française. *Questions de Communication*, 26, 39–54.

Dubois, F.-R. (2014). *Introduction aux Porn Studies*. Les Impressions Nouvelles, Brussels.

Dujarier, M.-A. (2008). *Le travail du consommateur : De McDo à eBay, comment nous coproduisons ce que nous achetons*. La Découverte, Paris.

Edelman, B. (2009). Red light states: Who buys online adult entertainment? *Journal of Economic Perspectives*, 23(1), 209–220.

Fayner, S. (2010). Down the tubes: How free streaming video threatens the porn industry. *MIT Technology Review*, August, 103–106.

Foucault, M. (1976). *Histoire de la sexualité I : La volonté de savoir*. Gallimard, Paris.

Gomez-Mejia, G. (2014). La pornographie amateur au prisme des "réseaux sociaux". *Hermès, La Revue*, 2(69), 129–131.

Hardy, S. (2008). The pornography of reality. *Sexualities*, 11(1–2), 60–64.

Jacobs, K. (2007). *Netporn: DIY Web Culture and Sexual Politics*. Rowman and Littlefield Publishers, Lanham.

Johnson, J.A. (2011). Mapping the feminist political economy of the online commercial pornography industry: A network approach. *International Journal of Media and Cultural Politics*, 7(2), 189–208.

Keilty, P. (2017). Carnal indexing. *Knowledge Organization*, 44(4), 265–272.

Kunert, S. (2014). Les métadiscours pornographiques. *Questions de Communication*, 26, 137–152.

Landais, É. (2014). Porn studies et études de la pornographie en sciences humaines et sociales. *Questions de Communication*, 26, 17–37.

McKee, A. (2016). Pornography as a creative industry: Challenging the exceptionalist approach to pornography. *Porn Studies*, 3(2), 107–119.

Paasonen, S. (2006). Email from Nancy Nutsucker: Representation and gendered address in online pornography. *European Journal of Cultural Studies*, 9, 403–420.

Paasonen, S. (2009). Healthy sex and pop porn: Pornography, feminism and the Finnish context. *Sexualities*, 12(5), 586–604.

Paasonen, S. (2010). Labors of love: Netporn, Web 2.0 and the meanings of amateurism. *New Media & Society*, 12(8), 1297–1312.

Paveau, M. and François, P. (2014). Un objet de discours pour les études pornographiques. *Questions de Communication*, 26, 7–16.

Preudhomme, S. (2016). Codes, contrôle et réappropriation autonome : Le pro-am comme système organisationnel singulier. *Revue française des sciences de l'information et de la communication*, 9, 1–14.

Rea, M.C. (2001). What is pornography? *Noûs*, 35(1), 118–145.

Ruberg, B. (2016). Doing it for free: Digital labour and the fantasy of amateur online pornography. *Porn Studies*, 3(2), 147–159.

Sarracino, C. and Scott, K.M. (2008). *The Porning of America: The Rise of Porn Culture, What it Means, and Where We Go from Here*. Beacon Press, Boston.

Szymanski, D.M. and Stewart-Richardson, D.N. (2014). Psychological, relational, and sexual correlates of pornography use on young adult heterosexual men in romantic relationships. *The Journal of Men's Studies*, 22(1), 64–82.

Tarrant, S. (2016). *The Pornography Industry: What Everyone Needs to Know*. Oxford University Press, New York.

Trachman, M. (2012). *Le travail pornographique : enquête sur la production de fantasmes*. La Découverte, Paris.

Vörös, F. (2015a). *Cultures Pornographiques. Anthologie des Porn Studies*. Éditions Amsterdam, Paris.

Vörös, F. (2015b). Le porno à bras-le-corps. Genèse et épistémologie des porn studies. In *Cultures Pornographiques. Anthologie des Porn Studies*, Vörös, F. (ed.). Éditions Amsterdam, Paris, 5–31.

Voss, G. (2012). "Treating it as a normal business": Researching the pornography industry. *Sexualities*, 15(3–4), 391–410.

13

Cultural Policies 2.0: Rebuilding the Intervention of Public Authorities

The transformations linked to digital technology affecting the cultural industries are numerous and significant in several respects[1]. They raise fears of an imbalance between English-language productions intended for the world market and local productions, which are more difficult to export, discover and get the attention of an audience. New digital platforms are emerging as powerful vehicles for global intermediation, shaping the contours of a new global cultural industry and dictating the form, nature and flow of digital cultural product flows. Several authors (Benghozi 2011; Benghozi and Benhamou 2008; Vlassis 2015) stress the importance of State interventions in the restructuring of cultural industries. However, fundamental questions remain as to how and at what level one should intervene in a context of rapid change and globalization. How can and should public authorities respond to these processes in order to define policies and regulatory frameworks conducive to the development of a cultural offer, which is certainly a vector of competitiveness, and also of diversity and creativity?

Our obejctive in this chapter is to understand the nature of these transformations and their impacts on cultural industries as well as the effectiveness of policy and regulatory instruments aimed at protecting and promoting the diversity of cultural expressions in Quebec in the Canadian context. We discuss the political and regulatory issues related to the transformations of cultural industries and then

---

Chapter written by Maud BOISNARD, Destiny TCHÉHOUALI and Michèle RIOUX.

1 Benghozi (2011) identifies the following changes: 1) the multiplication of cultural supply; 2) the transformation of the business models of culture as a result of the convergence between the content and telecommunications sectors, with the emergence of new players; 3) the new role of the consumer, which changes the nature of works and the cultural sector; and 4) the multiplication of business models.

introduce possible solutions for revisiting cultural policies. We adopt a political economy approach that is limited here to a reflection on the digital transition issues of cultural industries with particular attention paid to the objective of promoting and protecting the diversity of cultural expressions in the digital age.

13.1. The transformation of cultural industries; regulatory challenges

Transformations brought about by digital technology can increase access to culture tenfold, but they can also become real threats to the diversity of cultural expressions if they are not controlled and directed towards the common good through appropriate and adapted cultural policies. It thus seems appropriate to rethink and adapt policies to the digital age (Beaudoin 2014; Guèvremont *et al.* 2013), the question is: how can States reaffirm and achieve a re-territorialization of public policies affecting culture in order to support the development of a diversified, exportable and competitive local/national digital cultural offer in the context of a globalized and transnational competition. Musitelli (2014) considers that "[t]he devastating deployment of the digital ecosystem does not only challenge production methods, economic models and social practices related to culture. It raises an existential question for the public authorities in their regulatory function" (p. 312).

Measures and policies related to the protection of cultural industries are less effective in a context where the production and dissemination of cultural content is increasingly taking place without territorial and regulatory barriers. Thus, the notion of *promotion* becomes more relevant without making the notion of *protection* obsolete. What concrete actions can ensure effective promotion of the diversity of cultural expressions in the digital age? What would be the ways to re-invent protection mechanisms in a context of liberalization and digitalization of cultural industries? Moreover, does diversity emerge from the multiplication of market supply and free trade, or would it be the responsibility of public policies (Mattelart 2009)? Currently, State responses seem ambivalent. Several countries have become aware of the urgent need for action and are undertaking major legislative reforms, relying on an interventionist approach. This is the case of the Quebec and Canadian governments, which have begun a process of reviewing their approach to cultural policies, noting the obvious limits of the regulatory framework in place (questioning quota systems, remuneration of creators and rights holders, private copying, etc.).

In Quebec and Canada, one of the most important challenges is to ensure a dynamic and coherent articulation of digital strategies and cultural policies (including regulations that affect cultural industries). This alignment, which is crucial for the future and the influence of the country's cultural industries, has not been achieved and raises important issues. To develop a genuine cultural policy, it would be necessary to develop concerted actions and multi-level intergovernmental synergy to ensure effective networking between the various cultural and digital policies and strategies of provincial and federal governments[2]. In general, national economic policies and digital strategies do not integrate cultural issues and conversely, cultural policies and measures do not adequately address, when they attempt to do so, the issue of digital opportunities and threats.

While Quebec and Canada are ahead of the rest of the world in this regard, it is essential to define and implement this in concrete terms, as the various players have developed the habit of working in silos. Quebec has developed a digital cultural strategy based on enriching the supply of digital cultural content and the distribution/accessibility of content. This initiative is interesting, but it has emerged in the absence of a comprehensive digital strategy for Quebec, specifying the place of culture within it. The Ministry of Culture and Communications (Quebec) (MCCQ) has implemented a process to renew cultural policy, but how this policy will be concretely linked to the province's overall digital strategy remains to be seen. Canada, for its part, has adopted a digital strategy that aims to facilitate online access to Canadian content and Canadian artistic and cultural achievements. Canadian Heritage has a new vision, "A Creative Canada", but nothing is yet very specific about modernizing the programs, policies, institutions and laws that structure the field of culture in the digital world. However, this vision incorporates the idea of networking, in particular by creating closer links between Canadian Heritage and Canadian Innovation, Science and Economic Development. On the contrary, without addressing the major concerns of the various cultural players, who expected to see the unveiling of a real cultural policy articulated with regulatory changes – particularly with respect to telecommunications and broadcasting laws – and the conclusion of an over-the-counter agreement with Netflix that could be followed by other similar agreements, much remains to be done to ensure the coherent meshing of the various elements of this vision. Taking the high degree of convergence of the telecommunications and broadcasting sectors into account, the integration of these two laws into a single law on electronic communications would make it possible to address the specific challenges of technological convergence, such as the issue of net neutrality.

If the terrain is complex, a dynamic articulation of digital economic development strategies and policies or laws affecting cultural industries is a necessary step to ensure the future of cultural industries in Canada as well as the diversity of cultural expressions. This necessary step will depend on the Canadian government's ability to continuously reflect and act on the laws and measures that would allow for dynamic adaptation to the rapid changes affecting both telecommunications and broadcasting.

---

2 *Plan culturel numérique du Québec*, *Stratégie numérique du Québec*, *Stratégie Canada numérique 150*, etc.

13.2. Priority issues and possible solutions

13.2.1. *Financing culture*

We know that new business models related to the economic "platformization" have devastating effects on the revenues of cultural industry players in Quebec and Canada, while new players, such as digital platforms, digital cultural service providers and telecommunications/Internet service providers, benefit.

Under current regulations, Canadian distributors must contribute to supporting local content through the *Canada Media Fund*. To date, the Canadian Radio-television and Telecommunications Commission (CRTC) has refused to regulate online services and exempted digital media[3]. In *Politique culturelle pour l'ère numérique* (Cultural policy for the digital age), Stursberg (2016) provides a useful diagnosis that positions itself to adapt specific measures to support the creation and distribution of different types of Canadian content by proposing the creation of a cultural diversity fund that would not distinguish between "old" and "new" broadcasters, as well as tax fairness measures for digital actors, such as Netflix, who are not subject to the same tax conditions as those imposed on other online programming broadcasters available in Canada.

This situation also fuels a debate about the contribution of Internet service providers, which reap considerable benefits from broadband services and generally allow the circulation of flows of digital cultural content and services. We argue that the current laws should be amended to redefine the different services and establish new rules of the game, including more equitable contribution modes to ensure the participation of all players. A fund for culture and discoverability could replace the various funds that currently exist, and all companies that benefit from the flow of digital cultural products should contribute to this.

13.2.2. *Digital taxation*

The issue of the taxation of digital players is a headache for public authorities, whether in Quebec, Canada or elsewhere in the world. Indeed, new transnational players use relocation and tax optimization strategies to avoid the rules in force or to avoid having to contribute to national mechanisms to support the creation and financing of culture in the countries where they operate. In particular, the latter may

3 In the context of Canadian broadcasting laws, Netflix is not considered a broadcaster or television, even though it offers the same subscription services as a broadcaster or cable channel, with the only notable difference that it does so online.

choose to declare their activities in countries where tax regulations are more advantageous to them, in order to have a very marginal tax rate, thus putting countries in a situation of regulatory competition in an area where cooperation is still underdeveloped.

As far as sales taxes are concerned, the difficulty is to define the location of the transaction (by the offer – the company – or by the consumer demand – the consumer). Whether it is income or consumption tax, tax authorities have the right to take measures, provided that they do not create discriminatory effects on markets. But do they have the capacity to collect these taxes? Following the example of other countries, particularly in Europe, Canada could impose sales taxes on online purchases by Canadians from foreign companies, given that these transactions are an increasingly important part of the economy. In Europe, the European Commission has issued a directive to tax multinationals. Quebec has made an effort to discipline foreign companies and as of January 9, 2019, according to *Revenu Québec*[4], 76 foreign digital service companies have registered for the QST (Quebec Sales Tax).

13.2.3. *Telecommunications regulation and net neutrality*

In an environment of convergence of sectors, respect for Internet neutrality must be ensured. According to Wu (2003), the principle of Internet neutrality must ensure equal treatment of all data flows, thus excluding any form of discrimination against the source, destination or content of information transmitted over the network. Today, the convergence between telecommunications networks and the content that flows through them means that the current regulatory framework and policies for telecommunications and broadcasting are at the heart of the debates on net neutrality.

Internet service providers (ISPs) have the ability to implement practices that undermine the principle of net neutrality by focusing on their own content or service offerings, slowing down certain bandwidth-intensive uses, such as video-on-demand, and developing new business models that promote multi-speed Internet, with priority being given to transporting certain services and applications for a fee. Canada should strengthen and proactively monitor this issue.

4 The complete list of the 76 suppliers outside Quebec and the operators of a digital platform for the distribution of goods or services that are registered in the QST file is available online on the *Revenu Québec* website: https://www.revenuquebec.ca/fr/entreprises/taxes/tpstvh-et-tvq/situationss-particulieres-liees-a-la-tpstvh-et-a-la-tvq/fournisseurs-hors-quebec/liste-des-fournisseurs-hors-quebec-inscrits-au-fichier-de-la-tvq/.

There is a dynamic of rivalry that uses bandwidth as a strategic weapon to discriminate on the Internet, specifically through bandwidth and data flow management. ISPs consider that this practice is necessary to make the investments related to the development of new infrastructure profitable and consider that they alone bear the costs of innovation, network capacity expansion and infrastructure maintenance, while at the same time, companies such as Netflix, which act as builders and content providers, benefit from networks and use an increasing share of bandwidth with the overwhelming supply of content they put online. Large ISPs may also enter into agreements with content providers whose services require high bandwidth consumption in order to provide users subscribing to these services with better Internet access in return for a higher price. Thus, a cultural policy 2.0 should provide for the regulation of the maneuvers of telecommunications companies and content providers that clog the "network of networks" in order to defend the general interest.

13.2.4. *Competition regulation, anti-competitive practices and dominant positions*

Whether in relation to "internalization" and economic "platformization" or because of the rise of the *cloud* and artificial intelligence, the process of economic concentration and the emergence of dominant positions for the benefit of digital giants is an unavoidable fact. Anti-competitive practices have been the subject of several prosecutions of various types. For example, the Competition Bureau of Canada underscores the importance of an innovative digital economy that allows fair and healthy competition and allows Canadian companies to compete at home and abroad. The Bureau has already closely monitored Google's behavior between 2013 and 2016[5] and, in general, continues to monitor the digital market.

Until now, the regulation of cultural industries has been based on a set of measures and policies that apply to a well-defined and well-delimited territory. However, with digital technology, we are witnessing the arrival of new players offering deterritorialized and desegmented (or convergent) services. This results in several types of regulatory asymmetries. Telecommunications operators are subject to a number of obligations to deploy the physical network infrastructure and territorial meshes in order to cover a given territory. Broadcasters are subject to different obligations and regulations regarding the broadcasting of content. Cultural actors are involved in different activities, ranging from the creation to the dissemination of artistic and cultural works. In addition, digital players are often exempted from most of these regulations because of the innovative nature of their

5 In 2013, the Competition Bureau of Canada launched a survey to examine Google's practices related to online search, search engine advertising and online display advertising.

activities. In a world of convergence where dominant players are emerging, acting in several market segments simultaneously, the question of the convergence of laws and policies is once again raised.

In a context marked by porous borders between sectors and territorial boundaries, public authorities must find a way to level the playing field, with a vision that integrates the objective of finding ways to contribute to the development of a rich and innovative cultural environment. The drafting of a single law, covering all electronic communications and taking into account the cross-border and globalized dimension of digital cultural networks and products, is an interesting avenue, particularly if it integrates the Internet and the new players, such as transnational platforms, which play an important role, sometimes positive and sometimes negative, in the transformations underway. The public authorities must ensure that they maximize the benefits of their activities while reducing the costs and dangers of their expansion. A strengthening and better articulation of mandates for market surveillance and the fight against anti-competitive practices would also bode well.

13.2.5. *The importance of data: algorithms, metadata and discoverability in support of the diversity of cultural expressions*

Until a few years ago, local content quotas were an important element in protecting cultural industries. Today, nothing is less certain. Data and algorithms, at the heart of the digital transition of cultural industries, can promote a diversity of online cultural epressions. However, they can also lead to a standardized cultural offer by excluding the successful works or flagship products of high-profile artists, to the detriment of the discovery of new talent and access to a real diversity of content. In reality, we do not really know the dynamics of the discoverability of digital cultural products and their interaction with "physical" cultural products.

To be discoverable in the digital age, it is necessary to take into account the presence, visibility, recommendation and "consumption" (or actual discovery) of cultural products on digital platforms. What are the levels of presence, visibility and recommendation of local content in national and foreign catalogues of platforms such as Netflix, Spotify, iTunes/Apple Music, Google Play, Amazon Prime Video, or on emerging alternative/national platforms? Which of these platforms support the discoverability of a critical mass of local cultural content and which regulatory and policy provisions can serve as a lever to increase the discoverability of local content, both in the digital environment in general as well as on transnational platforms that are gaining in popularity and power? Would the development of "local" platforms be a necessary and effective means of financing and discovering local cultural products? These questions would require documentation and research on the transformations underway.

As paradoxical as it may seem, the fact is that in a world where data and computing power are multiplied, governments and local actors seem to lack strategic weapons and evidence to take their place in a globalized market that marginalizes them[6]. The production of discoverability indicators, which can document the discoverability of local products on the supply and consumption side, would provide policy-makers and cultural industries with data essential for public and private action to ensure a digital transition of the affected economic sectors[7].

13.3. Conclusion

Public action must achieve a better articulation of three worlds that evolve according to different logics: the worlds of trade, culture and digital. Digital technology is often perceived as an extra threat to the cultural sector in addition to the threat of trade liberalization. It is a transformer and amplifier of trade exchanges and business models that dictate new realities, affecting cultural actors and audiences as well as their relationships and interactions. However, digital technology can help to better link the worlds of commerce and culture, which are evolving according to different logics.

The transformations underway are far from over and, with future technological changes, we can only predict that, if trends continue, Canada will be in a situation of dependence – even marginalization – on companies such as Google (Alphabet Inc.), Amazon, Apple, Netflix and many others that, in just a few years, have developed market power that now allows them to impose themselves everywhere with new cultural services. These companies, regardless of the policy and regulatory responses from countries like Canada, will remain key players in shaping the future of the global economy and cultural industries. In this context, Canada should review legislations on the subject matter every five years to allow for the dynamic adaptation to rapid changes in both telecommunications and broadcasting.

---

6 As Lessig (2000) explains, the law of cyberspace depends on how it is coded. However, as far as algorithms are concerned, the development of their code is under the control of multinational web companies, which may even suggest that they can be used or oriented in such a way as to create discrimination and asymmetries both in the way they access a diversity of online cultural production and in terms of competition and the dominant position of platforms vis-à-vis local distribution companies (O'Neil 2016).

7 In 2017, the CEIM (*Centre d'études sur l'intégration et la mondialisation* – Center of studies on integration and globalization) created a laboratory to develop a discoverability index.

13.4. References

Beaudoin, L. (2014). Convention sur la protection et la promotion de la diversité des expressions culturelles : impacts et enjeux du numérique, Report. Organisation internationale de la Francophonie, Paris.

Benghozi, P.-J. (2011). L'économie de la culture à l'heure d'Internet : le deuxième choc. *Esprit*, 111–126.

Benghozi, P.-J. and Benhamou, F. (2008). Longue traîne : levier numérique de la diversité culturelle ? *Culture Prospective*, 1(1), 1–11.

Benhamou, F. (2011). *L'économie de la culture*. La Découverte, Paris.

Guèvremont, V. *et al.* (2013). La mise en œuvre de la Convention sur la protection et la promotion de la diversité des expressions culturelles à l'ère numérique : enjeux, actions prioritaires et recommandations, Report. RIJDEC, Paris.

Lessig, L. (2000). Code is law. On liberty in cyberspace. *Harvard Magazine*. January–February.

Mattelart, T. (2009). Enjeux intellectuels de la diversité culturelle. *Culture Prospective*, 2, 1–8.

Musitelli, J. (2014). Postface. La diversité culturelle et le numérique : un nouveau défi pour l'Unesco. In *Diversité culturelle à l'ère du numérique. Glossaire critique*, Frau-Meigs, D. and Kiyindou, A. (eds). La Documentation française, Paris, 305–312.

O'Neil, C. (2016). *Weapons of Math Destruction: How Big Data Increases Inequality and Threatens Democracy*. Crown Publishers, New York.

Stursberg, R. (2016). *Cultural policy for the digital age. the centre for law, technology and society*. Available at: https://techlaw.uottawa.ca/sites/techlaw.uottawa.ca/files/culturalpolicyforthedigitalage.pdf.

Vlassis, A. (2015). Négociations commerciales récentes et industries culturelles : de l'affrontement politique à la réconciliation normative ? In *Un nouveau pont sur l'atlantique : l'accord économique global entre l'Union européenne et le Canada*, Deblock, C., Paquin, S., and Lebullenger, J. (eds). Presses de l'Université du Québec, Montreal, 261–279.

Wu, T. (2003). Network neutrality, broadband discrimination. *Journal of Telecommunications and High Technology Law*, 2, 141–179.

14

The Digitalization of Cultural Policies in France

With the spread of the "technological revolution" in society, digital technology is an increasingly important part of public intervention. Economic, education, health and security policies have gradually integrated the digital dimension of social issues, while public officials have sought to build new "instruments" (Hood 2006) to act in the "information society". However, the emergence of digital policies should not be considered univocally, as a simple adaptation of governments to the new technological environment: State intervention in turn contributes to building categories of understanding to think about the social world (Bourdieu 2012), in particular the "digital" category, as a set of causes to defend, as a sector of activity to support and regulate, or as a particular mode of action.

The emergence of new categories of intervention refers to a now classic issue in public policy analysis (Burstein 1991; Dubois 1999; Tissot 2007). The many studies that are part of it show how categories are institutionalized around new government structures (ministries, secretaries of state), networks of actors and principles of intervention. However, the transversal dimension of the digital revolution contributes to blurring the boundaries of these categories, which are antagonistically seized by the various government agents: it thus creates a tension between the omnipresence of the "digital" category and the dilution of its unity in multiple public policies.

This text focuses on the construction and competitive appropriation of digital technology in the French government space based on the case of the Ministry of Culture. The intervention of the cultural administration on the Internet is most often summarized as the protection of online intellectual property and its corollary, the

---

Chapter written by Anne BELLON.

fight against the illegal exchange and downloading of creation. In doing so, France's Ministry of Culture has been one of the first government institutions involved in the construction of Internet regulations since the mid-1990s, which aim to regulate online practices and define new obligations for digital actors. Digital cultural policy would thus extend the traditional objectives of supporting the creative industry, to the detriment of taking better account of the practices and logics of cultural exchange on the Internet. It is in the name of the particularities of the digital space that some activists, experts and politicians have been advocating – since the mid-1990s – for a reform of digital cultural action (Lessig 2004; Dulong du Rosnay 2016).

Since 2008, conflicts between two visions of digital challenges for culture in France were crystalized around the so-called "Hadopi" law, which was named after a new agency that was created and eventually revised: *Haute autorité pour la diffusion des œuvres et la protection des droits sur Internet (Supreme authority for the distribution and protection of intellectual property on the Internet).* Offering a historical perspective on these conflicts and empirical data based on a four-month observation at the cabinet of the French Ministry of Culture, we propose to study the way in which sectoral actors oppose each other around the definition of digital issues and the public policies that must respond to them. First, we will briefly review the history of digital technology at the Ministry of Culture, then we will present the various coalitions in struggle, and finally we propose reasons for the construction of a particular vision of digital technology in the French cultural administration.

14.1. Digital technology at the Ministry of Culture: a perspective

Far from the image of an "enemy" of the Internet that is sometimes attached to it, the Ministry of Culture is in fact a pioneering administration in the spread of the Internet in France in the mid-1990s, at a time when the bureaucracy was largely resistant to this new network, which was perceived as a competitor to the Minitel system (Schafer and Thierry 2012). The mobilization of agents convinced of the potential of the Internet, particularly within the Research Department and the IT Services Department, promoted the early connection of workstations, the introduction of electronic mail and the implementation of one of the first French government websites, culture.fr, in 1994. The ministry's digital action was then part of a digitalization policy launched in the 1980s, with the aim of setting up and making vast museum databases accessible from computer and telematic networks.

With the development of the Web, departmental services are developing interactive sites linked to heritage collections, with the aim of renewing ways of accessing knowledge and art. Experiments with "online museums" are being carried out in partnership with the main public cultural institutions. This action is implemented by real Internet "activists" within the administration. Often close to associations promoting the Internet and defending rights, they insist on the revolutionary dimension of technological transformations and, at the same time, wish to decompartmentalize administrative policy or even rethink the modalities of the State's cultural action.

In contrast to these experiments, the issue of copyright emerges, in parallel, as a particularly salient aspect of digital action in the ministry. This is due, in particular, to the international treaties – the World Intellectual Property Organization (WIPO) treaty in 1996 (Sell 2003) – and the European obligations – the Copyright Harmonization Directive in 2001 – which commit successive governments to reforming intellectual property protection on the Internet. In 2000, a *Conseil supérieur de la propriété littéraire et artistique* (Superior Council of Artistic and Literary Property – CSPLA) was created within the ministry, bringing together experts, professionals and consumer associations to discuss these issues. The institution produces many reports and runs consultations to think about the digital transformation of copyright policies.

Between 2003 and 2006, a first law was prepared and adopted after lengthy debates. The law *Loi sur le droit d'auteur et les droits voisins dans la société de l'information* (law on authors' rights and related rights in the information society – DADVSI), an act concerning copyright and neighboring rights, authorizes the use of technical locks by manufacturers and, above all, penalizes their circumvention (Derieux and Granchet 2010). In 2008, a new law was proposed by the Ministry of Culture, during Nicolas Sarkozy's five-year term, to strengthen the fight against intellectual property crime. The "Hadopi law" establishes a graded response to acts of illegal downloading, which can go as far as cutting off Internet access. These successive policies, which strengthen the control of rights holders and cultural industries over the modes of distribution and access to creative works, are, however, strongly contested.

On the one hand, many technical experts denounce inefficient and costly systems that are not adapted to the reality of practices and technological constraints. On the other hand, Internet rights advocates argue that these laws pose serious obstacles to the exercise of fundamental freedoms, including the freedom of communication. The Hadopi law is thus fought in the streets as well as in technical and political arenas. Its mechanisms are also partially censored by the Constitutional Council in order to better guarantee respect for online freedoms. Copyright policy thus exacerbates the tensions between the militant Internet and representatives of cultural industries, tensions that the ministry echoes around the challenges of reforming its action in the digital age.

14.2. Opposing coalitions

As we have just seen, the implementation of digital action in the Ministry of Culture has produced two increasingly divergent policies, supported by coalitions of opposing actors. The digitalization and dissemination of cultural heritage on the Internet is accompanied by a restriction on the dissemination of creative works online, in the name of copyright protection. The concept of *causal coalition* was developed by politician Paul Sabatier (1988) to study the mechanisms of political change. It highlights the importance of the beliefs and interests shared by a range of sectoral actors mobilized to defend new public policies. According to him, the transformation of public intervention is explained less by exogenous factors than by the dynamics of internal struggles between opposing "coalitions" and the structure of resources and supports they manage to mobilize at a given time. Far from forming a homogeneous group, cultural professionals have been divided several times when the definition of a new cultural policy was at stake (Surel 1997), particularly in the face of successive technological changes (fax, digitalization, video recorder, etc.).

It is proposed here to study the formation and (re)structuring of these coalitions, based on an observation of the negotiations conducted in the Ministry of Culture's cabinet, around a reform of digital cultural policy following the debates provoked by the fight against illegal downloading. Entitled "Act II of the cultural exception", the reform program launched at the beginning of François Hollande's five-year term (Socialist Party) in 2012 was supposed to respond to the strong political tensions that accompanied the implementation of the "Hadopi" mechanism. First, it involved the various professional groups and activists in the drafting of a report presented in autumn 2013 to the Minister of Culture, Aurélie Filippetti. Second, the report should have served as a framework for the drafting of a new digital law, a project led by the ministerial cabinet during 2014. Negotiations made it possible to see the emergence of two coalitions of actors: they were distinguished by their antagonistic appropriation of digital issues and the way they linked them to the objectives traditionally assigned to the State's cultural policy.

First, the 2012 political changeover brought former opponents of the Hadopi law, sometimes from the ranks of the Socialist Party or digital rights associations, into the cultural administration. The latter claimed positive recognition of exchange and remix practices on the Internet, or even the establishment of a legal license by the State for the unimpeded distribution of digital works. They also proposed that the protection of the public domain and the "creative commons" be enshrined in law in order to combat the increasing commodification of culture. Their conception of digital cultural issues was based on the convergence, in their view, of two objectives: on the one hand, the free flow of information has been promoted by the militant Internet since the 1980s (Coleman 2012, 2013); on the other hand, cultural democratization, the issue around which public cultural action has been built since the 1930s.

This coalition was formed around a handful of agents who were often isolated within the large cultural administration. They could be found, for example, in the ministry's "digital uses" department, while in the ministerial cabinet, this vision of the challenges of the Internet was relayed, albeit in an ephemeral manner, by the digital advisor Juliette Mant between April and August 2014 and, to a lesser extent, by the advisor in charge of arts education.

These public actors relied on "free culture" initiatives (Creative Commons France, Wikimedia) or digital rights associations (La Quadrature du Net) with which they regularly exchanged ideas, within the frameworks of informal meetings, as well as symposia or festive events organized by the ministry ("Hackathon of cultural data", "Digital autumn" project, etc.). They also developed collaborations with the Secretary of State for Digital Technology, or with the advisers responsible for digital technology in the Office of the Presidency and the Prime Minister, and finally, to a lesser extent, with the digital services of the Ministry of Education and Research. Together, they defended a transversal conception of digital policy at the service of Internet causes and ethics. The cross-sectorial coalition of Internet enthusiasts also aimed to compensate, through the creation of a support network within the government space, for the weakness of their position in various sectoral administrations.

Indeed, the members of this coalition were often newcomers to the ministry and therefore had few bureaucratic resources in a highly standardized space. Often younger than their colleagues (they are all under 40 years old), they were mostly former lawyers or activists, although some, but more rarely, were computer experts. As a result, they had little control over the codes of a bureaucratic policy that they were trying to subvert in the name of "digital revolution".

This was the opposite of the agents constituting the other coalition, supporters of a digital cultural policy at the service of the domestic creative industry. These included the sector advisors responsible for audiovisual, film, music or publishing in the department's office and the directors of the main administrative divisions. These senior civil servants often spent part or all of their careers in the cultural field, mostly in the administration or at the head of institutions supporting creativity. This "third cultural sector", at the crossroads of the public and private spheres, was composed of expert bodies (*Conseil supérieur de la propriété littéraire et artistique*), regulatory agencies (Hadopi or *Conseil supérieur de l'audiovisuel (Superior Council of the Audiovisual)*), as well as organizations for the redistribution of public subsidies (*Centre national de la cinématographie* or collecting societies). The trajectory of many of the ministerial advisers across these different institutions revealed the strong porosity of the boundaries between administration, public agencies and private companies in the cultural sector.

Senior officials also had many contacts with professional organizations. The strength of these cultural networks lied as much in the durability of these structures for the representation of artistic interests as in their ability to attract former members of the administration and mobilize the symbolic weight of artists' collectives in the struggle to define cultural policies. The circulation of sectoral elites thus encouraged the development of a common vision of digital challenges: among them, with the convergence of audiovisual media and telecommunications, the weakening of creative industries' business models, and the emergence of over-the-top players, the Internet revolution was above all perceived as a phenomenon destabilizing the existing equilibrium in a highly regulated sector (Chantepie and Le Diberder 2010). The main goal of this coalition was therefore to protect industrial players, particularly those facing competition from the GAFAs (Google, Amazon, Facebook, Apple), in the name of the "cultural exception". To do so, they advocated for an adaptation of regulations to the reconfiguration of the creative and cultural markets. According to them, it was also important to strengthen the means of the fight against piracy by consolidating the measures put in place with the Hadopi law – a graduated response, the fight against pirate sites and the increased legal accountability of technical intermediaries in the removal of illegal content. The digitalization of cultural policy then requires an increased use of regulatory instruments, whether in terms of taxation of new digital players or the introduction of new obligations and incentives (e.g. a charter with advertisers to combat streaming sites).

14.3. An industry policy instead of a user policy

Eventually, the asymmetric distribution of resources between the two coalitions is leading to the progressive marginalization of the promoters of Internet causes within the cultural administration. It can be observed, for example, in political arbitrations, most often in favor of the second coalition: the recognition of the public domain, which was first discussed in the drafting of the reform project in 2014, is thus gradually being abandoned. Similarly, the abolition of the Hadopi law, announced by the Minister of Culture in 2012, gives way to an increase in its financial resources from 2015 onwards. The ability of industrial actors to coordinate their efforts and solicit support from senior administrators and sector-specific political advisors is detrimental to the supporters of an Internet "users' policy", who have weak and scattered governmental relays. It leads both to the economic framing of the "digital" category in the cultural field (Schlesinger 2014), in the service of a reform of the regulation of creative markets, and the failure of a recognition of digital technology as an issue of democratization and renewal of cultural practices.

14.4. Conclusion

Far from destabilizing sustainably institutionalized public policy networks, the "digital revolution" therefore seems to have favored an instrumentalization of the "digital" category by sectoral elites, with largely unchanged policy objectives (Negrier and Teillet 2014): the defense of domestic creative industries, the affirmation of the "cultural exception" in international negotiations or the regulation of cultural markets by the State. However, this contribution makes it possible to qualify the vision of a homogeneous cultural administration, whose agents would unambiguously defend the reinforcement of the fight against piracy and the protection of sectoral balances.

In France, the development of digital policy at the Ministry of Culture is in fact durably marked by competing appropriations of the "technological revolution" under way, its meaning and the challenges it covers for the dissemination of culture and creativity in the information society. While policies for the digitalization and appropriation of heritage remain in the minority, their inclusion on the ministry's agenda can also benefit from the opening of new windows of political opportunity, the growing capitalization of expert resources within the coalition of "Internet enthusiasts", the restructuring of exchanges and the actors that constitute it.

However, the political alternation of 2017 seems to have accentuated a favorable balance of power for professional representatives of the creative industries: the positions taken by Minister Françoise Nyssen – in office in 2017 and 2018 – for strengthening Hadopi's capacity for action in the fight against illegal downloading and streaming, and Franck Riester's appointment as Minister of Culture – formerly rapporteur of the Hadopi law – in 2018 mark a sustainable dilution of digital technology in the defense of the sectoral actors. Cultural policy has therefore become "digital" by subsuming the digital environment to sectoral issues, more than it has allowed the emergence of a real digital policy for culture, encouraging the introduction of new logics specific to the Internet world into the ministry's action.

14.5. References

Bourdieu, P. (2012). *Sur l'État : Cours au Collège de France (1989–1992)*. Le Seuil, Paris.

Broca, S. (2013). *Utopie du logiciel libre. Du bricolage informatique à la réinvention sociale.* Le Passager clandestin, Paris.

Burstein, P. (1991). Policy domains: Organization, culture, and policy outcomes. *Annual Review of Sociology*, 17(1), 327–350.

Chantepie, P. and Le Diberder, A. (2010). *Révolution numérique et industries culturelles*. La Découverte, Paris.

Coleman, G. (2012). *Coding Freedom: The Ethics and Aesthetics of Hacking*. Princeton University Press, Princeton.

Derieux, E. and Granchet, A. (2010). *Lutte contre le téléchargement illégal : Lois Dadvsi et Hadopi*. Wolters Kluwer France, Paris.

Dubois, V. (1999). *La politique culturelle, Genèse d'une catégorie d'intervention publique*. Belin, Paris.

Dulong du Rosnay, M. (2016). *Les golems du numérique : Droit d'auteur et Lex Electronica*. Presses des Mines, Paris.

Hood, C. (2006). The tools of government in the information age. In *Oxford Handbook of Public Policy*, Moran, M., Ran, M., and Goodin, R.E. (eds). Oxford University Press, Oxford, 469–481.

Lessig, L. (2004). *Free Culture: How Big Media Uses Technology and the Law to Lock Down Culture and Control Creativity*. Penguin Press, New York.

Négrier, E. and Teillet, P. (2014). Le tournant instrumental des politiques culturelles. *Pôle Sud*, 41(2), 83–100.

Sabatier, P. (1988). An advocacy coalition framework of policy change and the role of policy-oriented learning therein. *Policy Sciences*, 21(2–3), 129–168.

Schafer, V. and Thierry, B. (2012). *Le Minitel : L'enfance numérique de la France*. CIGREF, Paris.

Schlesinger, P. (2016). The creative economy: Invention of a global orthodoxy. *Les Enjeux de l'information et de la communication*, 17(2), 187–205.

Sell, S. (2003). *Private Power, Public Law: The Globalization of International Property Rights*. Cambridge University Press, Cambridge.

Surel, Y. (1997). *L'État et le livre : Les politiques publiques du livre en France (1957–1993)*. L'Harmattan, Paris.

Tissot, S. (2007). *L'État et les quartiers. Genèse d'une catégorie de l'action publique*. Le Seuil, Paris.

PART 3

Digital Technology and Cultural and Communicational Practices

15

The Digitalization of Society and a New Form of Connected Sociability in Tunisia

This chapter aims to identify the links between digital culture, digital social networks (DSNs) and youth culture in the age of the digitalization of society. The construction of the figure of information and communication technology (ICT) users has been extensively discussed in information and communication sciences (ICS). Through ICS research, based on a double theoretical and empirical study focused on Mediterranean countries, including Tunisia, we have drawn up a panorama of the social uses of social web tools, which, according to Millerand, Proulx and Rueff (2010), refers to the emergence of new digital devices that are inseparable from the evolution of the Internet. This notion of social web (known as Web 2.0) has been addressed by ICS research (Pirolli and Cretin-Pirolli 2011).

In addition, the first objective of our study is to work on the construction and deconstruction of the notion of social web by researching the contemporary works that deal with the subject matter. We will see what lessons emerge from Mediterranean research on this social web in an increasingly digital society. Our second objective is to question the concept of digital humanities and see whether the discourse around this notion finds an echo in the Tunisian context.

Consequently, our issue addresses the new practices of DSNs in the Mediterranean. It focuses on the following questions: what are the communication issues of DSNs among young people[1] in the digital age? Can we talk about the widespread digitalization of our societies?

Chapter written by Alma BETBOUT.

1 We will also use the term *young people* to refer to the "Tunisian adolescents" in our study throughout this chapter.

15.1. Research purpose, hypotheses and working methodology

Digital culture, a set of social conventions, practices and uses related to digital technology, has developed over the past few decades, and has influenced all sectors and structured the evolution of society. In this respect, digital interfaces, touch screens and connected objects presented under the term "information and communication technologies" are nowadays "mediation instruments" for users (Pasquier and Jouët 1999). This mediation has thus fostered the emergence of new models of values, social relations and actions that transform our relationship with ourselves and the collective, and participate fully in the production of contemporary societies (Denouël and Granjon 2011).

Moreover, our study is in the tradition of the sociology of ICT use approach, and more specifically DSNs. The objective of this chapter is to examine the link between digital practices and social networks among young Tunisians. To this end, two hypotheses guide our investigation: the first is that the practices of digital tools refer to a new form of connected sociability and autonomy among users through connected objects, and precisely through mobile phones; the second is that the new usages of DSNs promote a reconfiguration of intergenerational ties among adolescents to distinguish themselves from their parents.

Our reflection will be based, on the one hand, on a survey we conducted using a paper questionnaire and in-depth semi-directive interviews with a population of[2] high school students aged 13–19 years in the city of Sousse[3], Tunisia, and, on the other hand, on an online survey of parents of[4] adolescents in the same geographical area, to which we received 34 responses. This empirical survey, which is part of our doctoral research (Betbout 2017), took place between December 2015 and May 2017. Our research involved a total of 201 people.

15.2. Research results

This study mainly led us to work with the actors. The desire to study the object from the participants' point of view led us to choose a participating method.

2 In four classes of different levels, 120 paper questionnaires were distributed. We ensured that our respondents understood the questions (open and closed). Then, we informed them of the confidentiality of the answers to reassure them and motivate them to engage.

3 City of the eastern region of Tunisia. The richness of its history makes it a must-visit place. Sousse is also an ancient port city, with a thousand artistic and cultural testimonies that make it an important reference point in terms of the historical events that have marked Tunisia.

4 We found it useful to obtain the views of parents of adolescents to understand their children's use and opinions on the subject, as the family environment is an explanatory variable for children's behavior.

We agree here with Goffman's comments, which speak of methodological interactionism. We were interested in these adolescent practices in order to understand the question of the appropriation of ICTs in a Tunisian society that, in the past, was increasingly marked by the place of technologies and the creation of a new youth culture around connected objects.

15.2.1. *Forms of online sociability among adolescents*

Traditional Tunisian society and Arab regimes have always operated on an authoritarian model (Laoukili 2011). This implies standards and rules of conduct that are imposed on everyone. This patriarchal social order has already been the subject of studies and analyses in anthropological and ethnographic research (Tlili 2002). However, it seems that, since 2011[5], Tunisia has experienced an evolution in socio-cultural relations between family members following the emergence of the digital social network Facebook. Indeed, ICTs are now part of their social and self-recognition practices (Pétiau 2011).

15.2.1.1. *Online friendly social skills*

The concept of *sociability* is well established today as an object of the sociological analysis of the social forms of relationships with others (Rivière 2004). Its use is necessary in multiple kinds of content. We speak of juvenile sociability, friendly sociability, family sociability, etc., as particular social forms of relationships with others. In her research on the practices of pre-teen adolescents, Céline Metton-Gayon (2004) writes that the Internet is a tool that participates in the process of "horizontal socialization: through their online practices, preteenagers develop a 'social world' shared with their peers" (p. 62). In response to questions such as "Does the use of Facebook influence your offline relationships? If so, explain in what ways", the opinions of adolescents are divided. Some people think that Facebook is changing social relationships. The most frequently cited responses are Facebook's role as an accelerator in creating friendly relationships:

> "Thanks to Facebook, I have a large list of friends that grows every day. Adding friends is convenient and easy, we comment, we like[6] pictures […] I think it's a powerful accelerator to have a friendship through Facebook" (Boy, 13 years old).

5 January 14, 2011. Il s'agit de la première révolution démocratique et sociale qu'ait jamais connue le monde arabe (The first democratic and social revolution has never been seen in the Arab world). Available at: https://www.herodote.net/14_janvier_2011-evenement-20110114.php.

6 This is a button embedded in Facebook that allows a user to express an interest in site content.

According to Kelly Cadec and Serge Proulx's (2015) reflection on the social representations of friendship on Facebook, the device accelerates and facilitates the friendship process for three reasons. First, Facebook brings out common areas of interest that would not be visible offline, as our respondent (15 years old) explains: "I was able to get to know people who have the same interests as me. We were able to schedule outings together". Second, the visibility of shared activities, common events and different sources of interaction (comments, sharing, likes, etc.) contributes to the development of certain forms of sociability. Third, the simple use of the tool is a meeting facilitator: "When I meet people on outings, as soon as I get home I add them as a friend on Facebook. Sometimes I add them instantly if I have the connection on my phone" (Girl, 13 years old).

According to Cadec and Proulx (2015), this observation applies to relationships with a low degree of friendship (beginning of relationship, knowledge, etc.). Indeed, mobile modes of communication and new computer technologies, combined with types of social agreements, have already begun to change the way people meet and interact. danah michele boyd (2007) notes that with the emergence of DSNs, adolescents have begun to adopt them as places to mark their identity and socialize with their peers. These DSNs are used by adolescents as a shared "social outlet" for their peers.

boyd's analysis focuses on the way in which social digital network sites can be understood as networked public spaces, which simultaneously represents the space built by networked technologies and the imagined community that emerges as a result of the intersection between people, technology and practice. She adds that teenagers are reshaping technology according to their goals. According to the researcher, as teenagers have learned to navigate digital social networks, they have developed powerful strategies to manage the complexity and social disadvantages inherent in these sites. Their strategies reveal how new forms of social media are being incorporated into daily life, complicating some practices and strengthening others.

If we talk about youth culture, Olivier Donnat (2009) states that there is undoubtedly a specific digital culture for young people. In any case, this is what the studies on cultural practices indicate. Through an analysis of the relationships that Tunisian adolescents have with the DSN, we have focused on studying these forms of connected sociability.

15.2.1.2. *Connected sociability through mobile telephony*

Some developing countries, notably Tunisia, consider that a massive adoption of ICTs can allow an "accelerated" catch-up of industrialized countries (Ben Youssef and M'Henni 2003). Thus, the number of mobile Internet subscribers in Tunisia was estimated at 7.8 million in 2018 (compared to 700,000 in 2011, 4.1 million in 2014 and 6.2 million in 2014[7]). In addition, the mobile phone[8] has been a powerful tool for peer sociability (Fize 1997) and has played an important role through the dissemination of writings, images and videos on DSNs in a country deprived of freedom of expression:

> "Thanks to the strong network coverage throughout Tunisia, we can be connected and reachable anywhere and at any time. This makes it possible to have this proximity and this link between friends. I think mobile phones and the Internet are the best inventions" (Girl, 19 years old).

Sami Zlitni and Fabien Liénard (2013) consider that mobile ICTs have played a major role in the organization and dissemination of information, and have promoted important discursive spaces in the support of populations during the Arab Spring:

> "Thanks to connected objects in general and phones in particular, I can connect in the public space. If I have any questions, I can ask my friends or go directly to Google or YouTube. No need to ask parents anymore. We can be independent and I think that's great" (Girl, 15 years old).

Adolescence is associated with the emancipation of the child, and the mobile phone plays a role in this process insofar as it allows a certain freedom at the same time as it maintains a link. This is what a father whose child uses a mobile phone tackles: "When I come home from work, I always find my son connected to Facebook. Within a certain acceptable limit, I find no problem with that, you just have to watch for excesses" (Father, 45 years old); "When my daughters come home from school, they straight away connect to social networks and I prepare dinner. I think it's a good compromise to spend time and stay in touch with their classmates while being at home" (Mother, 40 years old).

The traditional Tunisian family is, in fact, a conservative family that refers to well-established models of behavior. Minor children are not allowed to go out at night. The father has the authority and the mother has the role of educator in the

7 According to the website of the Ministry of Communication Technologies and Digital Economy of Tunisia: https://www.mtcen.gov.tn/index.php?id=332&date=4-2011&id=332&cHash=c9533bb2539d7328f2a24b5763c87705&L=0.

8 According to the African Manager website, 36.1% of Tunisians own a smartphone, 69% of whom use mobile Internet (4G); the main reason for this is mobility (https://africanmanager.com/tunisia-361-des-tunisien-possed-un-smartphone/).

religious and moral values to be transmitted. In this context, mobile technologies allow users to be with their families and maintain friendly relationships with peers outside the family circle. In addition, the interest of the DSNs is to facilitate a smooth evolution towards more autonomy.

15.2.2. *Sociability around hybrid writing*

With the advent of mobile telephony, usage changes regularly. Indeed, these are new territories where feelings of belonging and new spaces where the construction of young people's identity is manifested become affiliated. To be able to study the role that digital devices play in building social cohesion, we first examine contact training on Facebook. Then, we analyze the nature of the community's appropriation of digital social networks, as well as their place in the daily lives of adolescents.

15.2.2.1. *Sociability through mixed and hybrid writing*

The use of mobile devices and digital tools has become part of the adolescent environment. They have developed new cooperation practices. Marie-Claude Vetraino-Soulard (1998) speaks of "oralized writing" and suggests that a large number of interlocutors distance themselves from the rules of syntax and writing. Therefore, the expression resembles a transcription of oral speech. For example, here is a testimony[9] (Figure 15.1) from our survey:

Figure 15.1. *Short message in French between two friends on Facebook: "you're beautiful", "thank you, you too"*

> "Interviewer: What does 'pv qtv' mean?
>
> Yosr: It means we can talk in private whenever you want. *(on parle en privé quand tu veux)* [Laughs]
>
> I: Is it a coded message?

9 For the safety of the teenagers who were the subject of our investigation, we deleted the names and profile photos to ensure their anonymity.

Y: We are used to writing like that, for us it is not really a coded message.

I: Why do you write in abbreviations?

Y: To write faster. It is also the smartphone that makes it easier for us to do with its touchscreen" (Girl, 15 years old).

Reflecting on the statements by our respondents, "the requirement is to keep it short and quick, especially. To get to the essential, at the price of an astonishing exercise, which requires technical mastery" (Lardellier 2002, p. 126). Indeed, there is a group culture with its inventions and, in particular, its SMS language and its singular spelling, practices and representations: "To write '*bonne nuit*' (good night) we will write 'B8', a play on the pronunciation of *nuit*, and the number eight in French, *huit*; '*aujourd'hui*' (today), will be 'aujourd8', again another play on the pronunciation of the number eight. It's faster" (Girl, 16 years old).

According to Carole-Anne Rivière (2002), in the phonetic message, i.e. the message expressing sounds made to be heard, "writing becomes a pure decal of oral language and breaks with the constraints of form and respect for tradition" (p. 147).

15.2.2.2. *Sociability through the Latinization of the Tunisian dialect: between numbers and letters*

Another specific form of writing was observed among Tunisian adolescents in our survey. There are more letters in the Arabic alphabet than in the French alphabet. There are also different sounds in Arabic, or sounds that do not exist in Latin languages. As a result, Arab Internet users have created new language codes that will be used in the Tunisian dialect by associating a number with each letter of the Arabic alphabet (Table 15.1).

2	3	4	5	6	7	8	9
ا	ع	ث	خ	ط	ح	غ	ق

Table 15.1. *Letters of the Arabic alphabet associated with numbers*

Dialectal writing occupies an important place in the speeches and forms of digital writing among Tunisian adolescents.

Figure 15.2 is an example of a 15-year-old respondent's publication that illustrates our comments.

Sbe7 el 5ir ye jme3a chnowa jawkom
w ch3amlin??🖤🖤

Figure 15.2. *Screenshot of a respondent's Facebook wall*

The results of our study show unconscious encryption transgressing traditional writing, a diversion of spelling and typographical codes by young people. The latter mobilize a world of linguistic conventions that is distant from the language imposed on schools, although Tunisian society places great emphasis on learning classical literary Arabic so that it once again becomes the engine of communication. This can be explained by the dynamics created by these users to develop the language.

15.3. Conclusion

For decades, Tunisians have been accustomed to dealing with locked and censored information (Touati 2012). With the development of ICTs, they have grasped the importance of these places of socialization and these new tools in the creation of new spaces of expression. Indeed, each user builds his or her usage device according to his or her communication practices (Paquienséguy 2007), which are nevertheless accompanied by a homogenization of usage among adolescents. These young people are aware that Tunisian society is evolving, but this evolution is unevenly distributed among the generations. However, intergenerational relationships are not conflictual and there is no confrontational strategy either on the part of the children or on the part of the parents. On the contrary, we can talk about a logic of compromise. Young people show a desire for emancipation and the desire to distinguish themselves from their parents by integrating the constraints imposed by parental authority into their practices, but bypass them through an avoidance strategy by taking advantage of their private space to connect freely. From now on, this Tunisian society is modern, but – faced with the weight of social constraints – remains conservative.

15.4. References

Ben Youssef, A. and M'Henni, H. (2004). Les effets économiques des technologies de l'information et de la communication et croissance : le cas de la Tunisie. *Région et développement*, 19, 131–150.

Betbout, A. (2017). Pratiques de communication. Usages et usagers des réseaux socionumériques via le téléphone mobile en Méditerranée. Cas des adolescents tunisiens. PhD thesis, Université Clermont Auvergne, Clermont-Ferrand.

boyd, d.m. (2007). Réseaux sociaux numériques : vie privée, vie publique, what else ? Available at: https://www.danah.org/papers/KnowledgeTree-French.pdf.

Cadec, K. and Proulx, S. (2015). Les représentations de l'amitié sur Facebook. *Communication*, 33(2). Available at: https://journals.openedition.org/communication/5755.

Denouël, J. and Granjon, F. (eds) (2011). *Communiquer à l'ère du numérique. Regards croisés sur la sociologie des usages*. Presse des Mines, Paris.

Donnat, O. (2009). Les pratiques culturelles des Français à l'ère numérique. Éléments de synthèse 1997–2008. *Culture études*, 5(5), 1–12.

Fize, M. (1997). Les adolescents et l'usage du téléphone. *Réseaux*, 82/83, 219–230.

Laoukili, A. (2011) Emprise, résistance et dégagement : réflexions à partir des révolutions tunisienne, égyptienne, etc. *Connexions*, 1(95), 41–54.

Lardellier, P. (2002). *Le pouce et la souris : enquête sur la culture numérique des ados*. Fayard, Paris.

Metton-Gayon, C. (2004). Les usages de l'Internet par les collégiens. Explorer les mondes sociaux depuis le domicile. *Réseaux*, 123, 59–84.

Millerand, F., Proulx, S., and Rueff, J. (eds). (2010). *Web social. Mutation de la communication*. Presses de l'Université du Québec, Quebec.

Pasquier, D. and Jouët, J. (1999). Les jeunes et la culture de l'écran. Enquête nationale auprès des 6-17 ans. *Réseaux*, 1/2(92/93), 25–102.

Pétiau, A. (2011). Internet et les nouvelles formes de sociabilités. *Vie sociale*, 2(2), 117–127.

Pirolli, F. and Crétin-Pirolli, R. (2011). Web social et multimédia : propriétés d'une relation symbiotique. *Les Enjeux de l'information et de la communication*, 12(2), 73–82.

Rivière, C.-A. (2002). La pratique du mini-message. Une double stratégie d'extériorisation et de retrait de l'intimité dans les interactions quotidiennes. *Réseaux*, 2(112/113), 140–168.

Rivière, C.-A. (2004). La spécificité française de la construction sociologique du concept de sociabilité. *Réseaux*, 123, 207–231.

Stenger, T. and Coutant, A. (eds) (2011). Ces réseaux numériques dits sociaux. *Hermès, La Revue*, 59.

Tlili, F. (2002). Statut féminin, modèle corporel et pratique sportive en Tunisie. *Staps*, 1(57), 53–68.

Touati, Z. (2012). Presse et révolution en Tunisie : rôle, enjeux et perspectives. *ESSACHESS. Journal for Communication Studies*, 5(19), 139–150.

Vettraino-Soulard, M.-C. (1998). *Les enjeux culturels d'Internet*. Hachette, Paris.

Zlitni, S. and Liénard, F. (eds) (2013). *La communication électronique en question*. Peter Lang, Bern.

16

Digitalization and Knowledge at University: Study of Collaborative Student Practices

The question I propose to examine here is the following: how do university students' digital uses transform the knowledge they learn? This question will only be partially addressed, both because of the size constraints of the chapter and because I will approach it using a sociological survey that examines the question of academic knowledge more broadly. I would like to outline here some avenues for reflection that could be discussed and developed. In this short chapter, I will therefore first explain in which general framework I have worked, with which methodology, and then how I have addressed the question of the use of certain digital tools by students in their knowledge work. I will then present some suggestions for analysis based on these observations.

16.1. Knowledge as a result of collective work

This contribution is the result of a research project I conducted between 2011 and 2014 at a university in a major city in western France. My approach was to study, through sociological inquiry, the knowledge that is taught and learned at university. The idea was the following: knowledge at university is often considered as subjects that already exist, as things with an intrinsic existence, independent of what researchers or students do. On the contrary, I proposed to start from the following idea: knowledge is first and foremost the result of the work of several categories of people in universities, those who produce it through their research, those who teach it (it is sometimes the same people) and those who learn it. I rely on a "trick" by Howard Becker (1998):

Chapter written by Marie DAVID.

"Things are just people acting together. Physical objects, while real enough physically, don't have 'objective' properties. Neither do more intangible social objects. We give them those properties, for social purposes, by recognizing that they have them" (p. 69).

If knowledge, like everything else, is only "people acting together", then it is necessary to investigate who these people are (i.e. what categories are involved) and what concrete work these categories produce.

16.2. The survey on the knowledge taught and learned at university

This is what I realized during a field survey, in which I attended the courses of two training and research units (UFR): Science and Sociology. In Science, I took physics and chemistry courses. I focused on groups of first-year undergraduate students (called L1), and I went with them to class for a semester. I took the opportunity to observe not only interactions in class, but also outside: relationships with professors, with other students, work in university libraries, etc. I then conducted interviews with the students surveyed and with their teachers.

The focus of my research, the knowledge taught and learned at university, and my investigation therefore have no a *priori* connection with the digitalization of society. Only *a priori*, because one of the interests of inductive approaches (analyzed by Becker 1970, Glaser and Strauss 1967, or, in France, by Chapoulie 2000) is precisely not to decide in advance what we will find in the fieldwork.

16.3. The discovery of digital student practices

However, during the investigation, I noticed that L1 students in Science and Social Studies used certain digital tools such as social networks (such as Facebook) and collaborative storage spaces (such as Dropbox) to circulate information and documents between them[1]. It was a surprise for me to discover that L1 students were using these tools to exchange their course notes and other information. I understood this quite late in the survey year at the UFR of Science, because this use was not a practice that I had observed directly until this time (students do not go on Facebook during classes or to the university library). If this was a surprise, it is also because research on digital education does not address these uses. Although scientific studies

1 I had access to these tools in two ways: by registering on the open digital social networks used by students (such as unmoderated Facebook groups) and, for tools with controlled access, by asking students to register me.

of the use of digital technology by pupils and students have been increasing since the 2010s, they focus on showing the diversity of uses (Mercklé and October 2012) or their effect on test success (Burban, Cottier and Michaut 2013; Roche 2015). The issue of *working between students* via digital technology is not yet a specific subject under study.

It was during the interviews with Science students that I realized that this was a very common, banal practice: even though regular students meet each other every day at the university, they exchange information via digital tools.

Students use social networks, such as Facebook, and sharing platforms a little differently. The platforms (Dropbox in the survey) are used to deposit the note-taking that students have done in class. Digital social networks are used to exchange information. But which ones?

Exchanges within L1 students' Facebook groups can be grouped into three main themes: exchanges of course notes (transcripts written by the students of the teacher's course); information about the organization of courses and exams; and practical and festive information. Messages about exams also multiply one month before each exam period. But what difference does it make, from the point of view of knowledge, that students use these digital tools?

16.4. Digital uses and collective work of knowledge

The first effect noted from the use of these tools is the modification of student note-taking. The surveyed students know that they can obtain from others, via digital tools, the written record of all courses. However, in interviews, they say that they have difficulty taking notes in amphitheater classes (obviously in different ways depending on the students). Sharing allows the most anxious to reassure themselves (they can reread the lesson even though they themselves have not managed to write everything down) and allows the others to carry out parallel activities in progress. The "written trace" object live of the course, which one might think is an individual student's objective, thus becomes a collective objective, for all those who refer to the notes deposited on the platform, whether or not the written traces in question are faithful to what the teacher said.

This question of note-taking is not an incidental one: it is an important element in the definition of knowledge taken in by students. They do not learn directly what teachers say (even though they retain some of it): to prepare their exams, they work mainly from their course notes. If these are modified, it is the knowledge they learn that is also modified.

The sharing of digital tools also modifies the relationship to attendance. One does not have to be present to obtain the written content. Why do students still attend class? On the one hand, those who are diligent say that they attach great importance to their presence, because they think they will not be able to understand the contents simply by reading them in someone else's notes. In a way, this circulation of courses rehabilitates the professorial discourse: it is presented as essential to the understanding of knowledge. On the other hand, some students admit to skipping certain courses, those that are placed at a bad time for them (too early in the morning, for example), or those with "bad teachers" (see below).

Exchanges of information, questions and answers on digital social networks are intensified as the academic year progresses. They include the work requested by professors and that which students must produce. Part of the digital discussions is about defining the work to be produced. Indeed, the academic instructions always involve an element of uncertainty[2] that students must resolve: what is the precise length of the essay to be written? Is it absolutely mandatory to solve all exercises, or can we just do one part of them? Will the teacher agree to correct a work that was returned a few days late? What tools and sources can be used to facilitate the work?

Through the exchange of messages on Facebook, students adjust to each other and develop a form of non-binding collective response; non-binding, because no one is obliged to follow it. Even though there is no obligation on the teacher's part to accept the answer prepared by the students, he/she is all the more constrained because a large number of the students have reached an agreement. In other words, what digital exchanges between students change is their ability to agree, to limit uncertainty in the work to be done, to impose their definition of the work to be done, and in the way they must work with knowledge[3].

It should also be noted that the use of Facebook and Dropbox platforms displaces the knowledge circulation initiative. In a classic scheme, knowledge is held by the teacher, who transmits it to the students. In my observations, the professor does transmit knowledge to students, who take it in via note-taking and then circulate it outside of any professorial control. It is then a new knowledge that circulates, partly transformed by note-taking, which can be selective or distorted, and which teachers no longer have any control over.

2 Only the evaluated works are specified in the "Modalities of knowledge control", a regulatory document for all French university courses, and this, in a very imprecise way.

3 In a way, these negotiations between students, which sometimes lead them to reducing their professors' demands, can be compared to workers' negotiations to "goldbrick", as Roy analyzes (Roy 1952; David 2017).

The joint work of knowledge by students *through* digital tools represents a form of autonomy, since students take charge of the conservation and circulation of knowledge alone, without the intervention of professors. However, student self-nomination is often promoted as a condition for success in unity, but it is only rarely approached from this angle (David 2016).

In addition, the documents provided by teachers are circulated without their knowledge. These include documents that they choose to provide to one group of students, but not to others, or one year, but not the next.

> "For example, the thermodynamics handout – normally the teacher, he doesn't give it to us. It's only those who are at Polytech[4] who have the courses here, who have it. As a result, there is a friend who got it from a friend and put it on the Facebook group so that everyone can have the handout" (L1 Science student).

So, the professor of thermodynamics gave a handout containing his entire course written, but only to some students whom he considered more autonomous. However, this handout was made available by the students themselves to all the teacher's other groups, and even students with other teachers.

The digital tools they use allow surveyed students to compare their professors, by comparing the content they teach (or rather by comparing the student transcript of these courses). They say that comparing the content taught by different teachers allows them to better understand the course, but they also say that if they have a teacher who "explains poorly", they have an additional chance to understand. These comparisons feed into students' moral judgment of their teachers: the "good" and the "bad". By paralleling the notes taken in the courses of the different professors, the students develop a collective judgment on them. The most requested course notes are those of teachers designated as "good".

> "Above all, we can have interpretations other than that was taught in our class because we don't have the same teacher, for example, and then you say, 'Oh well, I understand better now'. As a result, it's easier. And so, right, we can get more details if my teacher doesn't explain something very well – there are students who have other teachers; they explain it to us so that we can understand. And inversely, me, the teacher I have in thermodynamics, they have her in point mechanics, so they don't really understand point mechanics" (L1 Science student).

4 The Polytech is an engineering school that is part of the university and whose first year courses are joined with those of L1 in the UFR of Science.

These comparisons also have an effect on the knowledge learned, because it is no longer only the knowledge transmitted by their teacher that students learn, but also that transmitted by other teachers.

The circulation of courses and the exchange of information take place outside the control of the faculty. It should be noted that the student networks I am talking about are deployed in parallel with the institutional networks made available by the university: their main characteristic is to precisely escape professorial control. Professors know that their students discuss among themselves on digital social networks, but they do not know what about. The teachers use it too, to convey messages: for example, they instruct a student to transmit information to others (such as a change of class or room time).

However, they generally ignore that the re-transcription of almost all their teaching by students is circulated. I note a paradox on this subject: when they talk about it among themselves, the surveyed professors (more those in Sociology than Science) say that they prefer not to give written courses[5] to their students; they prefer that they come to class and take notes. However, we have seen that these courses still circulate regardless of the decision by teachers themselves, or a version transcribed by students.

Finally, the student practices very quickly described here make it obsolete to reserve information, or documents, for only a selection of the students. Yet teachers continue to do so. Another possible solution would be to acknowledge and adapt to this change.

16.5. Digital exchanges, one dimension among others of students' collective activity

The scope of the changes related to the digital uses of students that I have just presented must be qualified. Exchanges related to learned knowledge and the ways it is worked are more generalized with digital social networks and collaborative platforms than without them: they involve more students. They are done almost instantaneously or in a very short time. They take place at a distance, outside the university premises. However, they do not constitute radical transformations in the way students work with knowledge.

5 Handouts or online documents that would transcribe all the course content.

These exchanges remain part of the general framework of interactions between students and their teachers. In particular, digital exchanges remain strongly embedded in the relationships established directly in the face-to-face interactions between students (even though this may seem paradoxical for exchanges that can take place remotely and anonymously).

Indeed, if we look at which students submit their notes to share them, or who answers the questions of others, we see that these are a small number of students. These are the ones who are very diligent in class (they are present almost all the time). They know each other directly and have direct exchanges with the teachers (and I know them too, since it is them who I see all the time during the investigation). They are, for example, the ones who will send emails to teachers to ask them questions or to negotiate (the date of submission of a job, for example). It is therefore the most assiduous students involved in university activities who are responsible for the circulation of knowledge and the digital exchange of information. Digital tools thus do not upset the relationship to knowledge or studies.

Students in the same group, who know each other, carry out a division of the work of learning knowledge among themselves, i.e. they divide up the different tasks to be done, which are not all considered as interesting or important. For example, I have observed in the classrooms the division of oral participation work. Note-taking is one of the tasks to be carried out in knowledge work, which can be assigned to a few members of the group, which is facilitated by digital tools. This is what these students are saying:

> "[…] so we have groups on Facebook, and there are several of them that distribute the work, and there are groups, whether it's the whole promotion or group 3 in particular, and we manage to stay organized, especially for the lecture courses" (L1 Sociology student).

> "We have a group on Facebook to put handouts or, for example, the courses that some… There are some courses where some [students] have not taken too many notes […]. We help each other. There is one who prints out the assignments from previous years and corrects them; […] so we really work with each other. So we really do a group work, we really help each other. By giving the handouts, by giving everyone's notes, for example, if I took notes on a class, but I'm not sure it's super complete, other people can add their notes, to see, to complete each other, etc. Some people scan their notes to help others" (L1 Science student).

Some Sociology students also tell me how they distributed the presence in class during a period of strike by university students, by instructing some of them to go to class while the others were on strike and then sharing classes via digital networks.

The division of labor between the members of a profession, or here of an activity such as learning knowledge, always has a moral component (Hughes (1971) refers to the moral division of labor). Not all tasks are as noble and are not assigned equally to all participants. For example, it is more often girls who are entrusted with note-taking work, as they are considered more reliable in this respect. In addition, not all participants are included in the same way, because they are not judged (morally) in the same way.

As a result, not all documents and information are systematically disseminated to everyone. Students report that they reserve them for students whose moral behavior they approve of. They build moral judgments about other students. There are two categories of people to whom all courses and information can be given: first, those who are usually diligent, who obviously work and who are likely to contribute themselves to the exchanges (e.g. those who will provide their own note-taking); second, those who have good reasons (reasons considered acceptable) for not coming to class, mainly those who are sick or have a job, but who are present whenever they can be.

Paradoxically, therefore, distance and dematerialized exchanges of knowledge are closely linked to being present in class (we have seen that they do not replace its importance), and because this presence allows the construction of relationships between students and the determination of "good" partners with whom it is possible to exchange.

The use – for the circulation of knowledge and the definition of what to learn – of digital tools is ultimately one element among others that contributes to the student perspective. This student "perspective" refers to how students define what they should do, in what order, in what way. As Howard Becker, Geer, Hughes and Strauss (1961) have shown regarding the work of medical students, students collectively define what is useful to learn or not and how they should use it[6]. It can be said that socio-digital networks or digital platforms contribute to the creation of the student perspective.

6 The students' perspective refers to both the level and direction they give to their efforts (Becker and Geer 1997). Based on the concept of *perspective* defined by Mead (1963), Becker *et al.* (1961) focus in their study of medical students on student group perspectives: "perspective […] are coordinated views and plans of action people follow in problematic situations" (p. 33). The definition of the *perspective* they use is specified as follows: "We use the term perspective to refer to a coordinated set of ideas and actions a person uses in dealing with some problematic situation, to refer to a person's ordinary way of thinking and feeling and acting in such a situation" (p. 34).

16.6. Conclusion

In conclusion, this chapter aimed to show, through a specific case, how the widespread digitalization of society could transform knowledge at university. By looking concretely at how students work with university knowledge, i.e. what they write, what they seek to learn, the exercises they do or do not do, we can see how they define, concretely, the knowledge they will learn. We then note that certain digital practices modify the conceptions of this work of knowledge. The knowledge worked is therefore not the same, because the conditions of this work have changed. This approach can be extended to the study of other areas of university knowledge: for example, how do professors work with knowledge to teach it? How do researchers produce knowledge in laboratories? (David 2017).

16.7. References

Becker, H.S. (1970). *Sociological Work: Method and Substance*. Aldine, Chicago.

Becker, H.S. (1998). *Tricks of the Trade: How to Think About Your Research While You're Doing It*. The University of Chicago Press, Chicago.

Becker, H.S. and Geer, B. (1997). La culture étudiante dans les facultés de médecine. In *Les sociologues de l'éducation américains et britanniques. Présentation et choix de textes*, Forquin, J.-C. (ed.). De Boeck Université, Brussels, 271–283.

Becker, H.S., Geer, B., Hughes, E.C., and Strauss, A.C. (1961). *Boys in White: Student Culture in Medical School*. University of Chicago Press, Chicago.

Burban, F., Cottier, P., and Michaut, C. (2013). Les usages numériques des lycéens affectent-ils leur temps de travail personnel ? *Sticef*, 20. Available at: http://sticef.univ-lemans.fr/num/vol2013/05-burban-cren/sticef_2013_NS_burban_05.htm.

Chapoulie, J.-M. (2000). Le travail de terrain, l'observation des actions et des interactions, et la sociologie. *Sociétés contemporaines*, 40(1), 5–27.

David, M. (2016). Pratiques pédagogiques et autonomie des étudiants de LI. *Inter Pares*, 115–122. Available at: https://halshs.archives-ouvertes.fr/halshs-01343114/document.

David, M. (2017). Les savoirs comme construction collective. Enquête au lycée général et en première année à l'université. PhD thesis, University of Nantes, Nantes.

Glaser, B.G. and Strauss, A. (1967). *The Discovery of Grounded Theory: Strategies for Qualitative Research*. Aldine de Gruyter, New York.

Hughes, E.C. (1971). *The Sociological Eye: Selected Papers*. Aldine-Atherton, Chicago.

Mead, G.H. (1963). *L'Esprit, le soi et la société*. Presses universitaires de France, Paris.

Mercklé, P. and Octobre, S. (2012). La stratification sociale des pratiques numériques des adolescents. *RESET. Recherches en Sciences Sociales sur Internet*, 1. Available at: https://journals.openedition.org/reset/129.

Roche, M. (2015). Les étudiants, le numérique et la réussite universitaire. Master's thesis, University of Nantes, Nantes.

Roy, D. (1952). Quota restriction and goldbricking in a machine shop. *American Journal of Sociology*. 57, 427–442.

17

Towards a Generalization of Digital Technology in Education?

Seeing the majority of people consulting their multifunctional phones on public transport, children communicating with each other by email while in the same room and young people's rooms turning into places where they watch, mostly individually, films, series and videos online for several hours a week (Thoër *et al.* 2015), there is no doubt about the importance of digital technologies in the information and communication practices of modern societies. Workplaces change with technological developments and living spaces change as new technologies are integrated, or traditional elements are connected to the Internet, as highlighted by the work on the Internet of Things (Saleh 2017), which is considered to be "at the heart of global anthropogenic technological transformation" (Noyer 2017, p. 2). Beyond environments, it is indeed human relations that are changing according to the uses of digital technologies, both in the workplace and in the private sphere, to the point of encouraging the implementation of strategies to manage their borders (Jauréguiberry 2014; Roudaut and Jullien 2017).

The rapid development of these technologies and their widespread use in society and daily activities are such that the questions raised by the evolution of "machines and people" (Linard 1990) are no longer reserved for science fiction, and Schwab (2017) considers that digital technology is at the root of a fourth industrial revolution. It is important here to understand digital technology, and the phenomenon of the transition to digital technology called "digitalization", not only as a reproduction technique that differs from analog, but also as a technological change that marks our daily environments and practices: "these are no longer tools at the service of old practices, but an environment in which we are immersed, which

Chapter written by Cathia PAPI.

determines and shapes our world and our culture" (Vitali-Rosati 2014). But what about a particular area of society, namely education?

In order to suggest possible answers to this question, we will first propose to anchor it in the field of educational sciences by briefly recalling the questions concerning the use of information and communication technologies (ICT) in teaching and learning. The issue that is raised will lead us to continue the reflection by focusing on two distinct cases of ICT integration and the evolution of techno-pedagogical practices: that of the international *Innovative School* program and that of *Ontario's e-Learning Strategy*. We will then come back to these two cases to come up with some elements of observations and discussion.

17.1. The place of technology in education: an old issue that is still relevant today

Each new technology is seen as full of promise in terms of educational change: whether it is to enable more massive teaching or – on the contrary – to individualize more, to promote accessibility or to learn more easily, there is no shortage of opportunities. Thus, in 1922, Edison already envisioned cinema as a means of revolutionizing education by considerably increasing the effectiveness of learning (Lebrun 2007). Nevertheless, research generally highlights that technologies which have been really and sustainably integrated into education are rarer than expected, and that they are generally those that conform to pedagogical practices prior to their emergence (Marquet and Dinet 2003; Papi and Glikman 2015).

Education thus seems to evolve more slowly than society as a whole. Indeed, despite political incentives that most often take the form of equipment financing, it is often noted that the use of technologies in the classroom is less common. The non-use of ICTs is generally explained by their lack of relevance (Kellner *et al.* 2010; Smith 2010; Tsatsou 2010), perceived risks of their use (Chaptal 2007; Larose *et al.* 2002), the instrumental conflicts that hinder them (Papi 2012) or the fact that the ideologies they represent run counter to the values promoted by individuals (Jauréguiberry 2014; Ritchel 2011; von Pape and Martin 2010), hence the succession between waves of hopes for techno-pedagogical innovation and the prevalence of rather traditional conceptions of courses and educational practices (Cuban 1983; Glikman 2002).

However, the fact that digital technology is tending to become widespread in modern societies[1], in most activities of daily life – both professional and social – for everyone from an early age, seems likely to break with the simple logic of introducing technologies on an *ad-hoc* basis and bring about a real change. To what extent, then, does the place taken by digital technology lead to changes in education?

Research shows that the social uses of technologies do not naturally translate into educational practices (Baron 2014; Fluckiger 2008; Papi 2015). We thus hypothesize that, although so-called digital technologies occupy an increasing place in society and are the source of pressure to integrate them into education, a generalization of digital technology can only take place within the framework of mechanisms (Papi 2014) that include not only technical but also pedagogical and well-articulated institutional dimensions.

We propose to introduce avenues for reflection based on two case studies in order to put forward a number of elements that make it possible to highlight certain obstacles and levers that are characteristic of the place of digital technology in education. We will therefore start by briefly describing the two projects concerned.

17.2. Field and survey methodology

Since 2007, programs called *Innovative Schools* have emerged, supported by Microsoft, which (in order to find out the effects) has funded research coordinated by Stanford Research Institute (SRI) International in collaboration with researchers located in the 12 countries in which a school was involved in this program. Each selected school wanted to improve education according to the learning considered necessary in the 21st Century, and could adapt this program according to its own objectives and the local and national constraints encountered. To do this, they were exposed to the "6i process" (Figure 17.1).

This process is similar to a project management process in which the needs or problems encountered are used to think about solutions, implement them and then evaluate their effects iteratively according to the limits or new challenges encountered. In France, the primary school selected to participate in the program had the objective of working on the organization of the school, its infrastructure, and the interactions between teachers, pupils and parents. In order to study the changes at work in this particular school, in 2009, we conducted interviews with the Microsoft

1 We do not ignore the digital divides that mark important differences in ICT infrastructure, equipment, use, skills and representations across and within societies, but we do not have room here to enter into these distinctions.

manager, the school principal and teachers who agreed to participate in the research: seven interviews in total. We also conducted three focus groups with students and observed 10 courses from different disciplines and levels.

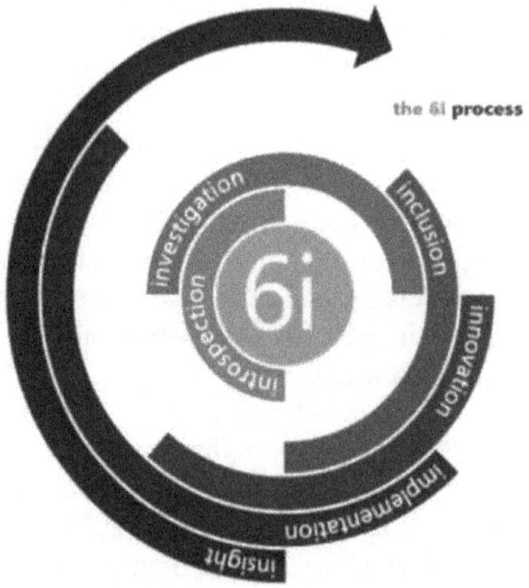

Figure 17.1. *6i Process (Microsoft Corporation, 2009) . For a color version of this figure, see www.iste.co.uk/george/digitalization1.zip*

2007 also marked the beginning of a provincial strategy for the deployment of digital technology in elementary and secondary education in Ontario. Indeed, the provincial Ministry of Education then decided to develop online education at the secondary level and the use of digital educational resources in elementary and secondary schools. To this end, teams were created within the ministry, and institutions were solicited to produce resources or support schools that had a provincial Learning Management System (LMS), which provided access to a Virtual Learning Environment (VLE); the Ontario Educational Resource Bank (OEB); and the Ontario Learning Community (OLC). From the mid-2010s onwards, the deployment of digital technology has been gradually linked to the desire to change education in order to promote the development of "21st Century skills" (critical thinking, creativity, communication, collaboration, learning to learn, global citizenship), again linked to digital technology, in that techno-pedagogical devices are considered so integrative that technology and pedagogy no longer seem to be considered separately[2]. In 2017, we conducted a survey to get an initial overview of the

2 It must be recognized that the integration of digital technology in education is no longer an objective in itself. In fact, in Ontario, 80% of students have already used a computer as part of their learning in kindergarten (Bennett 2017).

situation 10 years after the implementation of the e-learning strategy. To this end, we conducted interviews (46 in total) with people working in the Ministry of Education, consortia, school boards and schools (principals and teaching body). We also had the opportunity to observe two courses and participate in two meetings lasting a few days aimed at training and sharing within the community.

In both surveys, we were the only participating researchers, which allowed us to have a good knowledge of the fields that were explored. All the collected data were processed manually, according to the themes emerging in terms of techno-pedagogical practices and activities, leadership, training and support.

17.3. Towards techno-pedagogical evolutions but not without limits

The two cases studied are very different from each other. Indeed, on the French side, only one school participated in this project (the other eleven schools being located in other countries) supported by Microsoft and studied by the SRI. It should also be pointed out that Microsoft did not finance the equipment of schools and did not provide technology, but only supported the implementation of the 6i process. On the Ontario side, elementary and secondary schools across the province were encouraged to evolve with a variety of material and human resources at their disposal. In addition, the two surveys are eight years apart. However, there are many common points observed regarding the deployment of digital technology and the evolution of techno-pedagogical practices.

17.4. The development of active pedagogies that integrate digital technologies

In both cases, we found that students are encouraged to acquire the knowledge identified in the curricula, while developing 21st Century[3] skills through activities that made them work more in groups and use a greater variety of technologies than in traditional teaching. Many educational activities thus involve the consideration of various online resources[4], applications and technologies in a variety of situations.

3 For more details, see the Ministère de l'Éducation de l'Ontario (2016). Compétences du XXIe siècle. Document de réflexion. Available at: https://pedagogienumeriqueenaction.cforp.ca/wp-content/uploads/2016/02/Ontario-21st-century-competencies-foundation-FINAL-EN_AODA_EDUGAINS_Feb-19_16.pdf.

4 In the case of Ontario, beyond the resources, there are even entirely online courses that are offered in secondary education.

For example, with regard to written and oral language knowledge and skills, in the French primary school, students were invited to report on the dance performance in which one of their classmates participated by reporting, in groups, using the media of their choice (press article, radio interview, video). The work thus covered both the language and the use of technologies and applications related to the chosen medium (word processing, video editing or audio recording application, etc.) and involved developing collaborative skills between the students within each group. Similarly, in an Ontario elementary school, we were able to witness diction and writing work through a reading and transcription application. The students worked in pairs and answered questions by, when necessary, reading aloud the novel they were working on in class so that the quotations could be written automatically. After that, it was necessary to check that the transcription was correct. In both cases, students were encouraged to use technologies to facilitate written or oral language work, learning to work together, spreading out in different parts of the classroom so as not to disturb their classmates.

Observation of these activities, as well as others not mentioned here, has shown that, as research in the field has always demonstrated, the use of ICTs is far from innate, so much so that teachers must intervene to explain how applications that are more or less easily mastered by students work. It has also been observed that the unexpected or misunderstood behavior of some applications has caused astonishment, even amusement or irritation, and that some unrest has sometimes gripped the students concerned. Finally, for these and many other exemplary activities, it is important to note that it is not so much a question of pedagogical innovation as such, but rather of using modern technologies to rethink active pedagogy. To take just one example, the idea of having students write a press article did not wait for word processing. It was already in use in Freinet's pedagogy, with handwritten text that was later printed using old mechanical printing systems. However, current technologies offer new contributions in the sense that they not only enable a task to be carried out, but can also assist the teacher in certain functions.

Indeed, word processing can draw attention to potential errors to encourage verification before the teacher reads the text; similarly, the voice dictation system allows the student to identify his or her speech difficulties and seek to improve them without waiting for his or her reading turn, or being intimidated into doing so in front of the whole class. This allows teachers to devote more time to providing personalized support to groups or individuals. The pedagogical differentiation valued in both cases seems to be able to take advantage of digital technology in many ways. However, the introduction of a new application or technology arouses great enthusiasm, involving classroom management work to restore calm and redirect students' interest towards pedagogical activity, while waiting for its use to become commonplace. Thus, either such uses are repeated and gradually integrated into teaching and learning practices, or they remain exceptional and act as diversionary moments before being abandoned.

17.5. Non-generalized practices

Although different uses of technologies were developed in pedagogical situations that are often more active than in front-line teaching methods, it should be noted that this never concerns all of the practices implemented in a course or school. In other words, if the teachers who are most likely to give us interviews or welcome us into their classrooms implement original or even innovative practices, by including digital technologies, other teachers retain their ways of doing things or change them more slowly. It appears that, in an *a priori* surprising manner, some seem to have little knowledge of the dynamics at work, namely the 6i process in the French case or the "e-learning strategy" in the Ontario case. Others are more informed, but do not use what is available to them. For example, in Ontario, some teachers seem reluctant to connect to the VLE and have students connect with an identifier; they find this environment less user-friendly than others to which they had previously become accustomed. However, some seem to make partial use of it to satisfy a specific function, such as the students' work submissions portal. It would seem that non-usage thus does not come so much from a critical conception of the use of technologies in education such as the one potentially developed by researchers (George 2014), as from the perceived lack of relevance.

Thus, the overview actors point out that the VLE and the Ontario Educational Resource Bank (OERB) are used much more in high school, because of the access they offer to online courses, than at elementary level, where Google or Microsoft applications seem more attractive. In fact, the stakeholders interviewed report that, even though EAV and OERB are used less in elementary school than in high school, a variety of platforms or applications are called on, such that more pedagogical activities that include technologies are used in elementary school than in high school. One reason for this may be that in primary education, a teacher takes care of an entire class, which makes it possible to work in the form of projects integrating different subjects and technologies. We also observed this in the French case, where some activities were not only multidisciplinary, but also included students of different classes and ages in groups, allowing them to work harder on the skills they needed, which would seem difficult to envisage in secondary education.

17.6. Barriers and levers to the widespread use of digital technology in education

Although the added value of ICT uses in educational practices has not been scientifically proven, political will to develop them is often asserted, but often results in incentives or even financing for equipment that is used rarely or does not bring pedagogical change, as highlighted by research on the subject (Glikman 2002; Jacquinot-Delaunay 2008; Lebrun 2007; Linard 2003; Mangenot 2015; Marquet and Dinet 2003). In fact, techno-pedagogical innovations seem to be difficult to impose from above and generally come more from teachers from whom they will more or less spread, as Charlier *et al.* (2006) point out when talking about "enclave", "bridgehead" and "anchored practice". However, while the obstacles and reticences to changes in pedagogical practices and the inclusion of ICTs have often been studied, as we were able to highlight in the first section by referring to some work on non-use of technologies, the elements that are favorable to them are more rarely identified. Indeed, even though, in the two cases presented, generalization is not yet complete, it seems possible to identify key elements that have contributed to the emergence and some diffusion of new practices.

First of all, in order to not confine ourselves to individual practices, it seems favorable that the encouraged developments should be part of a clearly defined and defended vision at the institutional level. In other words, in order to not confine oneself to policies of less pedagogical importance, it is necessary to rely on a finely thought-out vision of education, taking into account all educational actors and phenomena, ranging from curriculum design to the evaluation of learning, including privileged pedagogical approaches. This implies starting by determining the real needs of education stakeholders and, in particular, of teachers, as well as the existing mechanisms and their limitations. This is what French schools were invited to do as part of the 6i process and what the Ontario Ministry of Education did by conducting a province-wide survey. Starting from the needs encountered in the field can help to somewhat limit the influence of industry on policy and, consequently, on equipment policies. However, some influence remains to the extent that industries in the field are seeking to create needs. In the French case, Microsoft was at the root of an initiative to support the emergence of new techno-pedagogical practices, in the hope that they would lead to the opening of new markets for these products. In the Ontario case, the training events of the various educational stakeholders were also venues for the presentation stands of various companies promoting their educational products.

Moreover, whatever the expected changes, it seems essential to involve the actors concerned from the outset so that they do not suffer the evolutions, but generate them themselves and can modulate them according to their knowledge of the field. Thus, within the framework of the French school, the principal and some teachers voluntarily submitted their applications to participate in the "innovative school" program. For the province of Ontario, the guideline is provided by the Ministry of Education, but it is Ontario's current teachers who are recruited for a period of time and trained to create educational resources that will be posted online, to teach online or to participate in the training and coaching of other teachers.

In fact, much more than the material investments made on an *ad-hoc* basis, it is in the field of support training that real investments seem necessary. These surveys show that regular support for school principals and the teaching body is essential if they are to change their techno-pedagogical practices, as Landry's work on media education in Quebec (Landry and Basque 2015) also highlights. This training can be envisaged in a multifaceted way during the initial training of teachers, then throughout their careers through moments of in-service or virtual training, participation in events promoting the sharing of practices or individual support for schools and teachers in their projects, in and outside the classroom, by other teachers who are experts in techno-pedagogical practices. Such training would also benefit from being accompanied by the development of a critical conception of these same practices so that they are not generalized beyond the framework in which they are relevant, as Craig and Amernic (2006) note regarding the use of slide shows.

17.7. Conclusion

While digital technologies are present in most everyday environments and activities in modern societies, their place is often more modest in education. In fact, teachers have not often been trained in their pedagogical uses, and their imagined and valued potentials are not apparent to the eyes of practitioners for whom they do not necessarily seem relevant. Similarly, young people, who are more familiar with these technologies than previous generations, do not transpose their social habits of research, communication, collaboration, etc., into their learning practices. The development of teaching and learning practices integrating digital technologies is therefore not self-evident and does not seem to be decreed either, as evidenced by the narrow scope of equipment policies, but involves complex mechanisms supported by a strong institutional vision and commitment as well as solid and critical teacher training to ensure sound practices.

Indeed, while various elements contributing to techno-pedagogical developments have been identified, the question of their relevance remains, insofar as there is a clear lack of research demonstrating – using generalizable data as evidence – the benefits of certain techno-pedagogical practices on learning. Beyond the idea of the generalization of digital technology in education, it is therefore necessary to question the carriers and scopes of such ambitions.

17.8. References

Baron, G.-L. (2014). Élèves, apprentissages et "numérique" : regard rétrospectif et perspectives. *Recherches en éducation*, 18(2), 91–103.

Bennett, P.W. (2017). Digital learning in Canadian K-12 schools: a review of critical issues, policy, and practice. In *Handbook on Digital Learning for K-12 Schools*, Marcus-Quinn, A. and Hourigan, T. (eds). Springer, Cham, 293–315.

Bissonnette, S., Gauthier, C., and Péladeau, N. (2010). Un objet qui manque à sa place : les données probantes dans l'enseignement. *Recherche et formation à l'enseignement : spécificités et interdépendance, Actes de la recherche*, 8, 107–133.

Chaptal, A. (2007). Usages prescrits ou annoncés, usages observés. Réflexions sur les usages scolaires du numérique par les enseignants. *Document numérique*, 10(3), 81–106.

Charlier, B., Deschryver, N., and Peraya, D. (2006). Apprendre en présence et à distance. *Distances et savoirs*, 4(4), 469–496.

Craig, R.J. and Amernic, J. (2006). Power point presentation technology and the dynamics of teaching. *Innovative Higher Education*, 31(3), 147–160.

Cuban, L. (1983). *Teachers and Machines: the Classroom use of Technology Since 1920*. Teacher's College Press, New York.

Fluckiger, C. (2008). L'école à l'épreuve de la culture numérique des élèves. *Revue française de pédagogie*, 163, 51–61.

George, É. (2014). Quelles perspectives critiques pour aborder les TIC ? *tic&société*, 8(1–2). Available at: http://journals.openedition.org/ticetsociete/1365.

Glikman, V. (2002). Apprenants et tuteurs : une approche européenne des médiations humaines. *Éducation permanente*, 3(152), 55–69.

Jacquinot-Delaunay, G. (2008). Accompagner les apprentissages : le tutorat "pièce maîtresse et parent pauvre" des dispositifs de formation médiatisés. In *L'université et les TIC. Chronique d'une innovation annoncée*, Jacquinot-Delaunay, G. and Fichez, E. (eds). De Boeck, Brussels, 179–222.

Jauréguiberry, F. (2014). La déconnexion aux technologies de communication. *Réseaux*, 186(4), 15–49.

Kellner, C., Massou, L. and Morelli, P. (2010). (Re)penser le non-usage des TIC. *Questions de Communication,* 18, 7–20.

Landry, N. and Basque, J. (2015). L'éducation aux médias dans le Programme de formation de l'école québécoise : intégration, pratiques et problématiques. *Revue canadienne de l'éducation*, 38(2), 1–33.

Larose, F., Lenoir, Y., Karsenti, T., and Grenon, V. (2002). Les facteurs sous-jacents au transfert des compétences informatiques construites par les futurs maîtres du primaire sur le plan de l'intervention éducative. *Revue des Sciences de l'Éducation*, 28(2), 265–287.

Lebrun, M. (2007). *Théories et méthodes pédagogiques pour enseigner et apprendre, Quelle place pour les TIC dans l'éducation ?* De Boeck, Brussels.

Linard, M. (1990). *Des machines et des hommes : apprendre avec les nouvelles technologies.* Éditions universitaires, Paris.

Linard, M. (2003). Autoformation, éthique et technologies : enjeux et paradoxes de l'autonomie. In *Autoformation et enseignement supérieur*, Albero, B. (ed.). Hermès-Lavoisier, Paris, 241–263.

Mangenot, F. (2015). Le numérique entre effets de mode et réelle innovation. In *Enseignement/apprentissage des langues et pratiques numériques émergentes*, Potolia, A. and Jamborova Lemay, D. (eds). Éditions des archives contemporaines, Paris, 1–14.

Marquet, P. and Dinet, J. (2003). Un cartable numérique au lycée : éléments de sa genèse instrumentale chez les enseignants et les élèves. In *Conférence EIAH 2003*. Available at: https://www.researchgate.net/publication/36380893_Un_cartable_numerique_au_lycee_elements_de_sa_genese_instrumentale_chez_les_enseignants_et_les_eleves.

Microsoft Corporation (2009). The Microsoft Innovation Schools Program. Year 1 Evaluation Report.

Noyer, J.-M. (2017). The internet of things, the internet of "everything": some remarks on the intensification of the world's digital folding. *Information and Communication*, 17(1).

von Pape, T. and Martin, C. (2010). Non-usage du téléphone portable : au-delà d'une opposition binaire usagers/non-usagers. *Questions de Communication*, 18, 113–144.

Papi, C. (2012). Causes et motifs du non-usage de ressources numériques. *Recherches et éducations*, 6, 127–142.

Papi, C. (2014). *Formation à distance. Dispositifs et interactions.* ISTE Éditions, London.

Papi, C. (2015). Digital spaces: between educational tools and student uses. *Procedia: Social and Behavioral Sciences Journal*, 174, 3757–3764.

Papi, C. and Glikman, V. (2015). Les étudiants entre cours magistraux et usage des TIC. *Distances et médiations des savoirs*, 9. Available at: https://dms.revues.org/1012.

Ritchel, M. (2011). A Silicon Valley school that doesn't compute. *The New York Times*, 22 October. Available at: https://www.nytimes.com/2011/10/23/technology/at-waldorf-school-in-silicon-valley-technology-can-wait.html.

Roudaut, K. and Jullien, N. (2017). Les usages des outils de réseau social par des salariés : des registres privés et professionnels individualisés. *Terminal*, 120. Available at: http://journals.openedition.org/terminal/1610.

Saleh, I. (2017). Internet des objets (IdO) : concepts, enjeux, défis et perspectives. *Information and Communication*, 2(1).

Schwab, K. (2017). *La quatrième révolution industrielle*. Dunod, Paris.

Smith, A. (2010). Home broadband 2010. *Pew Research Center. Internet and Technology*, 11 August. Available at: http://www.pewInternet.org/Reports/2010/Home-Broadband-2010.aspx.

Thoër, C., Millerand, F., Vrignaud, C., Duque, N., and Gaudet, J. (2015). "Sur le web, je regarde des vidéos, des séries et des émissions" : catégorisation et sélection des contenus de divertissement visionnés en ligne par les jeunes de 12 à 25 ans. *Journal of Media, Performing Arts and Cultural Studies*, 2(2), 191–207.

Tsatsou, P. (2010). Pourquoi certains n'adoptent-ils pas l'Internet ? L'influence de la vie quotidienne et de la culture de résistance en Grèce. *Questions de Communication*, 18, 63–88.

Vitali-Rosati, M. (2014). Pour une définition du "numérique". In *Pratiques de l'édition numérique*, Sinatra, M.E. and Vitali-Rosati, M. (eds). Presses de l'Université de Montréal, Montreal, 63–75. Available at: http://www.parcoursnumeriques-pum.ca/pour-une-definition-du-numerique.

18

French Pensioners Facing the Digitalization of Society

In France, the number of Internet users has increased since the democratization of the network some 15 years ago, reaching 87% of Internet users in 2016. While this growth has slowed since the late 2000s for the population as a whole, the use of retirees continues to grow impressively: while 12% of retirees were Internet users in 2006, they accounted for 61% in 2016 (Croutte *et al.* 2016). However, at the same time, they still correspond to the age group that is least likely to be connected (Charmakeh 2015).

Despite these various observations, it appears that the digital practices of this category of the population remain poorly studied in France in the fields of sociology and information and communication sciences, in a context where research focuses more on another age group, that of adolescents and young adults (Lobet-Maris 2011).

However, the relationship of the oldest generations to Information and Communication Technologies (ICTs) is a particularly rich field of research for the sociology of uses. Indeed, members of the baby boom generation, now young retirees, have seen computers, and their connected versions, gradually settle into their social environment over the course of their adult lives. Because of this particular temporality, their adoption of these ICTs has been voluntary or forced, or has not taken place, due to many socio-economic parameters that have their roots in the biographical trajectories of individuals, particularly in relation to gender or profession. This situation has therefore led to significant disparities in ownership and now raises the question of the integration of this category of people into digital

---

Chapter written by Lucie DELIAS.

culture, in the current context of the increasing digitalization of society, particularly with regard to services related to the management of daily life.

To address this issue, it is necessary to take into account social phenomena related to generation, as well as those related to age, which, like gender, "race" or class, determine a set of social representations from which specific forms of oppression may result. In the case of age, these oppressions are referred to as *ageism* (Butler 1969). In particular, the use or non-use of connected computing by retired people is linked to a set of social expectations, or even to forms of normative injunctions associated with their age and position in the life cycle.

While our research has allowed us to identify significant and varied uses by seniors, regardless of their skill level, we have chosen here to focus instead on the injunctions to integrate the digital world that weigh on them, as a group that constitutes one of the last frontiers of the Western "digital divide" that should be bridged. In this context, incentives to equip ourselves with connected computing and to "get started" come from different groups and institutions, such as the local social network or companies. The State, for its part, through the increasing digitalization of its services, tends to transform these incentives into a *de facto* obligation to participate in the digital world.

These injunctions are a theme that emerged strongly from our survey work, as part of ongoing doctoral research, for which 37 interviews were conducted with people of the baby boom generation living in the Paris region and mostly between 65 and 75 years of age, as well as observation sessions in three associations offering computer literacy courses for seniors and welcoming participants with varied socio-economic profiles.

This text, more than the final results, aims to provide an analytical framework and avenues for reflection on the integration of retired people into digital culture from a critical perspective. After the presentation of some theoretical points of reference, we will characterize the injunctions addressed to them from a social, identity and practical point of view, by developing more specifically the emblematic case of the dematerialization of public administrative services in France.

18.1. Contemporary digital culture and its implications for the identity and social integration of retired people

18.1.1. *Digital culture, seniors and "successful aging"*

As early as 2002, Serge Proulx proposed defining digital culture as a "new normative environment [...] made up of rules, procedures and protocols" (Proulx

2002, p. 189), broad and diffuse, guiding practices and conditioning forms of know-how, as well as know-how related to ICT.

As a result of developments in "Web 2.0", it can be assumed that this digital culture has evolved in two complementary directions. On the one hand, Internet usage has increased and has become "ordinary". The know-how and interpersonal skills associated with it no longer concern only a limited number of amateurs and their appropriation has become more and more common and essential. On the other hand, there is a growing standardization of the features of this culture, as companies that dominate the Web define how they use it based on their own standards and interests.

Internet sociology research has shown that the dominant contemporary digital culture has developed around exploration and participation (Pasquier 2018; Proulx 2017), each of these aspects requiring specific skills, necessary for Internet users to exploit their potential and, above all, to derive social benefits. For example, in the context of the development of a "Web Registration" (Casilli, cited in Proulx 2017), participation is a prerequisite for the use of many online services, implying that the user must be able and willing to create an ever-increasing number of accounts based on personal information. On digital social networks – but not limited to them only – participation takes the form of managing self-presentation and digital identity, which is difficult to avoid if you want to use these platforms. However, not all Internet users are able to master this socio-technical framework (Flichy 2008), and the theoretical models that define digital culture sometimes tend to assume the existence of a generic user, who is assumed to be not only willing to adopt their values, but is also competent with different interfaces.

Hélène Bourdeloie and Nathalie Boucher-Petrovitch (2014) showed in particular to what extent the model of expressivism, according to which "ICTs conceal expressive potentialities allowing individuals to perform their identity and, *ipso facto*, to reconfigure their socially assigned identity in favor of an individually shaped identity", presented limitations in explaining the relationship of older people to ICTs. Indeed, the ability of users to appropriate online modes of expression depends on the social relationships of class, gender and age that pre-date digital practices. According to the authors, an age-related social assignment produces tensions in the use of ICTs by seniors: on the one hand, a tension between wanting to appropriate technological objects without necessarily having the necessary skills to do so; on the other hand, a tension between the desire to "stay up-to-date" while remaining faithful to one's values (in particular, a significant number of seniors are very reluctant to proceed with self-exposure on digital social networks). Thus, for older people, the expressive model encounters two types of limitations: one related to skills – knowing how to use devices and navigate sites – and the other related to values – adhering to the norms of digital culture to be able to integrate it.

In addition, addressing the relationship of baby boomers to digital retirement also implies placing it in broader social expectations for this population group, namely those of "successful aging" and its corollary, "active retirement". The ideal of "successful aging" emerged in the 1970s in relation to the new category of the "Third Age" (Laslett 1989) and is rooted in a set of discourses derived from the social policies of old age (Lenoir 1979), gerontology and the mainstream media. According to this model, retirement is no longer a time of rest, but a time of discovery and development: seniors, who are now aging in better health, enjoy life outside the home through social, cultural and even political activities. In line with this idea, while older people have long been considered "outside of the modern world" (Caradec 1999), it is now expected that they will be interested in ICT and connected to the Internet.

In the same way as expressivism, the model of successful aging has been accused of being part of a neoliberal vision of individualism that promotes a rational individual and a "self-entrepreneur" (Voirol 2011). Certainly, successful aging has positive implications, since it promotes a better integration of older people into society, but it also tends to erase the fact that being an active and connected retired person does not depend solely on an individual's will (Katz and Calasanti 2015). As Bernadette Puijalon and Jacqueline Trincaz (2014) point out, when they analyze the discourses of magazines aimed at seniors, "since the means of action are within everyone's reach, aging appears as a neglect, a weakness. To stay young, it is enough to simply decide to stay young because 'old age is in your head'" (p. 69). Thus, the risks of sanctions and exclusion are significant for retirees who do not have the means or desire to comply with this model.

18.1.2. *The identity dimension of the use of connected computing: getting started and staying involved*

The increasing digitalization of society has the consequence, for individuals in general and retired people in particular, of associating the use of connected computing with social integration, in both the practical and symbolic sense. As Proulx (2017) points out, "gestures of participation in the digital world are for users the equivalent of an adherence to modernity". The Crédoc figures show that this symbolic association is constantly increasing as society's digitalization increases: in 2009, 54% of French people thought that Internet access was important to feel integrated into society, compared to 65% in 2016. Among seniors, these figures increased from 41% to 63% for those aged 60–69, and from 33% to 50% for those aged 70 and over (Croutte *et al.* 2016).

This aspect is particularly evident in our interviews with people with low digital autonomy, in modes of enunciation that seem to depend on the gender of the people surveyed. For retired men, who have often been very involved in their professional careers, trying to master connected computing is a way of feeling integrated into the world "as it is" when work can no longer play this role, as Gérard expresses it[1]:

> "I'll be near the cemetery the day I can't follow this anymore, it's over. No, but I'll say it, I'm already quite old, I'm over 70, so it may make you laugh, but it's true. And we feel it in many areas. I no longer have the activity level I used to have, I was certainly one of the bank's most brilliant wealth managers, but today I'm overwhelmed" (former asset manager, born in 1945).

Women, however, are more likely to express a sense of shame or guilt about feeling overwhelmed by ICTs and being "out of the loop". Geneviève explains that she is "not very proud" to admit, in her various social circles, that she does not use the Internet:

> "*So you feel some kind of pressure to get started?*
>
> Yes, that's right. Do you know how I recognize it? When I'm in an association or with other people, I don't dare say… I end up saying: 'Send me an SMS and not an e-mail, because I don't know how to do it'. So there's pressure. But its' true that I'm not very proud to have to say that I don't know how to use a computer. There are few people like me around my age" (former stay-at-home mother, born in 1941).

Karima (former caregiver, born in 1940) feels embarrassed to ask questions about ICT vocabulary she doesn't know, especially when she stops to ask us during the interview: "Tell me, what is WiFi? I look stupid…".

This identity dimension at play in the control of connected computing is validated and reinforced by the various incentives to "get involved" that the least autonomous retired people receive from their environment, in a more or less direct way. These injunctions may come from those around them – in particular, their adult children tend to offer them equipment without necessarily taking the time to explain how they work and how to support their uses – or from Web and technology companies that are beginning to realize the potential market of baby boomers and promote products that specifically target them.

1 All first names have been changed.

Among these different sources of injunctions to get online, we will focus in the following on the one that the State is setting up through the dematerialization of its administrative services. As it conditions access to rights and citizenship, the use of the Internet is in this case more of an obligation than an incentive.

18.2. E-government: a *de facto* obligation to use digital tools

18.2.1. *Outlines of the dematerialization of administrative services*

The dematerialization of public administrative services is not a new phenomenon. In France, the theme of e-government has met with some political success since the mid-1990s (Bacache-Beauvallet *et al.* 2011; Dagiral 2011) and has accelerated in recent years. The current government plans to completely dematerialize all administrative procedures by 2022, with the aim of "simplifying" the administrative system, as well as saving staff. Thus, a large part of the procedures related to the *Pôle Emploi* (French governmental agency which registers the unemployed, etc.), the *Caisse d'allocation familiale* (family-oriented sector of the French social security system) and the *Sécurité sociale* (French social security system) are already digitalized. On the contrary, online tax returns are becoming more widespread and will affect the entire population within four years. Persons who can justify a lack of connection or an inability to complete the online procedures may be exempted, but the government has not yet specified the details of the procedure, in particular the criteria to justify this inability[2].

In addition, there has been an increase in the dematerialization of many administrative tasks in everyday life, such as sending and paying energy or telephone bills, which, unlike cultural or leisure services accessible online, are essential for users. It is mainly the dematerialization of this type of service that gives retired people the feeling that they have to integrate into the digital culture, whether they like it or not. Thus, a whole semantic field of obligation, often expressed in terms of fatality, is found in the discourse of the interviewees questioned on their use of the Internet, as Adam expresses it:

> "Yes, but the thing is, I don't like it, but my friends, they said to me: 'You have to!' […] I'm very resistant too, I said, 'No, no, no!' But at the same time I see that now everyone needs it. Even to complete the document [for retirement], you need it, so you can't say no" (former kitchen helper, born in 1951).

2 See in particular: Gouvernement.fr (October 2, 2017). *Le Grand Plan d'investissement 2018–2022*. Available at: https://www.gouvernement.fr/action/le-grand-plan-d-investissement-2018-2022.

While it is Adam's friends who push him to become an Internet user, it is Patricia's daughter who manages to convince her. In both cases, the arguments of the relatives are validated by the fact that the use of the Internet is now inevitable:

> "*So this computer, it was your daughter who gave it to you, and you accepted it even if you didn't really like it initially.*
>
> Well, at the time she tried to convert me, she did well. She said to me, 'Mom, nowadays you can't do anything without computers'. I now see, when you call to request paperwork, the first thing they say is: 'Do you mind if we send it to you by email?'" (former teacher, born in 1950).

18.2.2. *Working class pensioners and digital dependency*

This increasingly important dematerialization of administrative services tends to create a context of "digital dependence" (Beauchamp 2012). Like the "car dependency" in some territories, a fully digitalized environment makes users dependent on the Internet connection to access certain essential resources. This digital dependence makes people who are in a situation of digital non-use more vulnerable, in the broad sense understood by Fabien Granjon (2010), as "all practices and individuals whose characteristic is to have a material 'incapacity' and/or a practical 'incapability' to benefit from the economic, social and/or cultural potential that can be offered by the use of connected computing".

Non-use is more common among people with low (although to a lesser extent) educational and economic capital (Granjon *et al.* 2009); non-users are therefore not exclusively "seniors", but age tends to amplify this phenomenon. Thus, the situation is particularly delicate for retired people from the working classes, as shown by our observations in introductory Internet courses for "seniors".

First, to explain their motivations for participating in introductory courses, almost all retired people from the least privileged classes cite as a priority that they need to learn how to carry out administrative procedures online, while middle and upper class retired people more often mention leisure activities or the desire to carry out new digital-related projects as ways to spend their free time.

This can be explained by the fact that, while public authorities continue to dematerialize their services, very few concrete solutions are currently proposed to overcome the closure of counters and support non-users of the Internet. It is then the local associations that take over to try to train the most disadvantaged retired people, without always having the necessary means to do so. First, empowering less competent people would require several hours of intensive training per week, where most courses offer two to three hours of weekly lessons; on the contrary, taking steps on behalf of users, and thus accessing their passwords and personal information, raises obvious ethical issues related to confidentiality.

In addition, there is the management of symbolic violence generated by situations of digital dependence, which is experienced on a daily basis by these users. This is what Sylvain, responsible for cultural and social activities in an association in a popular district of Paris, describes. One of their roles is to help retired people in the neighborhood to fill out their administrative documents, knowing that they often have an immigrant background and sometimes have difficulty mastering French:

> "I remember a gentleman who couldn't read and write, who had probably never been to an administration unaccompanied, who always made someone call someone for him to get a piece of paperwork, and who, by doing so, had perceived the workings of the process, what it took to get the paperwork. He knew phone numbers, but I had to explain to him that it doesn't work that way anymore… He said: 'But yes, retirement is 3960, I know, I know', I told him: 'I'm just explaining to you that things will move faster with the Internet'. The guy collapsed, he thought, 'Dammit, one more thing I'm not going to understand'. That's the message being sent back to people".

Thus, age and socio-economic situation are cumulative and are at the origin of a condition of dependence and vulnerability produced less by the lack of skills of individuals than by an often unsuitable digital environment.

Patrick, also elderly and one of the interviewees whose profile corresponds more to being "resistant" to digital culture, also points to the generational dimension of this phenomenon. In a cynical but nevertheless revealing way, he expresses his perception of a foreign position he occupies vis-à-vis the more recent generations, defined by their familiarity with digital culture:

> "*So you don't do taxes on the Internet yet, but maybe you will?*
>
> It's imminent. They classify age, there's still a tolerance for old people like me. It's a kind of demographic extinction… our age group will disappear, and then there will only be people who are supposedly digitalized" (former press corrector, born in 1950).

18.3. Conclusion

With regard to integration into contemporary digital culture, seniors therefore encounter both diffuse social injunctions, directly linked to the "successful aging" model, and forms of *de facto* obligations arising from administrative dematerialization processes.

Thus, this brief overview, although covering a relatively small sample of urban retirees, made it possible to analyze the particular interactions between age, generation and social class in the context of the digitalization of society. The relationship of retired people with digital culture, far from being anecdotal, is proving to be a fruitful entry point for studying normative injunctions to participate in the digital world.

18.4. References

Bacache-Beauvallet, M., Bounie, D., and François, A. (2011). Existe-t-il une fracture numérique dans l'usage de l'administration en ligne ? *Revue économique*, 62, 215–235.

Beauchamps, M. (2012). Espace urbain et stratification sociale. *RESET*, 1. Available at: https://journals.openedition.org/reset/139.

Bourdeloie, H. and Boucher-Petrovitch, N. (2014). Usages différenciés des TIC chez les seniors au prisme de l'âge, du genre et de la classe sociale. *tic&société*, 8(1–2). Available at: https://journals.openedition.org/ticetsociete/1433.

Butler, R. (1969). Age-ism: Another form of bigotry. *The Gerontologist*, 9(4), 243–246.

Caradec, V. (1999). Vieillissement et usage des technologies. Une perspective identitaire et relationnelle. *Réseaux*, 17(96), 45–95.

Charmarkeh, H. (2015). Les personnes âgées et la fracture numérique de "second degré" : l'apport de la perspective critique en communication. *Revue française des sciences de l'information et de la communication*, 6. Available at: http://journals.openedition.org/rfsic/1294.

Croutte, P., Lautié, S., and Hoibian, S. (2016). Baromètre du numérique. Report, Centre de recherche pour l'étude et l'observation des conditions de vie (Crédoc), Paris.

Dagiral, E. (2011). Administration électronique. *Communications*, 1(88), 9–17.

Flichy, P. (2008). Technique, usage et représentations. *Réseaux*, 148–149(2), 147–174.

Granjon, F. (2010). Le "non-usage" de l'Internet : reconnaissance, mépris et idéologie. *Questions de Communication*, 18. Available at: https://journals.openedition.org/questionsdecommunication/410.

Granjon, F., Lelong, B., and Metzger, J.-L. (eds) (2009). *Inégalités numériques. Clivages sociaux et modes d'appropriation des TIC*. Hermès-Lavoisier, Paris.

Katz, S. and Calasanti, T. (2015). Critical perspectives on successful aging: Does it "appeal more than it illuminates"? *The Gerontologist*, 55(1), 26–33.

Laslett, P. (1989). *A Fresh Map of Life. The Emergence of the Third Age*. Weidenfeld & Nicholson, London.

Lenoir, R. (1979). L'invention du "troisième âge". Constitution du champ des agents de la gestion de la vieillesse. *Actes de la recherche en sciences sociales*, 26–27, 57–82.

Lobet-Maris, C. (2011). Âge et usages informatiques. *Communications*, 1(88), 19–28.

Pasquier, D. (2018). Classes populaires en ligne : des "oubliés" de la recherche ? *Réseaux*, 208–209(2), 9–23.

Proulx, S. (2002). Trajectoires d'usages des technologies de communication : les formes d'appropriation d'une culture numérique comme enjeu d'une "société du savoir". *Annales des télécommunications*, 57(3–4), 180–189.

Proulx, S. (2017). L'injonction à participer au monde numérique. *Communiquer*, 20, 15–27. Available at: https://journals.openedition.org/communiquer/2308.

Puijalon, B. and Trincaz, J. (2014). L'injonction normative au "bien vieillir". In *Vieillesses et Vieillissements. Regards sociologiques*, Hummel, C., Malon, I., and Caradec, V. (eds). Presses universitaires de Rennes, Rennes, 61–72.

Voirol, O. (2011). L'intersubjectivation technique : de l'usage à l'adresse. Pour une théorie critique de la culture numérique. In *Communiquer à l'ère numérique*, Granjon, F. and Denöuel, J. (eds). Presses des Mines, Paris, 127–157.

19

From the Digitalization of Society to the Production of a Biomedicalized Food Culture

This chapter presents some of the conceptual elements and ideas that inform my doctoral research. From a perspective rooted in Cultural Studies, I observe the development of what I theorize as "biomedicalized food culture", made possible by, among other things, the digitalization of society. This research is part of the critical literature emerging from the field of critical studies on food (see, for example, Brady *et al.* 2012; Koç *et al.* 2012), which focuses on theorizing unequal relationships, exclusionary regimes or the normativities and stigmatizations that contribute to the production of contemporary knowledge on food as well as the links between food and bodies.

First, I will present some of the theoretical foundations underlying my critical thinking, largely inspired by the work of Clarke *et al.* (2010) on the biomedicalization of society. I will then define what is meant by "biomedicalized food culture", by referring to some examples to illustrate how it is deployed and materialized in a whole set of knowledge, practices, discourses, etc., by which "healthy" food and contemporary bodies are defined. In so doing, I will present how digitalization contributes to the development of this particular food culture. I will conclude by briefly presenting some of the issues related to how, through this biomedicalized food culture, "healthy" food and the links between food and bodies are redefined.

Chapter written by Myriam DUROCHER.

19.1. The biomedicalization of society

The theorization of biomedicalized food culture is inspired by the writings of Clarke and his colleagues (Clarke *et al.* 2000; Clarke *et al.* 2003; Clarke *et al.* 2010) for whom the biomedicalization of the social field participates in extension of its medicalization[1] and a change in the distribution of biomedical knowledge, reconfiguring the ways in which it deploys and informs its relationship with the living. For Clarke *et al.* (2003), the addition of the prefix *bio* to the term *medicalization* refers to the new possibility of transforming living organisms, both human and non-human, through technoscientific practices and technologies, such as bio-technologies, molecular biology and genomics. These practices make it possible to start from the living itself (e.g. an individual's tissues) and then transform it or even generate new forms of living (e.g. synthetic biology). For Clarke *et al.* (2010), biomedicalization is characterized by different interrelated processes[2] that contribute to redefining the ways in which bodies, health and life itself are understood. While the medicalization of society has fostered the emergence of knowledge and practices aimed at *controlling* medical phenomena such as diseases or injuries, biomedicalization focuses on the transformation of the body through technoscientific interventions from the very beginning. Biomedicalization, thanks to the innovations proposed by the technosciences, opens the door to a desire to improve life according to a preventive logic informed by the urgency of anticipation.

This biomedicalization of society takes place in a biopolitical context which, for Rabinow and Rose (2006), favors a mode of governance of life through life itself. The resulting governance strategies are based on the "objectifying" characterization of living organisms, i.e. the development of a whole set of techniques, strategies and systems for categorization and classification based on the measurable and evaluable characteristics of living organisms. It is also in this context that new forms of

1 For Clarke *et al.* (2000), the medicalization of the social field refers to the expansion of the jurisdiction of medical practice and its authority across society, generating a new form of social control not only through the medical institution, but also through the development of a medicalized relationship with the living body.

2 For Clarke *et al.* (2010), biomedicalization is achieved through a set of co-constitutive processes: 1) the co-constitution of new knowledge, technologies, services and capital through a new biopolitical economy of medicine, health and disease; 2) the intensification of the importance given to health, particularly oriented towards ideals of improvement through technosciences and the development of increasingly personalized surveillance tools and practices; 3) the technoscientific transformations of biomedical practices where interventions for treatment or improvement are increasingly supported by technosciences; 4) the transformation of the ways in which biomedical information is produced, disseminated and used; and 5) the bodily transformations that occur from within rather than through the addition of external elements.

subjectivity are produced, where injunctions to self-responsibility and health care intersect, with a view to prevention and risk management:

> "In this context, individuals move from being passive 'profane' patients to being active consumers responsible for their own biomedical future. Whether it is about reducing risks through self-monitoring and lifestyle changes, or submitting to expert testing and control, the onus is on the individual to take what is constructed as crucial biomedical decisions that affect their health" (Clarke *et al.* 2000, p. 23).

Fostered by the increased presence of computer and information technologies that transform the ways in which bodies are understood, mobilized and worked upon, biomedicalization allows the diagnosis, treatment and transformation of the biological from its very materiality, through the adoption of measures deemed appropriate:

> "Health itself and the proper management of chronic illnesses are becoming individual moral responsibilities to be fulfilled through improved access to knowledge, self-surveillance, prevention, risk assessment, the treatment of risk, and the consumption of appropriate self-help/biomedical goods and services" (Clarke *et al.* 2003, p. 162).

In doing so, individuals are encouraged to act and become active consumers, responsible for their health.

19.2. The emergence of a biomedicalized food culture

The notion of *culture* in the expression "biomedicalized food culture" is inspired by the work of Stuart Hall (1980) and is therefore part of a Cultural Studies perspective. Here, culture must be understood as being (re)produced through practices that incorporate and materialize what structures or modulates it. "Culture" is therefore observed in the deployment of a set of knowledge and practices, such as the establishment of policies, programs, phenomena related to popular culture, media, and economic, medical and other practices. The methodological and analytical view I take of the development of this biomedicalized food culture is inspired by this definition, which means that I identify and observe a set of heterogeneous practices and discourses that today help to define what and how contemporary "healthy eating" is understood.

To name but a few examples, I observe the deployment of this biomedicalized food culture across the field of popular culture while information about functional foods is numerous. Functional foods are defined and characterized by association between certain health benefits and the ingestion of specific molecular bioactive components that are presumed to have the potential to reduce the risk of chronic disease (definition taken from the writings of Kim 2013 and Scrinis 2012; see, for example, "*Les fruits de mer protégeraient les aînés du déclin cognitif*" (seafood will protect seniors from cognitive decline) (*La Presse canadienne* 2016)).

This biomedicalized food culture is also deployed in the field of biological, biochemical or nutritional sciences, multiplying the production of knowledge while questioning the links between food and bodies according to a logic and desire to act on biological materiality. This is the case, for example, with the new field of nutrigenomics research, promoted by the Department of Nutritional Sciences at the University of Toronto, which explores the relationship between genes and food intake. Nutrigenomics attempts to understand how an individual's genetic variations and particularities influence physiological responses related to the ingestion of certain nutrients, with the potential aim of understanding (and potentially preventing) the risks of chronic disease development[3]. The presentation of the research conducted in this field promotes the advances that can be expected in weight loss and the supposed prevention of diseases such as diabetes, obesity, certain types of cancer, etc.

Technological advancements are also actively contributing to the development of this biomedicalized food culture, as increasingly precise and personalized monitoring tools have been designed. This is the case, for example, of the "MyFitnessPal" calorie meter, which, thanks to a food database that systematically calculates the calories ingested, offers to help its users lose weight. The personalization and commercialization of technologies that are designed to produce knowledge that unites the body and food operates in a different way with uBiome Inc. The company offers tools and knowledge for analyzing microorganisms, such as bacteria and viruses, that make up an individual's biological materiality in order to diagnose their state of health and propose a diet corresponding to their body composition (Johne 2017).

These examples are too few to demonstrate the multiplicity of recurrences involved in producing this biomedicalized food culture and the biochemical and

---

3 University of Toronto website: http://boundless.utoronto.ca/impact/should-your-dna-determine-whats-for-dinner-nutrigenomics-el-sohemy/. The University of Toronto has distributed promotional signs in the downtown area with the following question: "Should your DNA determine what's for dinner?"

biospecific knowledge that emerges. These elements may not seem to be linked at first glance since they seem to be coming from a multitude of distinct domains and produced by heterogeneity of actors in various places. Nevertheless, they highlight how the practices and discourses of "healthy eating" seem to present points of convergence in terms of their ways of producing and mobilizing food and bodies.

Through the production of knowledge that constitutes contemporary "healthy eating", knowledge about the body is also produced. For example, it is possible to observe the emergence of "plastic" bodies, whose very materiality or trajectory would be considered as possibly transformed or modulated through the ingestion of specific nutrients. The idea of a "plastic" body is also closely linked to the idea of a machine-body, which must be "fed" in an appropriate way in order to maximize its potential and performance, following the metaphor of the machine that requires proper maintenance for maximizing its performance. The literature emerging from critical studies on nutrition allows us to reflect on the issues that arise when links that are too causal, reductive and "universalizing" are created between the ingestion of specific foods and supposed transformations of body components or functions (see, for example, Kim 2013; Scrinis 2013). Thus, through the establishment of a causal, decontextualized and universalized relationship between the ingestion of specific foods and bodies, new normativities by which bodies are understood are produced and the way bodies respond to ingesting foods is understood to be the same (Kim 2013).

These concepts such as "plastic" or "machine" bodies are particularly important in the context of the production and circulation of discourses that link aging bodies to food. Through these discourses, a conception of bodies emerges by which the aging process could be slowed down or even prevented, as if the act of "healthy" eating in itself could guarantee "successful" aging (Durocher and Gauthier in press)[4].

These are just some of the bodies that are produced, framed and oriented at the heart of this biomedicalized food culture. At this point, I want to start exploring its deployment modes from the forces that inform development. Thus, I conceive the widespread digitalization of society as one of the driving forces behind its biomedicalization. This echoes Clarke *et al.*'s (2010) theorization of the biomedicalization of society, which is understood to be made possible through the deployment and use of computer and information technologies, which allow

4 See the work of researchers in critical gerontology, such as Stephen Katz (2013) or, more specifically in relation to nutrition, Coveney (2006), who criticized the injunctions and normativities associated with so-called "successful" aging, which involves, among other things, maintaining good physical health and failing to consider the broader systemic and structural factors that can prevent an individual from aging "healthily" beyond their food intake.

transformations in the distribution and accessibility of biomedical knowledge, as well as in the means and tools developed to capture it[5]. This biomedicalized food culture therefore contributes, on the one hand, to the multiplication of informative content aimed at informing individuals about what constitutes contemporary "healthy eating", understood according to its biochemical components, and which are themselves linked to the components and body processes designed to be influenced by the intake of these nutrients. On the other hand, it participates in the development of control and intervention practices on living organisms based on food. This is, for example, the case for the development of a whole set of technologies that contribute to promoting personalized and real-time monitoring and control of what is ingested or the biological materiality of an individual.

Thus, as part of my doctoral research, I observe the modes and places of deployment of this biomedicalized food culture as well as the forms of knowledge it contributes to produce. In doing so, it is necessary for me to question how it is made possible and how it can be articulated in a society characterized by the omnipresence of the *media*, which inform the production and circulation of knowledge as well as the creation of particular practices, constitutive of contemporary "healthy eating". Through the exploration of this bio-medicalized food culture, I would like to ask how knowledge about bodies is produced that help define the ways in which they are understood and worked on. In doing so, I aim to identify the new norms that are then created, uniting the body and nutrition. I will conclude here with some of the critical questions that drive the ongoing research. Since biomediation marks a

5 It should be noted that I am exploring the development of this biomedicalized food culture informed by media theories (Hepp *et al.* 2015; Hepp and Tribe 2013; Lundby 2014), which focus on the co-constitution of changes that occur in both culture and the *media*. These theories question this interrelationship as today's society is permeated by the omnipresence of the *media*, participating in the production of daily communicational practices, knowledge, norms, values and emotions that constitute our reality (Krotz 2009). The branch of media studies that analyzes mediatization processes from a socio-cultural perspective (Durocher 2017; Hepp *et al.* 2015) conceives that the "tightening" power of the *media* is exercised and (re)produced through interaction, through the communicative practices that are at the basis of the constitution of culture. Media theories therefore aim to challenge the way in which *media* are developed and deployed in interrelationship with culture (Hepp *et al.* 2015). *Media* here should therefore not be understood as being limited to digital technologies and the use of interactive algorithms, but includes, more broadly, any technology that enables the establishment of communicative practices as well as the production and sharing of information. It is therefore possible to include in this definition both institutional media and *self-tracking* applications, blogs, etc. Thus, I will prioritize the name *media* in italics, with reference to its Latin origin, in order to distinguish it from the name that would refer to mass media (Bardini 2016). The theories of mediatization seem promising to me to reflect on the co-development of a biomedicalized food culture and the *media* that inform its deployment, in light of the contemporary biopolitical context.

change in the "distribution of biomedical information and knowledge and [in] the responsibilities of individuals to seize it" (Clarke *et al.* 2000, p. 29), how should we reflect on contemporary bodies, the intersection of injunctions to self-responsibility and self-care and the production of knowledge that contributes to "healthy eating"?

How should we think about bodies in their relationship to food, when they are subject to a set of surveillance techniques (e.g. blood tests to assess blood sugar or cholesterol levels, mobile applications to monitor the calories ingested or expended in real time, etc.) and categorization to help produce them as "healthy" or not? In this context, how is "being healthy" (re)defined?

19.3. References

Bardini, T. (2016). Entre archéologie et écologie. *Multitudes*, (62), 159–168.

Brady, J., Gingras, J., and Power, E. (2012). Still hungry: A feminist perspective on food, foodwork, the body, and food studies. In *Critical Perspectives in Food Studies*, Doc, M., Sumner, J., and Winson, A. (eds). Oxford University Press, Don Mills, 122–135.

Clarke, A.E., Fishman, J.R., Fosket, J.R., Mamo, L., and Shim, J.K. (2000). Technosciences et nouvelle biomédicalisation : Racines occidentales, rhizomes mondiaux. *Sciences sociales et santé*, 18(2), 11–42.

Clarke, A.E., Shim, J.K., Mamo, L., Fosket, J.R., and Fishman, J.R. (2003). Biomedicalization: Technoscientific transformations of health, illness, and U.S. biomedicine. *American Sociological Review*, 68(2), 161–194.

Clarke, A.E., Mamo, L., Fosket, J.R., Fishman, J.R., and Shim, J.K. (2010). *Biomedicalization: Technoscience, Health, and Illness in the U.S.* Duke University Press, Durham.

Coveney, J. (2006). Food and Aging. In *Foucault and Aging*, Powell, J. and Wahidin, A. (eds). Nova Science Publishers, New York, 61–73. Available at: http://catalog.hathitrust.org/api/volumes/oclc/61167795.html.

Durocher, M. and Gauthier, M. (2018). A food blog created by and for elders: A political gesture informed by the normative injunctions to eat and age well. *Interaction Design and Architecture(s) Journal*, 36, 75–92.

Hall, S. (1980). Cultural studies: Two paradigms. *Media, Culture & Society*, 2(1), 57–72.

Hepp, A. and Tribe, K. (2013). *Cultures of Mediatization*. Polity, Cambridge.

Hepp, A., Hjarvard, S., and Lundby, K. (2015). Mediatization: Theorizing the interplay between media, culture and society. *Media, Culture & Society*, 37(2), 314–324.

Johne, M. (2017). Go with the gut – at uBiome Inc., science meets business opportunity. *The Globe and Mail*, 7 April. Available at: https://www.theglobeandmail.com/report-on-business/go-with-the-gut-at-ubiome-inc-science-meets-business-opportunity/article32676714/.

Katz, S. (2013). Active and Successful Aging. Lifestyle as a Gerontological Idea. *Recherches sociologiques et anthropologiques*, 44(1), 33–49.

Kim, H. (2013). Functional foods and the biomedicalisation of everyday life: A case of germinated brown rice. *Sociology of Health and Illness*, 35(6), 842–857.

Koç, M., Winson, A., and Sumner, J.M. (2012). *Critical Perspectives in Food Studies*. Oxford University Press, Don Mills.

Krotz, F. (2009). Mediatization: A concept with which to grasp media and societal change. In *Mediatization: Concept, Changes, Consequences*, Lundby, K. (ed.). Peter Lang Publishing, New York, 21–40.

La Presse canadienne (2016). Les fruits de mer protégeraient les aînés du déclin cognitif. *La Presse canadienne*, 11 May. Available at: https://www.lapresse.ca/vivre/sante/nutrition/201605/11/01-4980484-les-fruits-de-mer-protegeraient-les-aines-du-declin-cognitif.php.

Lundby, K. (2014). *Mediatization of Communication*. Walter de Gruyter, Berlin.

Rabinow, P. and Rose, N. (2006). Biopower Today. *BioSocieties*, 1, 195–217.

Scrinis, G. (2012). Nutritionism and functional foods. In *The Philosophy of Food*, Kaplan, D. (ed.). University of California Press, Berkeley, 269–291.

Scrinis, G. (2013). *Nutritionism: The Science and Politics of Dietary Advice*. Columbia University Press, New York.

University of Toronto (n.d.). Should your DNA determine what's for dinner? University of Toronto. Available at: http://boundless.utoronto.ca/impact/should-your-dna-determine-whats-for-dinner-nutrigenomics-el-sohemy/

Conclusion

As we have seen from the chapters of this first volume, the dimensions of "the digital" that have been discussed are inextricably linked to each other. Numbers, digitalization, quantification, Big Data, algorithms, digital social media and platforms – all these terms refer to changes at work and the process of "digitalization of society" today. However, it is impossible to decide whether these are developments or a revolution, continuities or ruptures, "simple" changes or major mutations. As can be seen from the chapters, many analyses suggest continuity in some respects, as well as elements in favor of certain breaks, unless it is primarily a question of an acceleration of more or fewer recent trends. The answer to these questions also depends, of course, on the objects studied and the temporality of the observations.

C.1. The example of digital platforms and changes at work

Let us take the subject on which we are working in the context of funded research, namely the places and roles of new intermediation services in the changes in culture and media in the digital age[1]. Thanks to the creation of digital platforms, these new services offer new forms of intermediation (web-based services, no advertising, premium services, low-cost subscriptions, etc.) that compete with "traditional" distributors of information and cultural products. These new services, often resulting from the communication industries (IT, telecommunications, the Web), rely on financial capacities much greater than those of the cultural industries

Conclusion written by Éric GEORGE.

1 Research project funded by the Conseil de recherches en sciences humaines (CRSH), with Arnaud Anciaux (Université Laval, Quebec), Anouk Bélanger (UQAM, Montreal) and Michel Sénécal (Université TÉLUQ, Montreal).

to obtain exclusive broadcasting rights on cultural products (Latournerie 2001; Benhamou and Farchy 2014). In addition, some of them have little or no tax liability or specific regulatory framework to follow, while traditional distributors contribute to the financing of television production and must take into account legislative and regulatory requirements, such as the 1991 Canadian Broadcasting Act (Sénécal and George 2018). But what roles do these platforms play in the current transformations of culture and media?

A first analysis shows that their place is much more significant downstream than upstream of cultural sectors (Ménard 2014). They are mainly present in the distribution/circulation of products. Above all, they seek to structure the formation of the social uses of ICTs and related cultural practices. To do this, they create platforms, new media forms, which offer various modes of referencing/recommendation, some of which are quite traditional (based on the categories: "new", "popular", "award-winning") and others more "innovative" (algorithms and preferences such as "you have already loved..."). However, these new players tend to also be present in the production sector, at least in the audiovisual sector. For example, the "scarecrow", Netflix, promised to invest C$500 million in Canada over five years, compared to the $8 billion invested worldwide since 2009 (Claus 2017). But while it is certain that the control of broadcasting rights is absolutely central to ensuring that these platforms can offer a wide and diversified supply, it is less clear, in the long term, what the scale of investment in audiovisual creation will be.

In addition, there is often talk of "digital culture" surrounding young people. This notion refers to the development of practices related to the devices we are interested in. Nevertheless, the concept of digital culture is highly criticized, as it would continue to hide significant inequalities that would still be based on more traditional relationships (class, gender and race) (Octobre 2014). On the one hand, it is clear that the new digital activities are mainly carried out by "young people". The generation variable is therefore relevant when considering cultural practices related to the platforms of interest (Thoër *et al.* 2016). On the other hand, these "young people" continue at times to have relationships with more traditional audiovisual content, for example thanks to the television set, in a family context. But what about when they become adults, when they are financially independent, when they live together as a couple or when they have children? It seems impossible to know now. Only the realization of new research that gives a certain place to the "long term" will make it possible to move forward.

C.2. The importance of the "long term" in research

However, since the 1980s, the communication sciences and, beyond that, all social sciences have been marked by the importance of research that is micro, banal and everyday. On this subject, Georges Balandier wrote in 1983:

> "The most important (perhaps) thing in the vogue that multiplies expensive researches on everyday life is the recent movement of minds that has made the subject appear again in the face of structures and systems, quality in the face of quantity, experience in the face of the instituted. This strong trend affects much more than just the social sciences field, but it mainly affects it. From this point of view, it is not without interest to note that the sociology of everyday life (considering the relationship of the individual to lasting, repeated social impositions) successfully joins two of the disciplines celebrated over the last twenty years, social, cultural and historical anthropology (considering the relationship with the 'other') and psychoanalysis (dealing with the relationship between the individual and their own history). In all three cases, the subject's point of view is privileged – not necessarily an exceptional subject, but rather the 'ordinary' or 'banal'" (p. 8).

This tendency to focus on the banal and the ordinary in research has certainly been relevant insofar as it has provided evidence that challenges analyses that are too tinged with structuralism and that too often focus on the most important institutions in our societies. But didn't these choices also lead to a focus on the short term, or even on a certain "presentism"? So isn't there a great risk of seeing something new everywhere, for example in an age called the digital age? Wouldn't each sociotechnical innovation tend to drive out the previous ones? And, on a more theoretical level, wouldn't communication sciences be even more subject to this trend than other social science disciplines, while Gaëtan Tremblay (1998) reminds us that "the history of communicational thinking is [...] marked, oriented, at each of its stages, by technological advances" (p. 178)? This is before adding: "Like it or not, it must be noted that the technical factor is at the heart of the emergence and development of communication sciences" (p. 178). On the contrary, it seems to us that integrating the "long term" into research, as Armand Mattelart (1989, 1994, 1999) has done throughout his career, would greatly help us to consider the possible cultural, economic, political, social and technical changes related to digital technology.

Choosing such an option would also make it possible to rethink existing power relations when it comes to culture and communication. Admittedly, Big Data can be considered as the means that would – finally! – allow us to "reveal" consumers' preferences both in terms of taste in news topics and music, and in terms of literature or even television series. In addition, the communicative socio-technical devices grouped for a decade around the term "Web 2.0" are sometimes considered as new media that are likely to challenge traditional inequalities within cultural industries by giving part of the power back to the users of DICTs. While these analyses are interesting, they are nevertheless limited.

In fact, systematically and simultaneously emphasizing the short term and the micro in research often means ignoring socio-historical contexts, omitting the central place of capitalism and its forms in societies, and neglecting the power relations between social actors (Mattelart 2014). Thus, most Big Data is collected by companies that are highly dominant in their respective markets – whether it is Google (search for information and other services on the Web), Facebook (a digital social network with a "generalist" vocation), Amazon (online commerce), etc. They are analyzed by algorithms of which very little is known. These same companies have also benefited greatly from the various spin-offs (advertising revenues, data accumulation, provision of free content, etc.) resulting from the many activities of DICT users, highlighted since the 2000s, with the term "participatory Web" (Bouquillion and Matthews 2010), to reach the size they are now and the dominant position they enjoy (Smyrnaios 2017).

As in the past, in an era that we could call "pre-digital", audiences are not passive. This has been well documented in a number of studies over the decades, at least since Richard Hoggart's 1957 book *The Uses of Literacy: Aspects of Working Class Life*. However, as Ien Ang (1990) says, the *cultural studies* researcher working on these issues sometimes tends to become an "eloquent champion, the advocate of a consumer-centered cultural democracy. The public's activity can be proven, and the millions of ways in which it uses and interprets the media can be cited" (p. 247). With the multiplication of communicational socio-technical devices, the analysis of the culturalist researcher seems more relevant than ever, as the very modalities of the activity of receivers have diversified greatly over the decades, to the point where there are now more and more creators of content. Nevertheless, Ang (1990) added that, from the study of activity, it was impossible to conclude that there had been an increase in the power of the public, which seems to us to be an important clarification, whereas the cultural and communication industries have not been "dissolved in the digital age". On the contrary, the processes of industrialization and commodification still seem to be penetrating the culture, information and communication sectors more and more. This does not mean that there are no practices that resist in one way or another against the persistent domination of capitalism.

We will return to these issues in Volume 2 of this book. In particular, it will discuss different types of information production and social mobilization based on the development of uses of ICTs for socio-political purposes.

To be continued…

C.3. References

Ang, I. (1990). Culture and communication: towards an ethnographic critique of media consumption in the Transnational Media System. *European Journal of Communication*, 2–3(5), 239–260.

Balandier, G. (1983). Essai d'identification du quotidien. *Cahiers internationaux de sociologie*, 74, 5–12.

Benhamou, F. and Farchy, J. (2014). *Droit d'auteur et copyright.* La Découverte, Paris.

Claus, S. (2017). Le débat sur la mondialisation culturelle à l'heure du "numérique" : le cas de Netflix au Canada. *COMMposite*, 19(2). Available at: http://www.commposite.org/index.php/revue/article/view/257.

George, É. and Sénécal, M. (2017). L'importance de la "longue durée" dans les études en communication à partir de l'analyse des industries culturelles. In *Temps et temporalités en information-communication : des concepts aux méthodes*, Domenget, J.-C., Pélissier, N., and Miège, B. (eds). L'Harmattan, Paris, 45–60.

Latournerie, A. (2001). Petite histoire des batailles du droit d'auteur. *Multitudes,* 2(5), 37–62.

Mattelart, A. (1989). *L'internationale publicitaire*. La Découverte, Paris.

Mattelart, A. (1996). *The Invention of Communication*, Translated by S. Emanuel. University of Minnesota Press, Minneapolis.

Mattelart, A. (1999). *Histoire de l'utopie planétaire. De la société prophétique à la société globale*. La Découverte, Paris.

Mattelart, A. (2014). De la difficulté à penser l'international au regard de l'histoire : leçons d'un itinéraire intellectuel. In *Critique, sciences sociales et communication*, George, É. and Granjon, F. (eds). Mare & Martin, Paris, 13–33.

Ménard, M. (2014). The concept of the industrial channel in the domain of culture, information, and communication: a French speciality? *Canadian Journal of Communication*, 39(1), 73–88.

Octobre, S. (2014). Les enfants du numérique : mutations culturelles et mutations sociales. *Informations sociales*, 1(181), 50–60. Available at: https://www.cairn.info/revue-informations-sociales-2014-1-page-50.htm.

Sénécal, M. and George, É. (2018). Les méandres des discours politiques sur la création culturelle et médiatique au Canada et au Québec : avant et après Netflix. *Création, créativité et médiations. Congrès de la SFSIC Actes vol. 2 : Modèles et stratégies d'acteurs*, 19–29. Available at: https://www.sfsic.org/attachments/article/3280/Actes%20vol%202%20-%20congrès%20SFSIC%202018.pdf.

Smyrnaios, N. (2017). *Les GAFAM contre l'internet. Une économie politique du numérique*. Institut national de l'audiovisuel, Bry-sur-Marne.

Thoër, C., Millerand, F., and Vrignaud, C. (2016). Regarder des séries en ligne : les formes de l'attachement chez de jeunes adultes québécois. In *D'un écran à l'autre : les mutations du spectateur*, Châteauvert, J. and Delavaud, G. (eds), L'Harmattan, Paris, 557–571.

Tremblay, G. (1998). Le lieu (virtuel) des sciences de la communication. *Loisir et société*, 21(1), 173–192.

List of Authors

Arnaud ANCIAUX
CRICIS
Université Laval
Quebec
Canada

Yanita ANDONOVA
LabSIC
Université Paris 13
Villetaneuse
France

Anne BELLON
CESSP
Université Paris 1
France

Alma BETBOUT
LCS
Université Clermont Auvergne
Clermont-Ferrand

Maud BOISNARD
CEIM
Université du Québec à Montréal
Canada

Philippe BOUQUILLION
LabSIC
Université Paris 13
Villetaneuse
France

Samuel COSSETTE
CRICIS, GRISQ
Université du Québec à Montréal
Canada

Marie DAVID
CENS
Université de Nantes
France

Lucie DELIAS
IRMECCEN, UTRPP
Universités Paris 3 et Paris 13
Villetaneuse
France

Myriam DUROCHER
CPCC
Université de Montréal
Canada

Éric GEORGE
CRICIS
Université du Québec à Montréal
Canada

Édith LAVIEC
GRESEC
Université Grenoble Alpes
France

Armand MATTELART
CEMTI
Université Paris 8
Saint-Denis
France

Jacob MATTHEWS
CEMTI
Université Paris 8
Saint-Denis
France

Maxime OUELLET
CRICIS, GRISQ
Université du Québec à Montréal
Canada

Robert PANICO
CREIS
IUT de Valence
Université Grenoble Alpes
France

Cathia PAPI
CURAPP-ESS
Université TÉLUQ
Montreal
Canada

Fabien RICHERT
CRICIS, GRISQ
Université du Québec à Montréal
Canada

Michèle RIOUX
CEIM
Université du Québec à Montréal
Canada

Julien ROSSI
COSTECH
Université de technologie de Compiègne
France

Rémi ROUGE
CRESPPA, LabToP
Université Paris 8
Saint-Denis
France

Destiny TCHÉHOUALI
CEIM
Université du Québec à Montréal
Canada

Geneviève VIDAL
CREIS et LabSIC
Université Paris 13
Villetaneuse
France

Index

G, H, I

K, L, M

N, O, P, R

S, T, U, W

Other titles from

iSTE

in

Information Systems, Web and Pervasive Computing

2019

ALBAN Daniel, EYNAUD Philippe, MALAURENT Julien, RICHET Jean-Loup, VITARI Claudio
Information Systems Management: Governance, Urbanization and Alignment

AUGEY Dominique, with the collaboration of ALCARAZ Marina
Digital Information Ecosystems: Smart Press

BATTON-HUBERT Mireille, DESJARDIN Eric, PINET François
Geographic Data Imperfection 1: From Theory to Applications

BRIQUET-DUHAZÉ Sophie, TURCOTTE Catherine
From Reading-Writing Research to Practice

BROCHARD Luigi, KAMATH Vinod, CORBALAN Julita, HOLLAND Scott, MITTELBACH Walter, OTT Michael
Energy-Efficient Computing and Data Centers

CHAMOUX Jean-Pierre
The Digital Era 2: Political Economy Revisited

COCHARD Gérard-Michel
Introduction to Stochastic Processes and Simulation

DUONG Véronique
SEO Management: Methods and Techniques to Achieve Success

GAUCHEREL Cédric, GOUYON Pierre-Henri, DESSALLES Jean-Louis
Information, The Hidden Side of Life

GHLALA Riadh
Analytic SQL in SQL Server 2014/2016

JANIER Mathilde, SAINT-DIZIER Patrick
Argument Mining: Linguistic Foundations

SOURIS Marc
Epidemiology and Geography: Principles, Methods and Tools of Spatial Analysis

TOUNSI Wiem
Cyber-Vigilance and Digital Trust: Cyber Security in the Era of Cloud Computing and IoT

2018

ARDUIN Pierre-Emmanuel
Insider Threats
(Advances in Information Systems Set – Volume 10)

CARMÈS Maryse
Digital Organizations Manufacturing: Scripts, Performativity and Semiopolitics
(Intellectual Technologies Set – Volume 5)

CARRÉ Dominique, VIDAL Geneviève
Hyperconnectivity: Economical, Social and Environmental Challenges
(Computing and Connected Society Set – Volume 3)

CHAMOUX Jean-Pierre
The Digital Era 1: Big Data Stakes

DOUAY Nicolas
Urban Planning in the Digital Age
(Intellectual Technologies Set – Volume 6)

FABRE Renaud, BENSOUSSAN Alain
The Digital Factory for Knowledge: Production and Validation of Scientific Results

GAUDIN Thierry, LACROIX Dominique, MAUREL Marie-Christine, POMEROL Jean-Charles
Life Sciences, Information Sciences

GAYARD Laurent
Darknet: Geopolitics and Uses
(Computing and Connected Society Set – Volume 2)

IAFRATE Fernando
Artificial Intelligence and Big Data: The Birth of a New Intelligence
(Advances in Information Systems Set – Volume 8)

LE DEUFF Olivier
Digital Humanities: History and Development
(Intellectual Technologies Set – Volume 4)

MANDRAN Nadine
Traceable Human Experiment Design Research: Theoretical Model and Practical Guide
(Advances in Information Systems Set – Volume 9)

PIVERT Olivier
NoSQL Data Models: Trends and Challenges

ROCHET Claude
Smart Cities: Reality or Fiction

SAUVAGNARGUES Sophie
Decision-making in Crisis Situations: Research and Innovation for Optimal Training

SEDKAOUI Soraya
Data Analytics and Big Data

SZONIECKY Samuel
Ecosystems Knowledge: Modeling and Analysis Method for Information and Communication
(Digital Tools and Uses Set – Volume 6)

2017

BOUHAÏ Nasreddine, SALEH Imad
Internet of Things: Evolutions and Innovations
(Digital Tools and Uses Set – Volume 4)

DUONG Véronique
Baidu SEO: Challenges and Intricacies of Marketing in China

LESAS Anne-Marie, MIRANDA Serge
The Art and Science of NFC Programming
(Intellectual Technologies Set – Volume 3)

LIEM André
Prospective Ergonomics
(Human-Machine Interaction Set – Volume 4)

MARSAULT Xavier
Eco-generative Design for Early Stages of Architecture
(Architecture and Computer Science Set – Volume 1)

REYES-GARCIA Everardo
The Image-Interface: Graphical Supports for Visual Information
(Digital Tools and Uses Set – Volume 3)

REYES-GARCIA Everardo, BOUHAÏ Nasreddine
Designing Interactive Hypermedia Systems
(Digital Tools and Uses Set – Volume 2)

SAÏD Karim, BAHRI KORBI Fadia
Asymmetric Alliances and Information Systems:Issues and Prospects
(Advances in Information Systems Set – Volume 7)

SZONIECKY Samuel, BOUHAÏ Nasreddine
Collective Intelligence and Digital Archives: Towards Knowledge Ecosystems
(Digital Tools and Uses Set – Volume 1)

2016

BEN CHOUIKHA Mona
Organizational Design for Knowledge Management

BERTOLO David
Interactions on Digital Tablets in the Context of 3D Geometry Learning
(Human-Machine Interaction Set – Volume 2)

BOUVARD Patricia, SUZANNE Hervé
Collective Intelligence Development in Business

EL FALLAH SEGHROUCHNI Amal, ISHIKAWA Fuyuki, HÉRAULT Laurent, TOKUDA Hideyuki
Enablers for Smart Cities

FABRE Renaud, in collaboration with MESSERSCHMIDT-MARIET Quentin, HOLVOET Margot
New Challenges for Knowledge

GAUDIELLO Ilaria, ZIBETTI Elisabetta
Learning Robotics, with Robotics, by Robotics
(Human-Machine Interaction Set – Volume 3)

HENROTIN Joseph
The Art of War in the Network Age
(Intellectual Technologies Set – Volume 1)

KITAJIMA Munéo
Memory and Action Selection in Human–Machine Interaction
(Human–Machine Interaction Set – Volume 1)

LAGRAÑA Fernando
E-mail and Behavioral Changes: Uses and Misuses of Electronic Communications

LEIGNEL Jean-Louis, UNGARO Thierry, STAAR Adrien
Digital Transformation
(Advances in Information Systems Set – Volume 6)

NOYER Jean-Max
Transformation of Collective Intelligences
(Intellectual Technologies Set – Volume 2)

VENTRE Daniel
Information Warfare – 2nd edition

VITALIS André
The Uncertain Digital Revolution
(Computing and Connected Society Set – Volume 1)

2015

ARDUIN Pierre-Emmanuel, GRUNDSTEIN Michel, ROSENTHAL-SABROUX Camille
Information and Knowledge System
(Advances in Information Systems Set – Volume 2)

BÉRANGER Jérôme
Medical Information Systems Ethics

BRONNER Gérald
Belief and Misbelief Asymmetry on the Internet

IAFRATE Fernando
From Big Data to Smart Data
(Advances in Information Systems Set – Volume 1)

KRICHEN Saoussen, BEN JOUIDA Sihem
Supply Chain Management and its Applications in Computer Science

NEGRE Elsa
Information and Recommender Systems
(Advances in Information Systems Set – Volume 4)

POMEROL Jean-Charles, EPELBOIN Yves, THOURY Claire
MOOCs

SALLES Maryse
Decision-Making and the Information System
(Advances in Information Systems Set – Volume 3)

SAMARA Tarek
ERP and Information Systems: Integration or Disintegration
(Advances in Information Systems Set – Volume 5)

2014

DINET Jérôme
Information Retrieval in Digital Environments

HÉNO Raphaële, CHANDELIER Laure
3D Modeling of Buildings: Outstanding Sites

KEMBELLEC Gérald, CHARTRON Ghislaine, SALEH Imad
Recommender Systems

MATHIAN Hélène, SANDERS Lena
Spatio-temporal Approaches: Geographic Objects and Change Process

PLANTIN Jean-Christophe
Participatory Mapping

VENTRE Daniel
Chinese Cybersecurity and Defense

2013

BERNIK Igor
Cybercrime and Cyberwarfare

CAPET Philippe, DELAVALLADE Thomas
Information Evaluation

LEBRATY Jean-Fabrice, LOBRE-LEBRATY Katia
Crowdsourcing: One Step Beyond

SALLABERRY Christian
Geographical Information Retrieval in Textual Corpora

2012

BUCHER Bénédicte, LE BER Florence
Innovative Software Development in GIS

GAUSSIER Eric, YVON François
Textual Information Access

STOCKINGER Peter
Audiovisual Archives: Digital Text and Discourse Analysis

VENTRE Daniel
Cyber Conflict

2011

BANOS Arnaud, THÉVENIN Thomas
Geographical Information and Urban Transport Systems

DAUPHINÉ André
Fractal Geography

LEMBERGER Pirmin, MOREL Mederic
Managing Complexity of Information Systems

STOCKINGER Peter
Introduction to Audiovisual Archives

STOCKINGER Peter
Digital Audiovisual Archives

VENTRE Daniel
Cyberwar and Information Warfare

2010

BONNET Pierre
Enterprise Data Governance

BRUNET Roger
Sustainable Geography

CARREGA Pierre
Geographical Information and Climatology

CAUVIN Colette, ESCOBAR Francisco, SERRADJ Aziz
Thematic Cartography – 3-volume series
Thematic Cartography and Transformations – Volume 1
Cartography and the Impact of the Quantitative Revolution – Volume 2
New Approaches in Thematic Cartography – Volume 3

LANGLOIS Patrice
Simulation of Complex Systems in GIS

MATHIS Philippe
Graphs and Networks – 2nd edition

THÉRIAULT Marius, DES ROSIERS François
Modeling Urban Dynamics

2009

BONNET Pierre, DETAVERNIER Jean-Michel, VAUQUIER Dominique
Sustainable IT Architecture: the Progressive Way of Overhauling Information Systems with SOA

PAPY Fabrice
Information Science

RIVARD François, ABOU HARB Georges, MERET Philippe
The Transverse Information System

ROCHE Stéphane, CARON Claude
Organizational Facets of GIS

2008

BRUGNOT Gérard
Spatial Management of Risks

FINKE Gerd
Operations Research and Networks

GUERMOND Yves
Modeling Process in Geography

KANEVSKI Michael
Advanced Mapping of Environmental Data

MANOUVRIER Bernard, LAURENT Ménard
Application Integration: EAI, B2B, BPM and SOA

PAPY Fabrice
Digital Libraries

2007

DOBESCH Hartwig, DUMOLARD Pierre, DYRAS Izabela
Spatial Interpolation for Climate Data

SANDERS Lena
Models in Spatial Analysis

2006

CLIQUET Gérard
Geomarketing

CORNIOU Jean-Pierre
Looking Back and Going Forward in IT

DEVILLERS Rodolphe, JEANSOULIN Robert
Fundamentals of Spatial Data Quality